Editors' Notes for Teaching

Literature

THE HUMAN EXPERIENCE

Editors' Notes for Teaching

Literature

THE HUMAN EXPERIENCE

Ninth Edition

Richard Abcarian and Marvin Klotz

Bedford / St. Martin's

New York ♦ Boston

Manufactured in the United States of America.

09876
f e d c b a

For information, write:
Bedford/St. Martin's, 75 Arlington Street, Boston, MA 02116   (617-399-4000)

ISBN: 0-312-44129-0

EAN: 978-0-312-44129-6

Preface

In this instructor's manual, we have tried to say something useful and illuminating about each of the primary works anthologized in *Literature: The Human Experience,* Ninth Edition, except those already discussed in the text. We do not expect instructors to agree with all of our interpretations—we would be surprised if they did. Where our analyses are not persuasive, we hope they will in any event be useful in giving the instructor something to disagree with. Mindful that questions asked by editors in introductory anthologies often baffle students (and occasionally instructors as well), we focus our analyses on the study questions that accompany all of the fiction, drama, and essay selections, as well as many poetry selections.

For convenience of reference, the manual is arranged by genre, and within each genre, alphabetically by author. Following each selection's title is a page reference corresponding to the text.

Richard Abcarian
Marvin Klotz

Supplementing Literature with Print and Multimedia Resources

Instructors who wish to supplement *Literature* with additional works may be interested in the print and multimedia materials available with the ninth edition.

For instructors who wish to incorporate research into their classes, our Web site links students and instructors to a wide variety of literary research materials, an interactive poetry tutorial, and reading comprehension quizzes for many of the selections in the book. Visit us at <bedfordstmartins.com/experience_literature>.

The *Robert Frost: Poems, Life, Legacy* CD-ROM is available to qualified adopters who would like to incorporate additional works by or about Robert Frost into their classes. This comprehensive CD-ROM includes searchable text of his poetry, comprehensive critical and biographical resources, and audio recordings of Frost reading sixty-nine of his finest poems.

Available on videotape are several full-length feature film versions of selected works in *Literature*. The acclaimed versions of these works include *Othello* and *A Raisin in the Sun*, among others.

For instructors who want to teach a longer work in conjunction with the anthology, Bedford/St. Martin's also publishes Case Studies in Contemporary Criticism, Bedford Cultural Editions, Bedford Shakespeare Series, and Case Studies in Critical Controversy. Titles in these series are available at a special price, shrink-wrapped with the ninth edition.

Titles available in the Case Studies in Contemporary Criticism series include *The Awakening, The Dead, Death in Venice, Dracula, Emma, Frankenstein, Great Expectations, Gulliver's Travels, Hamlet, Heart of Darkness, The House of Mirth, Howards End, Jane Eyre, A Portrait of the Artist as a Young Man, The Rime of the Ancient Mariner, The Scarlet Letter, The Secret Sharer, Tess of the D'Urbervilles, The Turn of the Screw, The Wife of Bath's Prologue and Tale*, and *Wuthering Heights*. Volumes from the Bedford Cultural Editions, the Bedford Shakespeare Series, and Case Studies in Critical Controversy include *The Adventures of Huckleberry Finn, Benito Cereno, The Blithedale Romance, Clotel, The Commerce of Everyday Life: Selections from* THE SPECTATOR *and* THE TATLER, *Evelina, The First Part of King Henry the Fourth, Life in the Iron-Mills, Oroonoko, The Rape of the Lock, Reading the West: An Anthology of Dime Westerns, The Taming of the Shrew, The Tempest, Three Lives, Twelfth Night*, and *The Yellow Wallpaper*.

Ordering Information

These and other resources are available to adopters of *Literature: The Human Experience,* Ninth Edition. To obtain copies or more information, contact your local Bedford/St. Martin's sales representative, or call Bedford/St. Martin's at 1-800-446-8923.

Contents

POETRY

DRAMA

ESSAYS

Editors' Notes for Teaching

Literature

THE HUMAN EXPERIENCE

Fiction

Chinua Achebe   Marriage Is a Private Affair   (p. 1277)

"Marriage Is a Private Affair" is one of those stories whose emotional impact should not be forgotten in the classroom. Many, perhaps most, readers will at the very least get a little choked up when reading the last two or three paragraphs of the story, and bringing up emotional moments in the classroom can provide a very powerful way into a discussion.

Identifying the source of this emotion—our happiness that this family will no longer be unhappily divided—can lead to a discussion of what it is that has blocked this happiness. It is impossible to blame the father solely, and students should not need much guidance to be able to see the way that tribal identification and religious belief reinforce each other and make both the father and his larger community unable to accept Nnaemeka's marriage to Nene. In the end, the father's desire to know his grandchildren trumps his desire for marriage within the tribe and his religious beliefs both in filial obedience and in women's "proper" role. What it means for Achebe that family is more important in the end than these other forms of community is worth discussing.

It is also worth returning to our frustration at the division within the family and our relief on its being overcome, in particular to the narrative aspect of our reactions. Discussing the conventions of these kinds of stories—of romance thwarted or close relatives estranged—can lead to insights about how fiction and drama play on our ideas about the ways the world should be. Their reaction to the end of "Marriage Is a Private Affair" can lead students to see that happy (and sad) endings draw their power not just from the stories that precede them but also from something within readers.

Sherman Alexie   This Is What It Means to Say Phoenix, Arizona   (p. 768)

This is a deceptively simple story. Victor, a reservation Indian, needs to travel to Phoenix, Arizona, to claim the body of his father. Without a car or money for transportation, he applies to the reservation tribal council for help. They give him $100.00, not enough for a round-trip, and suggest he find a friend who owns a car. He manages to find an old childhood acquaintance, Thomas Builds-the-Fire, who has a car and is willing to help if Victor will take him along. The heart of the story is their round-trip to Phoenix. What appears a rambling, on-the-road narrative becomes an exploration of the relationship between these two men within the context of their Native American heritage and history. We learn, through frequent flashbacks, about the childhood relationship between the two men. Thomas Builds-the-Fire has always been "a storyteller that no one wanted to listen to" (para. 16), something of an embarrassment to his deracinated fellow Native Americans, including Victor. Thomas was always chided for thinking too much, and as Victor soon discovers, it is a trait he has not lost. Thomas's thoughts focus on his identity and his history as a Native American, on the glory before and the degradation and humiliation after the coming of the white man.

Victor is uncomfortable with these reminders of who he is but, at the same time, powerfully drawn to them. During the Fourth of July fireworks of their childhood, it was Thomas who remarked on the strangeness of Native Americans celebrating the independence of those who had reduced them to utter dependence (para. 36). Victor's embarrassment as Thomas, the "crazy Indian storyteller" (para. 77), flirts with Cathy, the Olympic gymnast, dramatizes vividly how skewed his perceptions are. Cathy *likes* Thomas. Victor's growing respect for Thomas is apparent in the scene that follows, when he apologizes for the childhood beating.

By the time they return to the reservation, Victor's feelings toward Thomas have altered more profoundly than even he realizes. "Victor knew that Thomas would remain the crazy storyteller who talks to dogs and cars, who listened to the wind

3

and pine trees," he thinks. "Victor knew that he couldn't really be friends with Thomas even after all that had happened. It was cruel but it was real" (para. 179). Before they part, Thomas asks Victor to listen to one of his stories sometime in the future. Victor agrees with a wave of his arm and departs. Thomas drives home and enters his house, then "heard a new story come to him in the silence afterwards" (para. 193). Surely that story will tell of Victor's and other Native Americans' new willingness to hear Thomas's stories of their past and future.

We can surmise that the "This" of the title refers to the entire symbolic meaning of Victor and Thomas's journey. Victor's new openness to Thomas's stories suggests hope for the future. Indeed, Victor's attempt to make up for the shame he feels over his attitude toward Thomas is revealing. In giving Thomas half his father's ashes, he seems to be not only honoring Thomas's sense of "tribal ties" (para. 181) but also signaling his own new awareness of them.

The tone of this story is worth examining for the way in which Alexie infuses his serious theme with a great deal of humor. The humor begins in the very first scene, with Victor's appearance before the tribal council. The council's response to Victor is the patronizing "Now, Victor," as though they are addressing a child. When Victor is embarrassed to be seen talking to Thomas at the trading post, the narrator dryly remarks, "Victor felt a sudden need for tradition" (para. 24). Thomas tells a very funny story about the two Indian boys who wanted to be warriors (para. 43) and about his dream of standing by the falls in Spokane (para. 123). Much of the humor arises from the inability of both Thomas and Victor to be somber about themselves and their very serious concerns.

The unintrusive and natural way in which the social/political theme runs through the narrative helps create a tone of comic seriousness. Victor's treatment by the tribal council suggests the way in which the Bureau of Indian Affairs has reduced Indians to powerlessness and treated them like children. Thomas's remark on the Fourth of July celebration is a casual, matter-of-fact observation. So is his comment to Cathy about the U.S. boycott of the 1980 Olympics: "Sounds like you all got a lot in common with Indians" (para. 88).

Finally, the omniscient narration is largely unobtrusive and nonjudgmental, though at a number of points, the narrator makes quiet but oracular comments. He interrupts the story of the fireworks celebration to comment that "Years later, they would need much more" (para. 40). The story about Thomas's attempt to fly concludes with the admiring comment: "Everybody has dreams about flying. Thomas flew" (para. 137).

Isabel Allende   And of Clay Are We Created   (p. 1498)

Allende's story tells a tragic story, and students will feel the tragedy of the little girl, Azucena, quite directly. What discussion can bring out is why Allende tells this tale — what it is might want readers to feel (and think) other than sadness.

A good way to get at Allende's possible larger ideas is to point students to the other main emotional reaction they should have to the story, that is, frustration. This frustration may be directed both at the inability of The Republic (a fictional country representative, it should be made clear to students, of the South American countries Allende grew up and reported in) to marshal its resources to save Azucena and the others trapped in the mud and at the distance from which citizens (in the figure of the narrator) see events unfold. Recognizing their frustration while reading the story should help them see that "And of Clay Are We Created" does more than tell a tragic story: it indicts those who might have averted the tragedy as well as pointing out how distanced the privileged and the outside world are from these kinds of events (and the larger, national, man made catastrophes).

A comparison to Milcha Sanchez-Scott's *The Cuban Swimmer* (p. 1486) might help students see the ways in which writers use the death of young characters to create sympathy and draw attention to social ills. If your class does not read the play, discussion of this literary convention could begin from a rereading of the moment when Azucena tells Rolf Carlé that she is trapped not just by rubble and mud but by "the bodies of her brothers and sisters clinging to her legs." The image of the young, trapped by circumstance, is a powerful image for the curtailing of possibility facing future generations under certain political and economic circumstances.

James Baldwin Sonny's Blues (p. 704)

The power of this story on the theme of drug addiction among black jazz musicians in the ghetto derives from Baldwin's skillful weaving of the past into the present narrative. Raised in housing projects, the narrator and his younger brother, Sonny, have taken dramatically different paths. The narrator has become a math teacher, while Sonny is a jazz musician and heroin addict. They have drifted out of each other's lives. The newspaper account of Sonny's arrest is the first step in the narrator's journey through the past that will end in an emotional reconnection with his estranged brother. Sonny "became real to me again," he says (para. 2). As Sonny reenters his life, the narrator undergoes a gradual awakening that turns his aloofness and alienation from his own history into a homecoming of the emotions. This transformation is foreshadowed in the narrator's encounter with Sonny's addict friend as he leaves his classroom (paras. 8–48). The friend, like Sonny, represents everything that offends and baffles the narrator: an aimless, squandered life. "I hated him," the narrator says (para. 9). By the end of their conversation, the narrator declares, "I didn't hate him anymore" (para. 42).

The journey toward a reconnection with the past, on both a personal and a historical level, is a painful and common theme in African American literature. It appears in two well-known short stories, Charles Chesnutt's "The Wife of His Youth"and Ralph Ellison's "Flying Home." Baldwin's narrator retains an emotional bond with his past, evident in his choosing to live in a "housing project" (para. 47). Yet he has assimilated middle-class values so thoroughly that all he can think of when Sonny tells him he wants to be a musician is "concert pianist" and "classical music" (para. 89). When Sonny tells him he plays jazz, the narrator's response is, "Can you make a living at it?" (para. 107). The narrator fails to understand what LeRoi Jones (Amiri Baraka) points out in his book *Blues People* (1963):

> Blues is the parent of all legitimate Jazz and it is impossible to say exactly how old blues is — certainly no older than the presence of Negroes in the United States. It is a native American music, the product of the black man in this country: or to put it more exactly the way I have come to think about it, blues could not exist if the African captives had not become American captives.

The narrator's understanding of Sonny — the passion he feels for jazz and his addiction to drugs — is deepened when he observes the revival meeting. He remarks on the futility and hypocrisy of religion, but is astonished at the transforming power of music: "As the singing filled the air the watching, listening faces underwent a change, the eyes focusing on something within; the music seemed to soothe a poison out of them, and time seemed, nearly, to fall away from the sullen, belligerent, battered faces. . . ." (para. 151).

In the long dialogue that follows the revival meeting, Sonny attempts to explain to his brother how heroin makes him feel. It is an astonishing scene, with the narrator near panic as his brother calmly and thoughtfully talks about the connection among drugs, suffering, and creativity for many jazz musicians. As the narrator listens to the music at the end, he experiences an epiphany, a swelling realization that Sonny's blues captures and in some mysterious way makes bearable the sorrows of African American life.

Toni Cade Bambara The Lesson (p. 136)

This is not a story whose theme is likely to elude the reader. It is given sharp and direct expression by Sugar: "I think . . . that this is not much of a democracy if you ask me. Equal chance to pursue happiness means an equal crack at the dough, don't it?" (para. 51) The visit of the narrator and her friends to Fifth Avenue's FAO Schwarz — probably the most expensive toy shop in the world — under the direction of the severe Miss Moore is a lesson in the best and profoundest sense of the term, for the narrator and Sugar (at least) can never again, we may surmise, see the world as they used to. The seeming simplicity of narration conceals an impressive artfulness. In the most general way, the language of the narrator strikes one as well-nigh perfect for a bright African American child. Within her limited world, she is tough, cunning, and skeptical of anything or anyone that smacks of pretentiousness, especially the middle-class sort. More specifically, the artistry of the opening paragraph is impressive in accomplishing the necessary exposition: the narrator's disdain, her shrewd perceptions of people and events, and the vivid evocation of her neighborhood.

The climactic scene, when the children enter FAO Schwarz, is just as artfully handled. In the narrator's confused feelings, her inexplicable sense of shame and her anger at feeling shame, we see beneath the tough exterior a frightened and insecure child. She feels as much a confused outsider in this symbol of white affluence as she did when she and Sugar crashed the Catholic church. It is worth noting, incidentally, that this reference to the Catholic church is followed by and thus effectively juxtaposed with the reference to "Mama Drewery," presumably some sort of neighborhood witch lady.

The last paragraph of the story embodies fully the title's significance. Although Sugar articulates the economic awareness that the trip awakens, Miss Moore stares at the defiant Sylvia, hoping to generate a response from her brightest student. And Sylvia, refusing to publicly acknowledge that she has learned anything, privately reveals the potency of the lesson by determining to "think this day through." Sugar can "run" if she wants to, but Sylvia will become forever converted from her complacent satisfaction, because "nobody gonna beat me at nuthin."

Robert Olen Butler Jealous Husband Returns in Form of Parrot (p. 1061)

This story was published in Butler's 1996 short story collection, *Tabloid Dreams*. All the titles in the volume Butler took from actual tabloid stories, titles meant to catch our eye as a supermarket cashier rings up our purchases. Most of us would probably let out a quiet, superior chuckle at the preposterousness of these lurid headlines proclaiming events we know could never be. Butler sets himself the daring task of fashioning his stories from these titles, titles such as "Woman Uses Glass Eye to Spy on Philandering Husband," "Woman Struck by Car Turns into Nymphomaniac," "Every Man She Kisses Dies," "Help Me Find My Spaceman Lover," and "Titanic Survivors Found in Bermuda Triangle." *Tabloid Dreams* would seem to be a collection of comic stories—or farces. There is indeed a great deal of comedy in Butler's tales—but all of them are serious, as "Jealous Husband Returns in Form of Parrot" brilliantly demonstrates.

You could argue that the very conception of the story is inherently hilarious: a deceased husband, transmogrified into a parrot, is bought from a pet store by his widow, carried home (his own former home!) in a cage, where he is kept in the den (he notes that his cage sits where his pool table used to), from which, if he positions himself just right on his perch, he can see down the hallway to the master bedroom and, if his wife leaves the door open when she takes her lovers to bed, "I can see the space at the foot of the bed but not the bed itself." He can hear the sounds of lovemaking but he can't quite see. "And they drive me crazy" (para. 15). As a man, it is easy to imagine what he might have felt called upon to do. As a parrot, he can only flap his wings and squawk and fluff up. A very funny scene. The juxtaposition of the husband/parrot accounts for much of the comedy throughout. "Are you a man or a mouse?" He is neither: he is a parrot!

Butler achieves complexity using language in interesting ways. The protagonist/parrot, linguistically speaking, is a double personality, capable of thinking with the full complexity and richness of human language, but speaking only with the limited language of a parrot. Compare, for example, the hilarious scene when the parrot/husband lashes out at the "cracker" (parrot language) whom his wife has brought home (para. 23) with what we might call the many passages of interior, human language that reveal the story of a weak, jealous husband, who could never quite win the love and respect of a wife who preferred rough and rowdy men. The pathetic husband, like a character in one of Chaucer's ribald tales of sexual betrayal, who ludicrously falls out of a tree as he spies on his wife in bed with a lover. The pathetic husband who, even as a parrot, fears that the cockatoo Gordo would break his heart.

The pathos is intensified by the parrot/husband's insight into his own weaknesses and timidity. When the pain of seeing his wife bed down with other men becomes unbearable, he resolves to "to let it go" and "just fly away," in a passage that takes on a kind of poetic fervor, but ends in farce when he smashes into a window pane (para. 19).

One reader has called "Jealous Husband Returns in Form of Parrot" "one of the saddest and most disturbing stories I have ever read." There is much to be said for this judgment, especially in light of the conclusion. The moment the parrot/narrator sees his wife naked after she has finished with her latest lover, the story gathers the momentum and urgency of an epiphany. Only now, for the first time, he see his wife's vulnerability, her need for something more than he could give to the woman he always loved and still loves. He is overwhelmed by the realization that he has done something "bad," that he is a "poor baby," and, most bitterly, that he "can never say what is in my heart to her. Never." At the end, he sees himself with bitter clarity—a weak man who can never be anything else, but determined to fly "even though I know there is something between me and that place where I can be free of all these feelings. . . ."

Raymond Carver   What We Talk About When We Talk About Love   (p. 1037)

Two married couples sit drinking gin in a sunlit kitchen as they discuss the subject of love. The conversation is dominated by Mel McGinnis, a cardiologist, and focuses on his assertion that "real love was nothing less than spiritual love." His wife, Terri, challenges him to account for the kind of love exhibited by Ed, her previous lover, who physically abused her. Mel flatly rejects the possibility that love and violence could be connected. Terri insists that Ed loved her "in his own way"; Mel condescendingly responds by accusing his wife of being masochistic. The hostility between Mel and Terri gives the story its tension. Married four years, the glow of new love has clearly given way to a bit of the contempt bred by familiarity. Yet they do care for each other. One kind of love.

Nick, the narrator, and Laura, his wife of a year and a half, contribute little directly to the discourse, mostly asking questions or making brief comments. Their significant contribution to the definition of love is not in what they say but in what they do. If Mel and Terri's relationship is adversarial and their weapon irony, Nick and Laura's is nonverbal, as demonstrated by the loving physical gestures that punctuate Mel's ramblings. Another kind of love.

Early in the story, when Mel appeals to Nick and Laura to support his assertion that Ed's behavior could not be called love, Nick responds, "I think what you're saying is that love is an absolute," and Laura says, "I don't know anything about Ed, or anything about the situation. But who can judge anyone else's situation?" Perhaps the theme of the story is to be found in the implications of these comments. There can be no single, absolute definition of love. The attempt to impose such a definition is an exercise in futility—and arrogance.

Nick begins the narrative, "My friend Mel McGinnis was talking. Mel McGinnis is a cardiologist and sometimes that gives him the right." In retrospect, we can read this line as irony. Clearly, Mel does not have any superior insights about love, notwithstanding his implied claim that he does because he spent five years in a seminary. Still bothered by Terri's insistence on being at Ed's bedside when he died, he dismisses all suicides as ignorant. Utterly lacking in self-awareness, he is unable to perceive any parallel between Ed's overt violence toward Terri and his own anger toward her. Although he dominates the conversation and brooks no disagreement, he grandiosely declares, "I don't know anything, and I'm the first one to admit it."

The story of the old couple injured in the auto accident presents a particularly difficult case of love for Mel. He cannot understand why the old man would be depressed because he was unable to *see* his wife. Perhaps Mel is baffled because the act of seeing is physical and thus inconsistent with his belief that love is spiritual. Perhaps the overwhelming realness of the old couple's suffering and the intensity of the old man's depression over not being able to see his wife force Mel to realize how fatuous his pontifications about love have been.

Begun in sunlight and animated conversation, the story closes with the two couples enveloped in darkness. All of them are a little drunk, Mel no doubt more than the others, since he has been drinking the most. Unable to penetrate the mystery of love or cope with the pain of living (when Terri offers him a pill for his depression, he declines with the comment, "I've taken everything there is"), Mel transforms his depression into anger about his ex-wife.

The grim ending is underscored by what appear to be a complex set of literary allusions. When Mel suggests that maybe he won't call his children and that they should just go eat, Nick replies, "Sounds fine to me . . . Eat or not to eat. Or keep drinking, I could head right out into the sunset," seeming to echo Hamlet's famous question, "To be or not to be." Laura's response indicates that she surmises Nick's meaning. Perhaps there is even an echo here of Ernest Hemingway's Nick Adams and other Hemingway heroes, such as the old man in "A Clean, Well-Lighted Place," who bury their pain in drinking and eating. Curiously, virtually the last words uttered in the story — Terri's "Now what?" — seem to echo a celebrated line from another story narrated by a Nick, the Nick Carraway of Fitzgerald's *The Great Gatsby*. Contemplating the moral disaster of the past and the bleak future, Daisy Buchanan asks, "What'll we do with ourselves this afternoon? . . . and the day after that, and the next thirty years?" The final words of Carver's Nick seem to offer little hope for the future of love.

Kate Chopin   The Storm   (p. 992)

This story was probably written in 1898 or 1899, shortly after Chopin's remarkable novel *The Awakening* was accepted for publication. Apparently, she never tried to publish "The Storm." It is doubtful that any reputable magazine would have printed it.

Until recently, if Kate Chopin was remembered at all, she was cited as one of those local colorists who flourished during the second half of the nineteenth century and made, through their colloquial style and regional sketches, a valuable contribution to the development of literary realism. But Kate Chopin was a startlingly accomplished realist born a generation too early. Consequently, her novel was almost universally condemned for its relatively frank expression of female sensuality. The reading public of 1900 would have been scandalized by "The Storm," which now strikes one as good-natured and sensible about the possibilities of unsanctioned sexuality — sexuality that not only doesn't injure anyone but actually heightens the commitment and affection between the wives and husbands in the tale.

Perhaps, to the modern ear, the language of the sexual encounter between Calixta and Alcée, counterpointed by the obtrusive erotic melody of the storm, might seem rather hothouse and literary. But one earnestly wishes to forgive the author for that minor excess in view of the refreshing attitude toward sex she dared to express. Note that the characters are equals — the women, as much as Alcée, enjoy and profit from the encounter. None victimizes, none is victim. Calixta is delightful and charming to her apprehensive husband when he returns. Alcée urges his absent wife to extend and enjoy her vacation. And Clarisse is charmed at the extension of the vacation from conjugal life that provided the first free breath since she married. "So the storm passed," the author concludes, "and everyone was happy."

Sandra Cisneros   The House on Mango Street   (p. 147)

The family in this story is large (four children and the parents), it is Latino, and it is poor. But it is, above all, a family — bound together by a love that protected the children from the vicissitudes and strains of a childhood upset by frequent moves and the social stigma of being poor, dramatically conveyed in the nun's comments near the end of the story about the narrator's home. The family has no choice but to endure indignities and exploitation. When water pipes break in their flat, they can only flee (perhaps without paying the rent) to another house. But in spite of all, they remain a cohesive family, dreaming a dream of a better time and a better house, but always realistic about their prospects. The Mango Street house is something of a shambles, far from the dream house the family envisions, but a small step closer to that dream than the flat on Loomis. As the final paragraph makes clear, the narrator will continue to believe in the dream — but the possibilities of attaining it will be tempered by a healthy and protective sense of realism.

Stephen Crane   The Bride Comes to Yellow Sky   (p. 93)

This comical story depends for its effect on widespread awareness of some "myth of the West" that was popularly manifested at the turn of the century in countless pulp magazines, and that remains enshrined in the long tradition of motion picture westerns. Scratchy, of course, is a kind of caricature of the last of the fearless gunmen; he fights for the sheer pleasure of it (but only when drunk these days). Another remnant of that mythic western scene—Sheriff Jack Potter—provided Scratchy with his only foil. Only Potter would issue forth to meet the rampaging Scratchy, and presumably, the two of them kept alive an idea about the code that governs behavior in a wilderness unspoiled by a stifling civilization.

But from the outset, the story details the steady encroachment of the "East" on the mythic "West" of Scratchy and Potter. In the first paragraph, as the train speeds to the West, the countryside, quite logically but also symbolically, is "pouring eastward." The train is described as one of the finest products of civilization: the coach has "dazzling fittings," "sea-green figured velvet," "shining brass, silver, and glass," and "wood that gleamed as darkly brilliant as the surface of a pool of oil." The ceiling featured "frescos in olive and silver." The porters and waiters on the train recognize Potter's type and patronize him unmercifully. The epoch of which he is a tiny remnant is clearly passing. Perhaps the strongest evidence of that passing is his errand. He has married and, consequently, has made the symbolic transition from mythic fearless sheriff-gunman to settled householder. He is preoccupied, as the train moves closer to Yellow Sky, with the feeling that he has betrayed the townspeople by marrying without their permission, hence robbing them of some vaguely defined status that depended on his more innocent state.

Section two, beginning twenty-one minutes before the train is due at Yellow Sky, opens with a microcosmic society present at the Weary Gentleman saloon. Crane's description of the speaking habits of the patrons establishes a social order, and the presence of the drummer represents one more incursion of the mercantile East. When the news comes that Scratchy Wilson is once again on a drunken rampage, that sense, rather pathetic now, of a raging wild West is established. But the information makes "an obvious cleft in every skull in the room" save the stranger's. (One might pause to make some points about Crane's habitual use of extravagantly witty figurative language.) The response to the danger is hopelessly timid; those who know Scratchy either disappear or take shelter behind bolted doors and the metal-lined bar. Scratchy is looking for a fight—but no one (since Potter is out of town) is prepared to give it to him.

We meet Scratchy at the beginning of section three, but first we meet his "maroon colored flannel shirt, which had been purchased for purposes of decoration, and made principally by some Jewish women on the East Side of New York." The origin of that shirt is a devastating comment on Scratchy's romantic rage. And Scratchy finally takes that rage to the one place in town likely to respond to it, rather than wait until it flickers into sobriety. Potter's house, however, is deserted, and Scratchy turns away frustrated, until by happy accident Potter and his new bride circle the corner. The moment is saved, and it is charged with meaning. As the two men face each other, the bride becomes "a slave to hideous rites." But Potter is unarmed. Scratchy can't believe it, but so it is. And when Potter informs Scratchy that he is married, Scratchy cannot comprehend. "No!" he cries. But it is true, and rather meaningfully, Scratchy remarks slowly, "I s'pose it's all off now." Discovering the antecedent to "it" is essential. That "it" must be a complex of attitudes, a code of behavior, that takes no account of sheriffs' wives. And ". . . in the presence of this foreign condition he was a simple child of the earlier plains." There is nothing left for Scratchy as he disconsolately shuffles away through the heavy sand, the last of a breed that cannot exist without at least one other to recognize its existence.

Vijay Dan Detha   Untold Hitlers   (p. 1505)

Students may find the style of "Untold Hitlers" confusing, but the climactic event will certainly strike a chord with them. Starting discussion from the impact of the cyclist's death—and the reaction of the men on the tractor to it—could give students a place from which to begin to figure out the author's use of recurrent phrases and images as well as the sharp turn he makes in his last paragraph.

From the story's repeated insistence on the humanity of the men who go to the city to pick up their new tractor to the recurring appearance of birds of prey, the story prepares us for an event that will test the categorical division between civilized and savage. While at first students may not see this aspect of the story, framing it in terms of foreshadowing (a term taught in every high school English class) might help them think about these curious repetitions: in a way different from the typical narrative foreshadowing, this is a kind of foreshadowing by theme, transmitted through symbol.

Connecting the savage competition between the farmers and the cyclist (also foreshadowed in the back-and-forth in the tractor-dealer's office) to the horrors of genocide and slaughter may feel like a stretch to some students. One way to work with this objection is to read carefully the ways in which the author anticipates it. "This one doesn't compare," the narrator says in the penultimate paragraph, but of course it does. A brief discussion of the ways these Hitlers are "untold," as the title describes them, can also contribute to students' understanding of the author's point about the similarity of acts of savagery, large and relatively small (yet still horrifying). Finally, if time allows, it is worth talking about point of view in "Untold Hitlers," as the story makes interesting use of it, shifting subtly between characters but placing readers for most of the narrative in the ultimately uncomfortable position of identifying with killers; talking about what this strategy means for the reading experience and for the significance of the story would be an ideal place to end discussion.

Chitra Banerjee Divakaruni   Mrs. Dutta Writes a Letter   (p. 752)

The opening paragraph of this story is a model of story-telling skill. In describing an action, Mrs. Dutta's reaction to her alarm going off, Divakaruni tells us much about her main character: she is a woman trapped in a life she cannot adjust to. Two months into this life of apparent ease and comfort provided by her son and daughter-in-law, she cannot sleep well. When she finally manages to silence the fallen alarm clock, she hears herself breathing, "a sound harsh and uneven and full of guilt" (para. 1).

Despite her own ambivalence and the doubts of her friend, Mrs. Basu (as we learn in the flashback midway through the story), Mrs. Dutta, driven by the ancient wisdom that "blood is blood," has yielded to her son's entreaties and moved from her native Calcutta to Sunnyvale, California, to be cared for in her old age. As the narrative slowly unfolds, we come to learn the source of Mrs. Dutta's sleeplessness and guilt. Removed from her native land to a strange and profoundly different culture, she begins to wither like a vine transplanted to inhospitable soil. Every custom, every belief about family relationships—everything that is bone-deep in her—is dramatically different in this new, alien culture. But she clings to her cultural practices and beliefs—what else can she do?—and so sets herself on a course that disrupts her new and westernized family. Mrs. Dutta's points of reference and comparison are all to the culture she has left behind, including her "uneasy pride" in a daughter-in-law who, unlike Mrs. Dutta herself, is fair enough to "pass for an American" and who reads the *Wall Street Journal* (para. 6).

The passage in which Mrs. Dutta reflects on the different meanings of illness powerfully suggests how deeply and inescapably she is dominated by her old world culture. In Calcutta, she remained "the center of the household" even when she was ill in bed. Illness brought with it a satisfying reaffirmation of her importance to the family. In Sunnyvale, by contrast, no one was inconvenienced by her falling ill. "There was, therefore," she realized, "no reason for her to get well" (para. 32).

The narrative moves very slowly, punctuated by Mrs. Dutta's "mind letter" to her friend, which charts the changes the accumulating details of her distress and doubts are creating. Her early drafts have all the optimism and cheery conviction one would expect under the circumstances. After such a momentous move, it is not easy to admit to doubts, especially to her best friend who herself questioned the wisdom of the choice. The climax occurs near the end when Mrs. Dutta overhears the argument between her son and daughter-in-law. She cannot see the family from the corridor where she is standing, only "their shadows—enormous against the wall where the table lamp has cast them . . ." (para. 106). She is shocked, of course, to hear that her presence is threatening to destroy the family. More shocking yet, however, is the final image: "All the shadows on the wall shiver and merge into a single dark silhouette." She "stares at the silhouette, the solidarity of it" (para. 117). It is an epiphany, a sudden realization that she has glimpsed a "solidarity" that excludes her.

The denouement is the final version of the letter she has been struggling to write. She need not worry whether it is blotched with tears, because this letter contains no pretence. It is true and honest. Whatever the letter means — Mrs. Dutta herself concedes that she cannot define "happiness" and "love" — she does know that the reasons that led to her give up her home and move to America were simplistic and naive. She knows also that only in her native land will she have any chance of discovering happiness and love.

Students might want to look at the possibility that one dimension of the story involves a competition between a mother and a daughter-in-law for control. Certainly, Shyamoli resents her mother-in-law's attempts to control the kitchen and the laundry as threats to her prerogatives as wife and mother. And while it might be argued that the struggle is not conscious on Mrs. Dutta's part, it remains central to the cultural conflict the story is about. Furthermore, Mrs. Dutta's attempts to exercise parental control over her married son (addressing him by his childhood nickname, for example) might be viewed by her daughter-in-law as threatening.

Harlan Ellison   "Repent, Harlequin!" Said the Ticktockman
(p. 429)

Over the centuries, scores of dreamers have published their blueprints for the perfect society when humans will finally achieve unalloyed happiness. It is in our own time, however, that modern science and technology seem to have placed that dream within reach. It is also in our own time that the most noteworthy anti-utopian works have been written. Extrapolating from the present, anti-utopian writers have created not the future they desire but the future that seems inevitably contained in the present.

The passage from Thoreau's essay (published in 1849) is, as the narrator of "Ticktockman" says, "the heart of it." Watching America become a mass urban society driven by a sense of manifest destiny and an uncritical commitment to bigness and progress, Thoreau insisted always on asking the question, "What is it all about?" "Men think that it is essential that the Nation have commerce," Thoreau wrote in *Walden* (1859), "and export ice, and talk through a telegraph, and ride thirty miles an hour, without a doubt, whether *they* do or not; but whether we should live like baboons or like men, is a little uncertain.' "Ticktockman" creates the society that Thoreau warned against, where the state has assumed virtually absolute power not only over the external affairs of its citizens but over their minds as well. It is an antiseptically and clinically efficient society in which means have been grotesquely transformed into ends and people into machines.

But even in such a society, the state is in danger because, while it may achieve near total control over the minds and affairs of the citizens, the impulse to question, to resist, to rebel is finally inextinguishable. In a *human* society, the Harlequin's escapades would be insignificant, "but in a society where the single driving force was order and unity and promptness and clocklike precision and attention to the clock, reverence of the gods of the passage of time, it was a disaster of major importance."

The Ticktockman, with all the sophisticated technological devices of the state at his disposal, finally captures the Harlequin and forces him, by some nameless techniques, to recant publicly. The totalitarian state triumphs — almost. For the final irony is that the great Ticktockman himself, compelled to deal with the disruptive rebel, commits the greatest sin possible in the society he dominates: He arrives late for work.

The structure of "Ticktockman" is simple but effective. The passage from Thoreau defines the issue and establishes the narrator's point of view as the context for the present action ("the middle"). The story then moves to "the beginning," providing brief scenes from an earlier time (i.e., our contemporary society) that explain how the world of the Ticktockman was able to develop. We are then returned to present action and the story concludes. This structure allows for maximum dramatic effect at the outset and yet makes it clear that the imagined world of the Ticktockman develops predictably out of the real world we live in.

The very banality of the Harlequin's name, Everett C. Marm, as well as the diffidence and weakness he exhibits in the scene with Pretty Alice, suggests that the Harlequin is simply an ordinary and nondescript human being—not a larger-than-life hero who has decided to assert his humanity. At the end, he has the courage to defy the Ticktockman by telling him to "get stuffed," but the scene immediately following describes his breakdown and recantation. This characterization of the Harlequin is central to the story's meaning: even in a thoroughly totalitarian society, the spirit of resistance and rebellion survives in ordinary people.

William Faulkner   A Rose for Emily   (p. 696)

Emily, daughter of the genteel but decayed Grierson family, is dominated by a tyrannical father until she is thirty years old. His leitmotif is the bullwhip he holds curled in his hand, with Emily somewhat to the rear. Doubtless the bullwhip intimidated a number of would-be suitors.

The story is told by a vague, disembodied "we," which seems to stand for the community and the complex set of moral imperatives that represented social order in the late nineteenth- and early twentieth-century South. The "we" voice seems to know everything that goes on in town—Emily's every act instantly becomes common knowledge.

The chronology of the narrative embodies Faulkner's typical and artful disorder. The story begins with Emily's funeral, and ends a short time later when "we" enter the closed-off room and discover the gruesome secret of the Grierson house. Now we know the source of the smell; now we know the reason for the arsenic; and, above all, now we understand Emily's eccentric rejection of all the town's approaches. But between the first and fifth sections, the narrative ranges through various periods in Emily's life, and we watch her suffer the fate of either her own or her father's exquisite choosiness. She is thirty years old at her father's death; the bloom of youth is faded. We may appreciate what it cost her to abandon her pride and go courting with Homer Barron—a Yankee, a vulgar construction foreman. But her need to be fulfilled—to be a wife and mother (so Faulkner tells us in interviews; see F. L. Gwynn and J. L. Blotner, eds., *Faulkner in the University,* University of Virginia Press, 1959)—is more powerful than her concern with what the town will think. The town, of course, thinks the worst—that Emily is sleeping with the Yankee (remember, this occurs about 1886)—and insists that something be done. Her distant relatives are sent for; the Baptist minister is forced to visit in order to set things right. Neither social force works. (We are told that the minister never went back—it would have been wonderful to listen in on the desperate conversation—his fumbling insinuations, her haughty and masterful rejection of his intrusion into her personal life. Faulkner leaves all that to the reader's imagination.)

And when, after all that Emily endured—her own sense of Homer's unsuitability, the appearance of cousins determined to save her from herself, the outrageous intrusion of the minister, the whole town's disapprobation—when, after all this, Homer declares (as he must have done) that their affair is over, is it unreasonable that Emily finally snaps? This time, she will have *her* way. Homer *will* stay with her, sleep with her.

Emily was born thirty years before her father's death, which occurred sometime before 1894, and dies at seventy-four. From before the Civil War through about World War II, Faulkner's fictional world was dominated by a kind of feudal nobility—the Sartoris family, the Stevens family (who turn up in the Yoknapatawpha saga along with the other nobles, the DeSpains and the Compsons). The mayor of Jefferson, Colonel Sartoris, mindful of her straitened circumstances, remitted Emily's taxes. It was illegal, but noblesse oblige. An earlier mayor, Judge Stevens, cannot bring himself to "accuse a lady to her face of smelling bad." This sort of chivalric behavior is scorned by the new people who attempt a more egalitarian stance. But Emily systematically faces them down. Even the poor druggist, who sells her the arsenic, quails before her aristocratic stare when he asks her how she intends to use it. Like the minister, he does not return to face her—he has the poison delivered. The "we" narrating the story is

fully aware of the aristocratic pretensions of the Grierson family—their upper-crusti-
ness is a prime factor in Emily's spinsterhood, and contributes the spice to the spectacle of her riding out with a Yankee construction worker.

The story was published in 1931, the same year as "Dry September" in which
Faulkner examines the character of Minnie Cooper—another neurasthenic spinster—
who regains the town's interest by accusing an innocent black man of raping her.
Both Minnie and Emily were of relatively good stock, an important consideration in
Faulkner's world. Their failure to flourish allows the townsfolk the luxury of feeling
sorry for them—surely the most galling of all perceptions. In both stories, the embittered women repair their own self-esteem by causing the death of a man.

Charlotte Perkins Gilman The Yellow Wallpaper (p. 997)

Like many of Poe's horror stories, with which Gilman's story has often been compared,
"The Yellow Wallpaper" is a study of a descent into madness. But whereas motives in
Poe's stories are often vague and mysterious or entirely personal, as in the case of
"The Cask of Amontillado," Gilman's is clear in assigning a social cause to her protag-
onist's disintegration: the suffocating role a patriarchal society imposes on women.

Patriarchal values are so deeply embedded in the narrator's psyche that she is
unable to recognize what is happening to her. Incapable of openly rebelling (as, say,
Edna Pointellier does in Kate Chopin's 1899 *The Awakening*, a novel on a similar
theme), Gilman's narrator turns her anger inward. Throughout her narrative, she
blames herself and constantly worries about discommoding her husband.

Both husband and physician, John is a potent representative of the oppressive
patriarchy. He attributes her nervous condition to her writing, an activity too stren-
uous for the frail mind of a female. He refuses to change the wallpaper that disturbs
her because "nothing was worse for a nervous patient than to give way to such fan-
cies" (para. 49). Impervious to the reality of his wife's condition, caught up in the
male arrogance that he knows what's best, John is unable to see what is happening to
his wife.

That descent is powerfully conveyed through the narrator's descriptions of the
wallpaper. Early on, she says that the curves on the wallpaper "suddenly commit suicide . . . and destroy themselves in unheard-of contradictions" (para. 33), this last
phrase an apt metaphor for her life. Later, the wallpaper seems to have no design; it is
a collection of "bloated curves," "columns of fatuity," an "optic horror" that dissolves
into "confusion" (paras. 96–99). From one of her windows she sees a garden that,
with its "deep-shaded arbors, the riotous old-fashioned flowers, and bushes and
gnarly trees" (para. 57), seems to symbolize an unfettered freedom to grow, which
she yearns for (a comparison of this garden with the immaculately designed and man-
icured garden in Amy Lowell's poem "Patterns" provides an opportunity to show
how the same "object," a garden, can function in very different ways as a symbol). As
she fantasizes the death of her husband at the end, we understand, in Emily Dickinson's words, that "Much madness is Divinest sense." Unable to directly confront John,
on the one hand, and unable, like John's sister, to believe in and accept the patriarchy's
values, the narrator "saves" herself through madness.

Below is reprinted an essay Gilman wrote in 1913 explaining the connection of
the story to her own life. It is an interesting piece for many reasons, not the least in
suggesting how an author uses autobiography for her art.

Why I Wrote "The Yellow Wallpaper"?

> Many and many a reader has asked that. When the story first came out,
> in the *New England Magazine* about 1891, a Boston physician made protest in
> *The Transcript*. Such a story ought not to be written, he said; it was enough
> to drive anyone mad to read it. Another physician, in Kansas I think, wrote
> to say that it was the best description of incipient insanity he had ever seen,
> and begging my pardon had I been there? Now the story of the story is this:
> For many years I suffered from a severe and continuous nervous breakdown
> tending to melancholia—and beyond. During about the third year of this
> trouble I went, in devout faith and some faint stir of hope, to a noted spe-

cialist, in nervous diseases, the best known in the country. This wise man put me to bed and applied the rest cure, to which a still good physique responded so promptly that he concluded there was nothing much the matter with me, and sent me home with solemn advice to "live as domestic a life as far as possible," to "have but two hours' intellectual life a day," and "never to touch pen, brush or pencil again as long as I lived." This was in 1887.

I went home and obeyed those directions for some three months, and came so near the borderline of utter mental ruin that I could see over.

Then, using the remnants of intelligence that remained, and helped by a wise friend, I cast the noted specialist's advice to the winds and went to work again — work, the normal life of every human being; work, in which is joy and growth and service, without which one is a pauper and a parasite; ultimately recovering some measure of power.

Being naturally moved to rejoicing by this narrow escape, I wrote "The Yellow Wallpaper," with its embellishments and additions to carry out the ideal (I never had hallucinations or objections to my mural decorations) and sent a copy to the physician who so nearly drove me mad. He never acknowledged it.

The little book is valued by alienists and as a good specimen of one kind of literature. It has to my knowledge saved one woman from a similar fate — so terrifying her family that they let her out into normal activity and she recovered.

But the best result is this. Many years later I was told that the great specialist had admitted to friends of his that he had altered his treatment of neurasthenia since reading "The Yellow Wallpaper."

It was not intended to drive people crazy, but to save people from being driven crazy, and it worked.

Nathaniel Hawthorne Young Goodman Brown (p. 82)

A good way to begin a discussion of this story is to explain briefly a fundamental tenet of Christian theology that underlies Hawthorne's vision. It is illustrated in the Old Testament story told in Genesis of how Adam and Eve, tempted by the serpent, disobeyed God and ate the forbidden fruit of the tree of knowledge of good and evil and thereby lost their primal innocence and happiness. Expelled from paradise into the world of toil, pain, and mortality, humankind henceforth lived in a state of sin until it was redeemed by the incarnation and sacrificial death of Jesus. Integral to this account is the belief that sin arose through free human agency, through the exercise of Adam and Eve's (and all their descendants') free will. For Christians, then, everyone is tainted by evil, freely chosen, but is capable of goodness and redemption. Young Goodman Brown is brought to grief because his experience in the forest overwhelms and destroys his faith.

The story opens at dusk as Brown bids good-bye to Faith, his wife of three months, as he sets off on a mysterious journey that will keep him away until morning. As he proceeds, the ordinary world of Salem gives way to the nighttime gloom of the forest, and the reality and innocence that Faith represents to Brown give way to ambiguities, doubts, and growing terror. He meets a traveler who looks like his father and carries a staff that "bore the likeness of a great blacksnake." The stranger says he has known all Puritan families, and once helped Brown's father and grandfather, even though Hawthorne tells us he looked "about fifty years old." It should be noted that the acts he helped in — publicly whipping a Quaker woman and setting fire to an Indian village — epitomize the religious intolerance and cruelty Hawthorne often associated with the Puritans. In this connection, it is also worth noting that Salem was the site of the notorious witchcraft trials in the 1690s, which resulted in the hanging, torture, and imprisonment of many citizens.

The dreamlike atmosphere intensifies, and by the time Brown sees Goody Cloyse and the other respected, pious citizens of Salem and overhears the conversation between the minister and Deacon Gookin, Brown becomes aware of the monstrousness of the errand he is on. When Faith's pink ribbons flutter down, he declares that "my faith is gone," convinced now that the world belongs only to Satan. Crazed with this knowledge, he rushes in a frenzy, blaspheming and raging, until he bursts forth upon the electrifying scene. Assembled into a single congregation before him are all the citizens of Salem, waiting for their minister. Standing on a rock before them, surrounded by four blazing pine trees, Satan delivers an extraordinary sermon that brings Brown's journey (and the story) to a climax. He then welcomes Brown and Faith into the communion of evil. No sooner does Brown call upon Faith to resist than the nightmare ends. It is morning and he returns to Salem.

The final three paragraphs bring the story quickly to an end. The function of the first of these paragraphs is twofold: to return Brown to the ordinary world in which the story opened (note the realistic specificity) and to prepare us for the final paragraph, in which the lasting and corrosive effects of the night are revealed. But before we come to that final summation of Brown's life, Hawthorne asks (as his readers no doubt will): "Had Goodman Brown fallen asleep in the forest and only dreamed a wild dream of a witch-meeting?" Hawthorne dismisses the question with "be it so if you will . . .," thereby making it clear that the story is about the inner world of Brown rather than the objective world of fact.

The concluding paragraph reveals the appalling truth about Brown's experience. He has confronted, as surely everyone must at one time or another, what Melville called "that great power of blackness" and is forever after dominated by its effects. Having been shown by Satan "the whole earth one stain of guilt, one mighty blood spot," he never for a moment questions the truth of his vision. Indeed, for Brown his vision is reality, and it slowly consumes his heart away.

Brown (like many other Hawthorne protagonists) has become the prisoner of a dehumanizing partial vision. He is so overwhelmed by this vision he can no longer accept what his own Christian doctrine teaches him: that humankind, while fallen and inherently evil, is made in the image of God and is next to the angels in the hierarchy of being. He turns pale when he hears the minister speak "of saint-like lives and triumphant deaths, of future bliss or misery unutterable" and so loses sight of those admirable human traits Hawthorne so often associates with the heart. Brown's heart disintegrates in a prison of gloomy despair and distrust where the hope and affirmation offered by saintly lives and triumphant deaths cannot penetrate. The pall of Brown's denial settles upon his entire family. He shrinks from Faith, who lovingly asked her husband not to leave on that fateful night, who skipped in joy and "almost kissed her husband on his return"; children and grandchildren bring neither joy nor innocence into his life. The final paragraph turns the remainder of Brown's long life into a sharply focused denouement, describing a man who loses his faith in humanity and thus in himself.

This story is a good one for discussing some important literary and technical matters. For example, students can be asked to speculate on why Hawthorne chose a nonrealistic narrative technique. One advantage, of course, is that it allows him to describe, in a single, terrifying night, an overwhelming vision of evil that realism could not accommodate. A protagonist in a realistic narrative might be brought to the same dark pessimism and despair as Brown, but it would require a very long narrative to make the change credible.

The story also affords good opportunities to discuss allegory and symbolism, the differences between them, and the way in which a great writer might use both (as Malamud also does in "Idiots First"). The name of Brown's wife, Faith, is obviously allegorical. "Faith" can almost always be read "my religious beliefs." On the other hand, the pervasive ambiguity in the story, particularly evident in Faith's pink ribbons, suggests the complexity of symbolism. In fact, the most persuasive argument against labeling it an allegory is the great number of varying interpretations the story has elicited.

Bessie Head   Looking for a Rain God   (p. 1354)

This story is based on an incident reported in a local newspaper. You might begin by asking students to characterize the economic lives of the characters. Obviously, they, and most of their fellow villagers, are subsistence farmers. What is likely to happen in south-central African societies when the crops fail? How do the social systems of such societies differ from those of modern western Europe and North America? Given the lengthy drought, is it absurd for this family to attempt to bribe a rain god? How, after all, can humans control nature? Their prayers were not effective. With their survival at stake, are they justified in seeking a more forceful method for controlling the rain? Many societies used sacrificial offerings to propitiate powerful forces. Some students may have read Shirley Jackson's "The Lottery" or Leslie Marmon Silko's "The Man to Send Rain Clouds" (in which the Christian funeral of an elderly Native American is combined with traditional Native American fertility rites designed to invoke rain). Others may be aware of anthropologist Sir James Frazer's study of "primitive" magic and religion, *The Golden Bough*. The Bible embodies several accounts of human sacrifice, notably the story of Abraham and Isaac (Genesis 22, where the sacrifice is averted by substitution of an animal) and the story of Jephthah and his daughter (Judges 11). The sacrificial and redemptive death of Jesus is Christianity's central thesis. In this context, is the sacrifice of the children wholly grotesque? And is the execution of the men a reasonable and sensible response?

We experience the children through a description of their games—they mother their dolls by constantly punishing them, an ironic insight into the texture of their own "good-for-nothing" lives. But their ironic preparation for assuming their own positions as village mothers proves futile. They are apparently good for something after all.

Ernest Hemingway   A Clean, Well-Lighted Place   (p. 107)

In "A Natural History of the Dead," Hemingway recalls the question asked by the explorer Mungo Park when, lost in the desert, he came upon a tiny plant: "Can that Being who planted, watered and brought to perfection, in this obscure part of the world, a thing which appears of so small importance, look with unconcern upon the situation and suffering of creatures formed after his own image?" Park's—and Hemingway's—answer was "surely not." "A Clean, Well-Lighted Place" reverses that response or, perhaps more accurately, renders the question irrelevant. There is no Being, benevolent or otherwise, to give the universe order. There is only nothing—not even "fear or dread."

This is what the old man and the old waiter know, and what the younger waiter does not know (because he has not lived long enough yet?). But even in a universe stripped of meaning, man needs to find order. As the older waiter recognizes, the old man finds that order and a sense of his own dignity at night in the clean, well-lighted café, itself an appropriate symbol of created meaning in a dark universe. The waiter's compassionate admiration for, and sense of kinship with, the old man is based upon a recognition that the old man has faced and accepted that true sense of nothingness that goes beyond fear and dread. For fear and dread imply uncertainty, an agitation of the soul, a response of the body and spirit to possibilities within or things outside. When those possibilities have ceased to exist, there remains only silence (the old man is deaf) and the need, in the dark of night, for light "and a certain cleanness and order."

Note Hemingway's use of the tacit in discussion of the old man's suicide attempt. By specifically eliminating one reason to commit suicide, the author creates in the mind of the reader a menacing host of dark and amorphous reasons for suicide that could never be successfully detailed.

Pam Houston   How to Talk to a Hunter   (p. 1075)

The collection in which this story appears is titled *Cowboys Are My Weakness*. The hunter in this story is one kind of cowboy—a macho, predatory male. The theme is clear enough, most succinctly described by the narrator's best friend when she says, "They lie to us, they cheat on us, and we love them the more for it." Since the story deals with a subject much discussed in many recent books and feminist forums, it is likely that students will want to focus on whether or not the story generalizes accurately and fairly: Is the relationship between the hunter and the narrator a common one? Is the characterization of the hunter as a liar and manipulator who will say anything to get laid a libel on all men? Or is such a charge unfair on the grounds that the author has created a specific individual, not a representative of a class? Likewise, should we view the narrator as unreliable, a bit self-serving?

Houston has consciously made certain choices about specifically technical matters in order to give the story a generalizing force: (1) neither the hunter nor the narrator is ever named, and (2) the prevailing tense is the future, conveying the sense that the specifics the narrator describes ("he'll give you a key . . .," "The next two hours he'll devote to your body . . .") are merely synecdoches for the narrator's (and many women's) common experiences with men. The future tense also creates a tone of predictive authority.

Readers may differ on the narrator's reliability. The hunter (and his sympathizers) might challenge her veracity and perceptions with the argument, "What do you expect from a rejected female?" The artistry of the story would lead us to argue otherwise. For one thing, the narrator has a certain distance and objectivity, evident in her sardonic humor and in her frequent admission that, in effect, she should know better than to believe what the hunter tells her. She is aware of his tricks and his lies on the concrete, personal level: his evasiveness about the answering machine and his crafty manipulation of language so as to avoid "using a gender-determining pronoun." Moreover, she has her "best female friend" to remind her what heels men are, as well as her "best male friend" to tell her essentially (but approvingly) the same thing. And, of course, she has the various bromides from college textbooks that elevate the learned behavior of the hunter (the male) to the level of genetic determinism: "A man desires the satisfaction of his desire; a woman desires the condition of desiring." She knows, rationally, that "love means letting go of fear" and that Patty Coyote, like the "mule deer" on the hunter's wall, "shares more with this hunter than you ever will." But there is nothing rational about the narrator's pursuit of the hunter. It is absurd that, knowing what she does, she participates so willingly and thrillingly in the final seduction. But the absurdity, of course, is *her* perception, for she after all is telling the story. It is she who imagines the scene's end, likening herself to her dog howling on a frozen night, "chained and lonely and cold."

Students should be urged to read the biographical note on Houston because the story is so clearly autobiographical. A couple of statements by Houston make the point even clearer. In the "Contributors' Notes" to *The Best American Short Stories: 1990*, Houston wrote:

> The first paragraph of "How to Talk to a Hunter" started out as a poem, which is one of the things that makes it different from all my other stories. I don't write poetry, so I was very surprised when it came out that way, and for half a second I thought maybe I could write poetry after all, but then I came to my senses and turned it into a story.
>
> Another thing that makes "Hunter" different from all my other stories is that it came to me all in a rush, ten straight hours at the computer, and after those first ten hours I never changed a word. I think that's mainly because it came out of my life's first moment of real desperation. I actually wrote the thing on Christmas Day. It is a story so frighteningly close to my own structures of fear and pain and need that I had to write in the second person, even though (and also because) second person is the most transparent disguise.
>
> Now what I like about the story is the rhythm the second person created, the cadence, the sound. I consider "Hunter" to be my gift from the great writing gods, and I know the whole thing by heart. I probably shouldn't admit this, but sometimes when I'm driving up the canyon late at night I recite it to the empty car.

Asked to define *cowboy* by a newspaper interviewer in 1992, she replied:

> This talk show host in Portland, Ore., asked me that. He brought in these five big, strapping guys and asked me to choose the *real* cowboy. I asked Cowboy No. 1, "What do you love?" He said,"I love my horse, ma'am." Cowboy No. 2 loved the rodeo. Cowboy No. 3 loved his horse and the rodeo, which left Cowboy No. 4 with nothing new to say. Cowboy No. 5 said he *liked* a lot of things. I chose him. He was the only one who couldn't use the word "love" in a sentence.

In the same interview, she explained one of the reasons she pursued outdoor and often dangerous activities: "You think I spent three summers leading hunters through Alaska because I like watching guys like David Duke shoot sheep? No. It was because if I didn't go with my boyfriend, somebody else would. I wanted to win."

Yu Hua   Appendix   (p. 354)

"Appendix" is a startling story. It is marked by a sudden turn of events and shift in tone. Helping students recognize the movement of the story—the reason the bottom seems to drop out of it—is crucial to helping them understand the significance of the moment it dramatizes to the narrator.

While the events that make up the plot of "Appendix" are far from typical, the kind of moment the story relates—the moment when a child realizes a parent is fallible and that the world is a dangerous place not just for children but for adults as well—is far more universal. The dramatization of this shared event in this specific story is sharpened by the suddenness of the turn that leads to the moment of realization. When the narrator realizes that his father is not "the strongest and most wonderful man" (para. 30)—when he sees that his father will not operate on himself as the heroic British surgeon did but instead, weeping, begs his sons to go get their mother—the sudden shift in his picture of the world is devastating. It destroys not just the narrator's picture of his father, who literally shrinks before his eyes, but his picture of their relationship and of himself. He is no longer a beloved son but becomes, instead, an appendix, a useless appendage, his father notes in the story's last line, that can kill you.

The movement from innocence to experience is connected in "Appendix" to the power of stories. The boys' sense of their father as hero is fueled by the story of the heroic surgeon who operates on himself, as the father says he would if he had to. However, the world's danger is downplayed in the story the father tells: an appendix can turn on you, but his story seems to say that heroes can handle moments like that. What the boys learn is that sometimes heroes fail. "Appendix," in the structure of its plot and concomitant shift in tone, dramatizes the impact of that recognition. The power of stories here is double-edged: they can shape attitudes, but they can also obscure realities. An important reality of experience—that the world is filled with dangers that people can't always heroically face down—is antithetical to the innocents' belief in the rightness and fairness of the world and in their own safety. That we are all in a way fatherless and unprotected—"bastards," in the father's term—is, according to "Appendix," something we all have to learn.

Shirley Jackson   The Lottery   (p. 416)

In formal terms, the impact of the story largely depends on the contrast between the holiday picnic atmosphere and the horrifying conclusion. Though the characters are rather flat, they speak for a variety of viewpoints: the rigid orthodoxy of Old Man Warner; the liberal, but dutiful, views of Mr. Summers, who can bend the ritualistic rules somewhat but never questions the value of the ritual; the ineffectual radicalism of Mr. and Mrs. Adams, who point out that some communities are thinking of giving up the lottery but do nothing to change their own community. As has been pointed out, the people of the village, through their acquiescent attitudes, are collectively the story's protagonist. Their mindless repetition of a traditional sacrifice, the efficacy of which and authority for which have been almost completely lost in antiquity, may be read as a satirical indictment of similar communal behavior in the face of less dramatic circumstances. Consider modern attitudes toward illegitimate birth, for example, or consider the sorts of social condemnation that one finds in letters written to newspaper advice columns.

This story is often referred to as a "scapegoat" story, but that seems unjustified by the events. There is no indication that the community's sins are expiated by the death of the sacrificial victim. The one particularly religious remark made by Old Man Warner, "'Lottery in June, corn be heavy soon,'" suggests that the rite is designed to guarantee fertility and is related somewhat to those sacrificial rituals that Sir James Frazer describes in *The Golden Bough*. Of course, fertility may very well depend on the ritual cleansing of the community from all sin, but the sacrifice, often human in ancient tradition (and some modern traditions as well), to ensure fertility is somewhat different. As a matter of note, some form of lottery (called *urim* and *thummim*) was used to inquire of God in the Hebrew Bible, and on one occasion (Joshua, chapter 7) was used to discover the identity of a transgressor, who was then put to death in order to free the community from the consequences of his sin.

James Joyce   Araby   (p. 102)

See the section "Reading Fiction," beginning on p. 6 of the anthology.

Franz Kafka   A Hunger Artist   (p. 398)

Whether the story is about religion or art (many modern artists have made a religion of art), it clearly embodies a fundamental dualism of matter vs. mind or body vs. soul; the artist represents mind or soul, and the impresario, the public, and, finally, the panther all represent the body. In his heyday, the hunger artist, in the grip of a vision like a writer or a religious martyr (and we note that his longest fast, like Moses' and Christ's, is forty days), is a commercial resource for the impresario and a spectacle to be scorned and disbelieved by the public. When the great change in public taste occurs, he becomes a minor diversion between more interesting events in a circus, even though his own vision and fasting ability remain unchanged. Finally, the hunger artist dies virtually unnoticed and is replaced by the panther, who—in his energy, physicalness, and "joy of life"—represents the very antithesis of the hunger artist.

But the story is complex. Possessed and consumed by a vision that the world exploits and cruelly jeers at, the artist is both pained and contemptuous that anyone could think he might cheat. He is doomed to be "the sole satisfied spectator of his own fast." And yet he remains dissatisfied, as if in dim recognition that the meaning his performance has for himself is inseparable from the interpretation his fellow human beings make of it. The strength of his artistry can compel people to look at him, but nothing he can do can compel them to grant him what he needs: understanding. The hunger artist is trapped in a bitter paradox: He is asking that life or society understand and honor non-life and death. The story explores, richly and ambiguously, the complex relationship between the artist (that is, any man consumed by a vision) and the world around him. Paradoxically, the very vision that cuts the artist off from life is what the artist offers to life. There is something sad in the death of the man of spirit and vision and something brutal in the exuberant and unthinking physicalness of the panther that replaces him.

The elaborate ceremony that caps the artist's greatest performance epitomizes the contrast between the artist and the public. When the public pays him its highest tribute, it understands him least. And these are the moments when he feels closest to "a performance beyond human imagination." The public alienation from him is emphasized when the fashionable young lady into whose arms the artist faints does all she can "to keep her face at least free from contact with the artist."

The symbolism of the cage is perhaps obvious enough, representing the imperfect isolation of the artist from the rest of the world. Ironically, the world restrains in a cage both the extreme of spirituality (the artist) and the extreme of physicalness (the panther).

Many critics see in Kafka's isolated and alienated heroes a reflection of his own life as a Jew in gentile Austria, his estrangement from his own domineering father, his tuberculosis, and his inability to sustain himself as an artist in a commercial society.

Jamaica Kincaid   Girl   (p. 750)

This single-paragraph story appeared in Kincaid's first book, *At the Bottom of the River* (1978), a collection based upon her childhood on the tiny island of Antigua in the West Indies. A mother is attempting to teach her daughter the essential rules a woman must learn if she is to find a future husband. In a tone sometimes solicitous but always didactic, the mother's rules and admonitions give the reader a richly detailed picture of a patriarchal society in which women must fashion themselves into packages attractive to men. There are numerous dos and don'ts a girl must learn—above all, that she must not behave in ways that will bring her the reputation of a "slut." "[Y]ou are not a boy," the mother sternly reminds her daughter. The implication seems to be not so much that the daughter misbehaves in the many ways her mother thinks she does; the daughter's denial seems to ring true. It seems more likely that the mother is reacting to a rebellious child who is determined to exercise some of the freedoms that boys enjoy. Learn the ways of women in our culture, guard your virginity and you will win a husband. Otherwise you will become unclean, the kind of woman a baker will not let near the bread.

Formally, the piece seems almost a dramatic monologue, except the girl does respond. The nearly uninterrupted flow of the mother's speech also seems to suggest a stream of consciousness, with the lilting cadences, parallelisms, and repetitions giving it structure and coherence.

D. H. Lawrence   The Horse Dealer's Daughter   (p. 1010)

As he frequently does in his work, Lawrence here emphasizes animality: Joe would marry, go into harness, be a subject animal; all the members of the family possessed a "curious sullen animal pride"; the horses pass "planting their great hoofs floutingly in the fine black mud, swinging their great rounded haunches sumptuously." And Mabel simply refuses to participate in the family's rational attempt to settle things. She will not answer questions about her intentions, and she is twice characterized as "mindless and persistent." She has few options. She can impose herself on her sister Lucy as a poor relation, or she can go for skivy, that is, become a servant girl. Neither of these is a viable mode for the sullen Mabel, so she chooses death.

This story is also the story of Jack Fergusson. He too is living in circumstances that are not viable. The dominant imagery of the story until its climax is the imagery of death, grayness, desolation, sickness, hopelessness. Jack is suffering from a bad cold as he tends his impoverished patients; he is losing, with the departure of the Pervins, his only resource of friendship; his sexual energies are dissipated on prostitutes. These two desolate lives, Jack and Mabel, come together at the pond.

Lawrence had originally entitled this story "The Miracle," thus pointing at the central event and its consequences. Mabel walks into the pond to kill herself, the physical description of the pond emphasizing its deathly nature. Jack, in great fear, walks into the pond to save Mabel, but slips under the deadly water himself. He recovers and delivers (literally and figuratively) Mabel and himself from the waters. It is difficult to avoid the symbolic nature of the event; the waters serve to kill Mabel and Jack and then serve as a sort of womb from which they are reborn into a new life.

The new life begins not with rational considerations but with a sort of animal passion. When Jack speaks to Mabel before the fire, "his life came back in him, dark and unknowing." "His will seemed to have gone to sleep." And he is powerless to withstand the erotic force of Mabel and the situation. "He looked down at the tangled wet hair, the wild, bare, animal shoulders." He had "no intention of loving her." But his intentions, his rational aspect, do not control here, and "With an inward groan he gave way, and let his heart yield towards her."

Although most of the story is realistically styled, Lawrence resorts to some breathtaking clichés at the end. One wonders whether he has lost control, or perhaps some ironic design, or whether the cliché is so submerged that it passes unnoticed. Consider these lines: "She lifted her face to him, and he bent forward and kissed her on the mouth, gently, with the one kiss that is an eternal pledge. As he kissed her his heart strained again in his breast. He never intended to love her. But now it was over. He had crossed over the gulf to her, and all that he had left behind had shrivelled and become void." And from time to time in the pages following, the tone seems painfully close to pulp magazine sentiment. The quality of the writing here might be used as the basis for a discussion of the difficulty of writing realistic love scenes. It might be a considerable challenge to locate any realistically rendered love scene in all of western literature, largely because the conversation of lovers is remarkably banal to those who overhear it.

Ursula K. Le Guin   The Ones Who Walk Away from Omelas
(p. 423)

This story is often categorized as science fiction, principally because Le Guin is a noted science-fiction writer. But in what sense does this story depend upon any of the usual characteristics of science fiction and fantasy? There are no futuristic machines, no supernatural manifestations, not even any remarkable events.

The author, in her headnote to the story (from *The Wind's Twelve Quarters* [New York: Harper & Row, 1975]), explains that the central idea for "this psychomyth, the scapegoat," came from an essay by William James, "The Moral Philosopher and the Moral Life." She concludes that headnote as follows: "Of course, I didn't read James and sit down and say, Now I'll write a story about that 'lost soul.' It seldom works that simply. I sat down and started a story, just because I felt like it, with nothing but the word 'Omelas' in mind. It came from a road sign: Salem (Oregon) backwards. Don't you read road signs backwards? POTS. WOLS nerdlihc. Ocsicnarf Nas. . . . Salem equals schelomo equals salaam equals Peace. Melas. Omelas. Omelas. Homme hélas."

The pastoral utopia of Omelas is not only inviting but seems quite within the realm of possibility. In recent years, numerous small colonies in the United States have sought to establish similar lifestyles—nothing about the social order of Omelas is so heroic or extravagant as to make it fantastic.

And as the narrator attempts to describe the people of Omelas, he or she scores a telling point. "The trouble is that we have a bad habit, encouraged by pedants and sophisticates, of considering happiness as something rather stupid. Only pain is intellectual, only evil is interesting. This is the treason of the artist: a refusal to admit the banality of evil and the terrible boredom of pain." In part, this is a valid statement. Most serious literature does not "describe a happy man, nor make any celebration of joy." The narrator does go on precisely to celebrate happiness—the state of people in a society with few laws, free of the military, the clergy, most machines, and, above all, guilt. But there is one small price—the unjust wretchedness of an innocent child. And Le Guin graphically displays that wretchedness, using the most sentimental of all objects—the bewildered and powerless child, aware of his punishment, desperately promising to be good, malnourished in a fearful dark closet, condemned interminably to this physical and emotional torture.

That miserable child, of course, not only represents the scapegoat carrying all the dark emotional detritus of Omelas, and thus purifying it, but also symbolizes all the tangible and intangible injustice that flows from the gratification of our own desires. And do we not, as do most of the citizens of Omelas, rationalize: unemployment is necessary to economic health; national boundaries must be policed to protect our wealth; low farm wages are shameful, but cheap food is desirable; too bad about the Holocaust, but that was not our problem; and too bad about apartheid, but that is not our problem. Are we not as amazed as the narrator of the story is at those who walk away from Omelas, at those who cannot accept personal gratification on those terms, at those who disrupt munitions plants, at those who pour blood over military draft records, at those who choose not to eat what they will not kill? Unlike the narrator, Le Guin denies that evil is banal, that pain is boring. How one deals with the perception of evil and pain crucially determines the moral quality of life.

Ma Jian   The Abandoner   (p. 1067)

To most western ears, this story will no doubt seem strange indeed, especially to those who know little about China except that its government is authoritarian, run from the top down by the Communist Party. Students should read the paragraph on Jian in the "Biographical Notes on the Authors" (p. 1573) to get some understanding of his background. If the world the vice-chairman inhabits, with its strict rules about the number of children permitted, enforced by a government official empowered to insert a coil into a woman's uterus to make sure she does not exceed the quota, seems fantastic, students need know something about the Great Proletarian Cultural Revolution initiated in 1966 by Mao Tse-Tung, chairman of the Communist Party. The superior value to a family of a male child over a female one, of course, cuts across time and civilizations and is still with us in many societies.

Jian's story is notable for its dry, businesslike prose, befitting a nameless bureaucrat/protagonist whose seemingly exclusive preoccupation is to abandon his retarded daughter so that he can have another chance for a male heir. The brisk, matter-of-fact prose makes his endeavors seem ordinary and rational. The vice-chairman is no hero or rebel; he does not question whether the government under which he lives is fair or just or right. He does his duty and obeys. One might argue that his very ordinariness and docility make all the more powerful the affirmation of life and love he finally opts for. From the time early on when he realizes that "each journey she took into the outside world was an opportunity to prove the resilience of her life force" (para. 9), his attempts to be a successful abandoner, many of them quite comic, creates a wholly "irrational" bond of love and compassion. At the end, Miamiao, his retarded, "useless" daughter, becomes the agent of his secular redemption.

Science (and government laws) coexist easily and naturally in this story with irrational fortune-telling: "Since the vice-chairman was blood Type A and had been born in the Year of the Rabbit, he was both stubborn and introverted" (para. 3). He knows that Miamiao suffers from a "chromosomal abnormality" (para. 5). But he readily consults fortune-tellers, including the lame Zeng, who lays out the major events of his life up to and including the age at which he will die. When Zeng's prediction about his forty-eighth year proves accurate, the vice-chairman decides to retire so that he can devote all of his time to abandoning his daughter. But something unforeseen, perhaps suprarational, begins to happen. Each time he tries to abandon his daughter, "he felt his attachment to her deepen" (para. 27). What began as a perfectly "rational" decision to rid himself of a retarded child ends, ironically, with that child showing him the meaning of his life. Needless to say, this is not an outcome that is of any interest to an authoritarian government.

Mutatis mutandis, Miamiao becomes for her father what Melville's Bartleby becomes for his lawyer-employer: the most unlikely agency of a moral transformation.

Naguib Mahfouz   Zaabalawi   (p. 111)

Mahfouz's story is set in modern Egypt, but it resonates with an ancient, archetypal pattern: a character sets out on a journey that becomes a quest for the meaning of life. The spur to undertake the quest may vary, but the actual journey always becomes a metaphor for a spiritual pursuit. In older versions, the protagonist undertakes the journey alone. Each stop or experience on the journey represents an important stage in his growing awareness and, ultimately, enlightenment. The medieval knight seeking the Holy Grail, Christian in John Bunyan's eighteenth-century allegory *Pilgrim's Progress* making his way to the Heavenly City, Young Goodman Brown in Hawthorne's eponymous tale passing ever deeper into the forest, even Jack Kerouc and his friends driving aimlessly in *On the Road*—all are variations on the pattern.

The narrator of Mahfouz's story lives in contemporary Egypt, and the story on the surface is "realistic": the narrator has a family, he travels through neighborhoods of office buildings and shops, he hears telephones ringing, and he describes the smells and sounds of the city. But beneath this surface realism the structure and events of the narrator's journey transform the story into an allegory. "[A]fflicted with that illness for which no one possesses a remedy" (para. 7), the narrator sets out on a journey to find Zaabalawi, a mysterious, fabled figure capable of performing miracles. But Zaabalawi is a figure, as he will learn, also derided and labeled a charlatan by some. Each of the protagonist's major encounters brings him closer not to a cure for his mortal illness but to an understanding of what matters in the journey of his life.

And those encounters move from the fully Westernized lawyer to the partly Westernized figure who provides a map to the calligrapher and musician, who represent authentic Egyptian culture.

The first of these encounters is with Sheik Qamar, a lawyer and old friend of the narrator's father. As the narrator enters the sheik's office, "A beautiful woman with the most intoxicating perfume" (para. 9) is exiting. He quickly realizes that the sheik, a business man, has little interest in his quest, or in Zaabalawi, for that matter. Whatever spiritual yearnings may have drawn Sheik Qamar to Zaabalawi in the past, he has long since yielded to the pleasures of the physical world. His luxuriously appointed office, his demeanor—everything about him suggests a man of the world. When he realizes that the narrator is not a potential client, he quickly sends him on his way.

The next encounter occurs at the Birgawi Residence, where Zaabalawi reputedly had lived. But the narrator finds the building decayed into a rubbish dump, fronted by the still-standing façade. The scene suggests the decay of a once-vibrant tradition. There, a seller of "old books on theology and mysticism," "a mere prologue to a man" distinguished by his "narrow, inflamed eyes" (paras. 22–23), plies his trade. The narrator's description of him seems to suggest someone so possessed by scholarly/historical studies that he has lost touch with the living power that Zaabalawi represents. Dispirited, the narrator briefly returns home, then sets out again. Now he seeks out another sheik who, while more sympathetic than the first one, draws a map of the district so that the narrator can begin a systematic search for Zaabalawi. The map merely bewilders the narrator.

His encounters with the calligrapher and the musician (paras. 37–74) bring him closer to his goal. Neither are merchants but, significantly, artists imbued with spiritualism. The calligrapher tells the narrator that Zaabalawi inspired his most beautiful drawings (para. 44), the musician reveals the connection between suffering and its cure (paras. 58–59). Both artists urge the narrator to continue his search — the musician sending him to seek out Hagg Wanas, a search that takes him to the most unlikely setting, the Negma bar.

There, the narrator has the climactic experience that ends his journey. He must get drunk before Hag Wanas will speak to him. He succumbs and with each drink falls ever deeper into a state of consciousness that he describes in words that echo those of many mystics who have tried to describe an essentially indescribable experience: a profound sense of contentment and oneness with the universe. Zaabalawi, Hagg Wannas tells the narrator, "will cure you if you meet him" (para. 106). The narrator's reward for his journey is not to find Zaabalawi and a cure to his illness. It is, as he realizes in the end, to have overcome any doubts about Zaabalawi's saintly existence. This end of the journey thus leads the narrator to a new beginning, announced by the final sentence.

James Alan McPherson   A Loaf of Bread   (p. 439)

In this story, McPherson examines, in a straightforward and stylistically plain narrative, a conflict that embodies many of the ambiguities and maddening dilemmas created by slavery and its heritage of racism. In a country that has seen successive waves of immigrants overcome the prejudices and legal disabilities placed on them and enter the mainstream of American life, the vast majority of African Americans have remained a species of permanent immigrant, all but forgotten until the repressed rage of being scorned and exploited, neglected and ghettoized, is ignited by a police beating — or the discovery that a local merchant is price-gouging.

Dealing with a topic that yields easily to melodrama (the good, struggling black versus the profiteer), McPherson avoids facile moral judgments by adopting a third-person narration so that both sides of the conflict can be examined with sympathy and some depth. Indeed, the nine sections of the story focus alternately on Harold Green and Nelson Reed, allowing us to see both of them as decent and ordinary men caught up in a conflict whose deepest origins neither is responsible for. "I did not make the world," Green protests (para. 4). "All my life I have lived on principle and I ain't got a dime in the bank," Reed angrily cries out (para. 94). There are no villains in this story — both men are right.

Harold Green, white and probably Jewish, clearly plays by the rules of the American economic system. His grocery store provides an essential service to the neighborhood, in return for which he earns a livelihood. He is a small businessman, not a social crusader. He is trying to earn a living, not change the world. He declares, and the narrative fully supports his assertion, "The businesses I run are always on the up-and-up" (para. 34) and argues convincingly that "I do not make a profit here because the people are black. I make a profit because a profit is here to be made" (para. 60).

Nelson Reed, black and a blue-collar worker, is an equally hardworking family man and good citizen. The discovery that Green's prices are higher in his Harlem grocery store than in his other store with a white clientele sparks a protest that thrusts Reed into a leadership role. Reed is no demagogue, out to build himself a power base, but a man sincerely outraged by the patent racist exploitation suffered by him and his people. Indeed, the event has a deeply personal effect on him, shaking his lifelong trust in God and forcing him to the realization that "The onliest thing that matters in this world is money" (para. 9).

The conflict, however, cannot be defined, much less resolved, by a rational and personal discussion between the two men. The protest has, willy-nilly, become a public political event that sweeps into its orbit a congeries of people and purposes and selfish interests that are beyond either man's ability to control or perhaps even understand: the black protesters, including "cynical young black men with angry grudges," the white liberals and "old-style leftists," "tape-recorder-bearing social scientists," and the hand-shaking politicians (para. 23). In a narrow sense, Green's explanations to Reed of why his prices are higher in the Harlem store make perfect economic sense and cannot reasonably be called gouging.

But in a larger and more significant sense, Green's figures and explanation of write-offs are swallowed up in the vast and tangled heritage of slavery and racism that is the story's context. Green did not create this context. The system of capitalism enables him to run a grocery store and, as his brother-in-law emphasizes in the analogy of the family wishing to sell an electric stove (para. 43), charge whatever the traffic will bear. Neither did Reed make this world. Yet somehow, as Reed and his people well know, African Americans have, from slavery right up to the present, been more often the victims than the beneficiaries of this created system.

One of the most dramatic moments in the story occurs during the meeting between the two men when Green responds to Reed's attack on his character by passionately declaring, "I am not an evil man!" (para. 43), then launches into a detailed explanation of the principles on which he conducts business, seeking Reed's approval each step of the way by appealing to him to "Place yourself in my situation." Adopting the Socratic method, Green attempts to elicit from Reed some understanding of what a reasonable profit is. But suddenly, the conversation is abruptly transformed by Reed's sense that he is being manipulated and insulted. "I ain't you," he cries out, and goes on to speak about his sharecropper father in Mississippi who died in debt to the company store (para. 77). A dialogue between two men over a specific issue at a specific time and place has been overwhelmed by the inescapable realities of the past. The dialogue perfectly captures the ironies of the story.

The final episode, the Saturday morning when Green gives away the store, brings the story to a dramatic, resonant end. Green opens the store in a lighthearted, happy mood, as if, after his initial anger and refusal, he has come to understand the rightness of his wife's plan. The customers and the pickets take everything free of charge. The giveaway seems to function as a pale, subdued version of a riot without its diffused focus and violence, although toward the end "there were several fistfights and much cursing" (para. 110).

In the denouement, when Reed returns to the store, Green harks back to their earlier conversation by asking, "Now will you put yourself in my shoes? I have nothing here. Come, now, Mr. Reed, would it not be so bad a thing to walk in my shoes?" (para. 117). Reed, responding "coldly," refuses the offer and tells Green only that he wants to pay for the loaf of bread his wife was given earlier. As Green's register rings up the fifty-seven cents for the loaf of bread, the story ends with Reed holding out a dollar. The abyss separating the two men seems unmediated except by the commercial transaction that will validate Green's actions as principled. The fact that the item is a loaf of bread, the staff of life and mainstay of the human diet, is perhaps a symbol of how antithetical to brotherhood are the values of the world that neither Green nor Reed made.

Herman Melville   Bartleby the Scrivener   (p. 370)

In the first section of the story, the narrator provides a leisurely description of himself, his business, and the general surroundings. He is genial, tolerant, a good Christian; his life has been governed by the belief that "the easiest way of life is the best." He has created for himself a comfortable and safe world with an equilibrium and predictability that embody the values he cherishes. Even the alcoholic Turkey and the dyspeptic Nippers fit neatly into this world, for their fits relieve each other and allow the narrator to be the generous and forgiving master without damaging his business profits. While the sight of Bartleby first shocks him, he quickly concludes that the young man will fit into this world quite easily. With Bartleby's first refusal to do his master's bidding, the lawyer's world begins to disintegrate, and the first section ends.

The second section begins with the narrator's first stunned amazement at this refusal, advances the story through a series of further refusals on Bartleby's part, and ends with the narrator's temporary and self-deceptive reconciliation to Bartleby's eccentricity. After all, he reminds himself (forgetting the "strange" feelings Bartleby has aroused in him), his scrivener is steady and usually dependable.

The third section opens with the narrator's discovery that Bartleby is living in his business chambers. No longer the self-confident employer of the first section, the lawyer slinks away from his own door. When he returns and surveys the miserable sum of Bartleby's worldly possessions, he is overcome with "a feeling of over-powering melancholy" that culminates in a vision of Bartleby's fate. The accurate foreshadowing of Bartleby's fate suggests that the narrator is beginning to discover that the bond that links humanity together is the antithesis of what he has supposed. Thus midway in the narrative, he stands uneasily poised between the world of the opening section and the world of Bartleby's negation. When Bartleby refuses to explain himself, refuses to accept the narrator's offer of charity, and refuses to leave, the baffled lawyer avoids this intransigent threat to his ordered world by fleeing, by moving away from Bartleby.

The final section brings the action to a swift conclusion. The narrator learns that the landlord has had Bartleby removed to the Tombs on a charge of vagrancy. There he turns his face to the wall and soon dies. In what seems a casual postscript, the narrator informs us that he subsequently hears a rumor about Bartleby's past: "That Bartleby had been a subordinate clerk in the Dead Letter Office in Washington . . ." Whenever he thinks over this report, the narrator continues, he can "hardly express the emotions which seize me." And, indeed, what better metaphor for the inability of one human being to break through the isolation of another than the Dead Letter Office? The very direction that the narrator's final reflections take brings home to him the unreality of the principles that have guided his life. His realization that Bartleby's condition represents the human condition, that his relationship with the scrivener is symbolic, is the final and most profound irony of this ironic tale.

Melville establishes a subtle bond between the narrator and Bartleby, a bond that gives the story a profound psychological truth and accounts for the narrator's ambivalence toward his recalcitrant employee. When Bartleby first appears, the narrator is struck by his "sedate" aspect, a trait that looms large in the narrator's early description of himself; he immediately installs Bartleby in *his* half of the divided office, as if in unconscious recognition of their strange kinship. As Bartleby becomes increasingly withdrawn, at a deeper level he is touching the narrator closely, for the narrator, too, has made his peace with the world through a deliberate withdrawal. He has elected not to engage in the more arduous and hazardous job of the trial lawyer, preferring, as his sinecure as Master in Chancery allows, to make a safe and comfortable livelihood by handling "rich men's bonds, and mortgages, and title-deeds." These documents, of course, mark the limits and define the nature of his withdrawal: They allow him to serve the world outside, thus keeping his withdrawal within the limits of the socially acceptable. He is increasingly fascinated and discon-certed by Bartleby precisely because Bartleby represents a tendency in himself, which, carried to its extreme, would destroy the guiding principles of his life.

The parallel is underscored, finally, by two striking details: one at the very begin-ning of the narrative, one at the conclusion. In the opening pages, the narrator dis-closes that subsequent to the events about to be related he lost his comfortable sinecure as Master in Chancery when a new constitution abolished the post. At the end of the narrative, we learn that Bartleby lost his clerkship in the Dead Letter Office for precisely the same reason. And if the coincidence strengthens the parallel, it rever-berates in yet another way, for the narrator's loss of the sinecure, with all the comfort and security that it signifies, foreshadows the more profound loss he is to experience when the meaning of Bartleby and his own relationship to the scrivener are finally revealed to him.

However one interprets the story, an analysis ought to take account of the perva-sive symbolism of walls and enclosures. Bartleby's desk faces "grimy back yards and bricks," he is isolated by a screen, the narrator alludes to Bartleby's "dead-wall rever-ies," Bartleby dies facing the prison wall, and the story is subtitled "A Story of Wall Street."

Some critics interpret the story as an autobiographical parable. Melville began his career with a number of quite successful South Sea romances, but by 1853, the year of "Bartleby," he had fallen out of favor with readers and critics, who found little of value in his more recent complex, symbolic works (*Moby Dick* was published in 1850). "Bartleby" is thus seen as a story in which Melville dramatizes his refusal to write the kind of fiction that would be a commercial success and his rejection of the entire commercial, money-making society that rewarded mindless "copiers." Carried a step further, "Bartleby" becomes a parable of the alienation of the serious writer in the modern world.

Pauline Melville   The Sparkling Bitch   (p. 454)

The narrator of this riveting story is not only omniscient but magisterial. The story of Charles Hay and his trophy wife Susan is told in a conventional, one might even say old-fashioned, narrative style: it moves from beginning to middle to end in a straight chronological line. There are only two characters. But the narrator is so firmly in charge of the world she has created, so *present* in the story with her detached yet passionate convictions and moral judgments, it would be reasonable to see her as a third character.

The opening paragraph says everything that needs to be said about Charles Hay: impatient with his wife, contemptuous of the country that his oil company has despoiled and its people, a predatory and thoroughly unlikable businessman. In dramatic contrast, his wife Susan is transfixed by the sight of a thirteen-year-old black boy casually dying of starvation behind a gas pump where the Hays have stopped to refuel their car. She is unable to move, kept there by what the narrator describes as "An irrational empathy." It is an arresting phrase. Can empathy ever be irrational, especially in the circumstances Susan faces? In any event, she finally manages to break the "spell" and leave the young boy. Five minutes after they resume their journey in their chauffeured car, they are held up by a native. When the driver informs him that the occupants have no money, he demands Charles's Rolex watch and then shouts at the driver, clearly a Nigerian native also, "You are telling lies . . . How do you think Nigeria is ever going to get ahead as a country if people like you tell lies. We will never get anywhere" (para. 12). It is a bizarre episode, a seemingly common criminal with a political agenda lecturing one of his countrymen as he robs the white passengers.

The middle of the story opens with the Hays back in their London home. The theme is advanced not so much by action as by Charles's feelings about the architecture of the financial district of London and the narrator's distinctly and tartly different views. Charles is entranced by the new architecture, which is all image and transparency, unlike the stolid and closed-in buildings of an earlier era. He is amused to note that "the more transparent the new buildings in the City of London looked, the shadier the dealings were that went on inside" (para. 14). The new buildings are "flirtatious" (para. 15), evoking the central role sex plays in the modern world of images and advertising. Charles loves appearances above all else. It is important to project the image of being environmentally responsible, not actually to protect the environment. Everything in the "Hay Oil" building is fake. And so, it turns out, is Charles's marriage.

The final section returns the focus to Susan, swiftly recounting her deterioration in the wake of her traumatic encounter with the starving boy: "After their return from Nigeria . . . a strange and powerful god emerged . . . , a god so extraordinary and attractive that she became bound to him and mastered by him" (para. 35). The encounter finally destroys her. She, in turn, shatters her cold husband's supreme moment as he basks in the glory of sitting at the "high table" at one of London's most significant image-making events. In the end, reality triumphs over image. The reality is that Susan's empathy was indeed "irrational" because in the face of the overwhelming and complex power of the white imperial world, symbolized by the architecture and business practices of the financial centers in London, a solitary white woman's empathy for a starving, thirteen-year-old black Nigerian boy is beside the point. It certainly will not change the behavior of the Charles Hayses of the industrialized world. The story, however, might change the way its readers behave.

26

Bharati Mukherjee Orbiting (p. 729)

Certainly one of the most stressful tribal ceremonies is the introduction of one's betrothed to his or her family for the first time. In this carefully nuanced story, Renata is understandably nervous about springing her new lover on her father and the rest of her family. The year since last Thanksgiving, we discover, has had more downs than ups—her brother is in the army; her fiancé, Vic, has simply abandoned her; her Uncle Carmine has had bypass surgery; her brother-in-law's difficult child by a first marriage will be a troublesome presence; her father is visibly aging. And she will top all that by introducing her new lover, Ro—an illegal Afghani refugee—to her unsuspecting Italian American family. Mukherjee knows what she is writing about. She married a Canadian, and left Canada as a result of the racism she felt; on a return visit to India, she was deeply troubled by the position of women in that society—in short, she knows intimately what it feels like to be a stranger in a strange land, as well as the tensions that form in conservative families when their unexamined social convictions are challenged. Renata's father and brother-in-law chat about sports— Ro, of course, doesn't know what they are talking about. Ironically, Ro is a sportsman—a squash player and a skier—not a spectator. Further, Ro is a cosmopolitan where the others are insular—yet Renata's family perceive him as a sort of greenhorn who doesn't know his way around. Again, ironically, Ro has been around: he has endured hardships the others cannot imagine, and survived.

Mukherjee provides some nice insight into cultural friction. Ro not only speaks differently but also holds his body differently. Renata (like Mukherjee) can feel her family's distress at this dark-skinned Moslem who doesn't drink alcohol or eat pork, but who has survived danger and lived with an intensity none of them has ever experienced. Renata's father's grandmother had emigrated from northern Italy and his most daring and exotic act was to marry a woman from southern Italy. "He made it sound as if Mom was a Korean or something." To stretch that tribal tolerance to someone like Ro is almost unthinkable. Yet Renata is secure in her choice and her feelings. By the end of the Thanksgiving dinner, she perceives Ro as a "scarred hero and survivor." Her father and brother-in-law "are children."

Some of your students may have lived through experiences almost identical to Renata's. Others will have endured parental displeasure over their friends' differing religious backgrounds or economic positions. It ought to be easy to generate a lively discussion of this story. Still others will testify to their parents' loving understanding. In any case, note that this story is not tragic—these are not star-crossed lovers, and Renata's parents are not going to excommunicate her, regardless of their distress.

Alice Munro How I Met My Husband (p. 1023)

Although it may seem to depend upon a surprising plot twist, this relatively straightforward story ought to be discussed for its insight into character and relationships. Note that the first-person speaker is remembering an experience from her fifteenth year. She was then an uneducated but intelligent and sensitive girl. We are given a number of clues that suggest a sort of native superiority to the middle-class housewife who employs her to keep house and look after the children. To begin with, she is a better cook than her employer. Further, she is gently contemptuous of Mrs. Peebles for buying canned goods rather than canning herself. Most of all, she (we may reasonably assume, like her mother) is amused that Mrs. Peebles considers herself "tied down" by two children and living in the country.

Having done poorly at school, she is content to be the hired girl—and discovers that the job is almost laughably easy compared to the workload the women bear in her own home, unequipped with modern appliances. Perhaps the nosey and gossipy neighbor Loretta Bird is a tad broadly drawn, but she, too, is recognized by Edie for what she is and deftly handled.

But Edie's nicest insight illuminates the relationship between servants and their employers. "They like to think you aren't curious," she ruminates. "They like to feel you don't notice things, that you don't think or wonder about anything but what they liked to eat and how they like things ironed, and so on." In short, employers would like to believe that their servants are robots of a sort—available to perform certain functions, but devoid of any human sensitivity of their own. Edie senses this, despite her youth and inexperience, and despite the Peebles's rather liberal behavior (she, after all, eats at the table with them). Hence her real terror when she is caught in Mrs. Peebles's fine dress by the romantic stranger who literally drops from the sky one day. She senses that her employer's attitude toward her would irrevocably change at this demonstration of her own humanity, curiosity, and daring.

Munro, of course, tricks us into rooting for Edie in the clichéd triangle completed by Chris Watters and his "fiancée," Alice Kelling. The rather faded Alice seems to be desperately pursuing Chris from one fairground to another; she quickly perceives Edie as a potential rival. That Watters is decent enough not to take advantage of Edie may seem a bit unreal; that the inexperienced Edie feels she has indeed been "intimate" with Chris is real enough. And she waits by the mailbox for the promised letter with all the romantic zeal of a fifteen-year-old — until her innate good sense persuades her to give it up. But by then, young Carmichael is smitten, and after a three-year courtship, at the respectable age of eighteen, Edie becomes his wife. We know how she met him, even if he doesn't.

We may smile at the bit of trickery that turns the plot but nonetheless admire Edie's character and insight into the foibles of the people around her.

Haruki Murakami On Seeing the 100% Perfect Girl One Beautiful April Morning (p. 143)

In this playful story, Murakami shines a gentle light on the universal, romantic notion — or dream — that somewhere in the world a perfect mate exists. It is, of course, a figment of the young imagination. The narrator, who tells us he is thirty-two, is perhaps a bit old for such a dream, which may account for his slightly self-deprecating and self-conscious tone. He muses about the perfect woman, aware that perfection is idiosyncratic and particular to every person and ultimately inexplicable. He sees her. He passes her by. Full of the idea and mental image of this woman, he imagines explaining to her "the complexities of fate" — the kind of endeavor only the love-besotted young have the boldness to tackle. He imagines that the encounter he yearns for would be "crammed full of warm secrets, like an antique clock built when peace filled the world" (para. 15). The metaphor resonates with all the fuzzy warmth the perfervid imaginings only the romantic young can conjure up. Then lunch, a Woody Allen movie (which any Woody Allen fan knows are mostly about failed and failing relationships), cocktails, and bed. That's the first fantasy.

As he approaches this hypothetical girl (note how seamlessly Murakami moves back and forth in time), he tries another fantasy: He will approach her with a question or a line to get things going. But, fearing rejection, he decides not to. Another encounter with her in front of a flower shop. More fantasy, this time an envelope containing "every secret she's ever had." But she disappears.

Except for the final sentence, the remainder of the narrative (a story within the story) begins with the ancient fairy tale formula "Once upon a time." The voice shifts to an omniscient narrator. It is a fable of perfect love — the uniting of the 100% perfect boy with the 100% perfect girl. But like characters out of a Nathaniel Hawthorne tale, the perfection of their love is pierced "by a tiny, tiny sliver of doubt" about whether it was "really all right for one's dreams to come true so easily." They have begun to distrust "miracles" and "fate" and begun to feel (again like many a Hawthorne character) that to be human they must somehow *earn* their happiness. So they part to test themselves, fall into an illness and awaken with their (romantic) memories erased. They have fallen out of the sleep of innocence, into the mundane world of everyday life. They experience love again, we learn, but not 100% love. In the coda to the story, fourteen years later, they pass each other but register only a faint recognition because, the narrator tells us, "their thoughts no longer had the clarity of fourteen years earlier."

Joyce Carol Oates Where Are You Going, Where Have You Been? (p. 1047)

This odd and troubling story has generated substantial critical comment. Oates testifies that the story's central episode is based on actual events reported in a 1955 *Life* magazine story about the rape-murders of three high-school girls committed by twenty-three-year-old Charles Schmid, who drove a gold car around Tucson, Arizona. Further, the epigraph "To Bob Dylan" highlights the difference between the music Connie and her friends enjoy and the clear-eyed, somber vision Dylan's lyrics often project. And critics point out the affinity of the story to the old popular ballad "The Demon Lover," which narrates the ruin of the good wife and mother lured to death and damnation by the blandishments of a satanic lover.

Add to these the numerous suggestive allusions to various folk- and fairy tales within the story. Is Arnold Friend some perverse Pied Piper? Does the pumpkin-like grinning face on Arnold's golden car (para. 35) suggest the magical coach that carried Cinderella to the ball? Do Arnold's "big and white" teeth (para. 83) suggest the wolf in "Little Red Riding Hood"? And does the image of the house as a "cardboard box I can knock down anytime" (para. 151) allude to "The Three Little Pigs"? Does his persistent trouble with his boots suggest that Arnold stands on wolf paws or cloven hooves?

In an introductory class, it might be better to delay these observations until the story has been discussed as an example of Oates's professed determination to write about "real people in a real society." Even then, it would be good if students (with a little prompting, perhaps) were able to find the allusions themselves. Attend also to Oates's *caveat* that the story has been "constantly misunderstood by one generation, and intuitively understood by another."

Your students will recognize that Connie inhabits two worlds—the constricting and disagreeable life within her family and the promising, exciting world of the mall, the movies, and the hamburger joints where she gossips with her friends and tentatively experiences her first episodes of romantic love with young boys she can control. Her romantic encounters are modeled on romantic films and the song lyrics of her favorite music—mostly sentimental clichés, assuredly not by Bob Dylan. She has no defense against the older Arnold Friend; he knows her world and crafts his blandishments for effect (the film made from Oates's story was titled *Smooth Talk*). But she has no insight into his world, and will become his victim.

No academic analysis of allusion, myth, folklore, or fairy tale is required. The story remains sufficiently realistic, even if Arnold does seem to have a supernatural awareness of events. Insisting on the story's allusiveness will create some interesting problems. How do Cinderella, who, after all, does get the prince, and Little Red Riding Hood, who, after all, is rescued in most versions, and the three little pigs, who, after all, are saved by the sturdy brick house of the wisest brother, figure in this story of a doomed young girl?

The more interesting question is: Why does Connie go out to Arnold and, presumably, to her rape and death? How accurate is Arnold's assertion (para. 151): "The place you came from ain't there any more, and where you had in mind to go is canceled out"? The world of moony fifteen-year-old adolescents is the place that Connie came from. It is a world where "all the boys fell back and dissolved into a single face that was not even a face, but an idea, a feeling, mixed up with the urgent pounding of the music. . . ." (para. 10). And where Connie had in mind to go is, doubtless, that shapeless happily-ever-after that followed the closing romantic embrace in her favorite movies.

Arnold points out to her: "This place where you are now—inside your daddy's house—is nothing but a cardboard box I can knock down any time" (para. 151). Ultimately, Connie has no protection—neither physical nor emotional—in a real world that nourishes the unimagined evil of smooth-talking Arnold Friend; her past is gone and her future is canceled out.

Tim O'Brien   The Things They Carried   (p. 1358)

"The Things They Carried" is one of almost two dozen chapters that constitute the novel *The Things They Carried* (1990), O'Brien's powerful book based on his experiences as a foot soldier in Vietnam. Although the title page describes the volume as a work of fiction and announces that "all the incidents, names, and characters are imaginary," O'Brien dedicates the book "to the men of Alpha Company, and in particular to Jimmy Cross, Norman Bowker, Rat Kiley, Mitchell Sanders, Henry

Dobbins, Kiowa." In another story, "On the Rainy River," the narrator identifies himself as Tim O'Brien and describes events closely based on the real Tim O'Brien's experiences.

Drawing heavily on his own experiences, O'Brien changes and shapes them according to his artistic purposes. As time passes and O'Brien's stature as a writer grows, we will learn more about the facts of his life, and critics and biographers will sort out what is literally biographical, what is not, and what cannot be known. Such information will give us greater insight into the way an artist transmutes the raw material of life into a work of polished art. But even then, we must keep in mind O'Brien's own paradoxical comment in "How To Tell a True War Story": "[I]t's safe to say that in a true war story nothing is ever absolutely true."

By 1968, the year O'Brien was drafted, serious resistance to the Vietnam War had developed. Many, for example, began to protest what they viewed as the class-based inequities of the draft, which allowed deferments to college students, mostly white and middle class, while the poorer lower classes, many of them black and brown, were being shipped off to fight. Others were questioning the political rationale for American involvement—the so-called domino theory. The nightly news tracked the war by reporting the military's celebrated "body counts"—the number of enemy killed each day. And as the war dragged on interminably, with higher and higher casualties and more and more troops committed to the conflict on both sides, politicians and generals tried to calm an increasingly angry and divided public with assurances that victory was at hand—that, in one of the era's memorable phrases, there was "light at the end of the tunnel."

The My Lai massacre occurred in 1968. At about the same time, the Orwellian logic of the war was unwittingly articulated by an American officer as he surveyed a Vietnamese village his troops had just destroyed: "It was necessary to destroy this village in order to save it."

"The Things They Carried" begins with a staple of sentimental war stories: the description of letters "from a girl named Martha" carried in a rucksack by a combat soldier, letters on which he builds romantic fantasies that sustain him as he moves through a jungle where his life might be snuffed out at any moment. What follows, however, is anything but trite or conventional. O'Brien's storytelling is complex and quite original. Lieutenant Cross's dreams about Martha punctuate a narrative that powerfully turns cataloging into a literary technique. Character, plot, and setting all emerge from the long lists of things enumerated in the story.

Each man's character is suggested in part by the concrete things he carries: Lieutenant Cross carries Martha's letters, Henry Dobbins carries extra rations, Ted Lavendar carries a supply of dope. There are also an extraordinary number of physical things related to combat that become a near crushing burden.

But *things* also has a metaphoric meaning for each of the men, which allows O'Brien to give his characters more individuality and the story greater complexity. In paragraph 2, for example, we are told that Kiowa "also carried his grandmother's distrust of the white man." Later, we learn, "They carried all they could bear, and then some, including a silent awe for the terrible power of the things they carried" (para. 12), and that "They all carried ghosts" (para. 17). Both the metaphoric and literal cataloging reach a passionate and lyrical climax in paragraph 31, which opens with the literal and the banal ("stationary and pencils and pens") and moves to the metaphoric in the kind of poetic parallelism reminiscent of the technique Walt Whitman uses in his poetry (they carried "The shared weight of memory," "the land itself," and "the sky"). The passage concludes with a powerful description of the men as virtual automatons, caught up in an event whose only meaning is survival, not the noble and heroic defense of the political ideals they have been called upon to defend. This passage echoes a famous one from Ernest Hemingway's 1929 antiwar novel, *A Farewell to Arms,* when Hemingway's disillusioned soldier-narrator reacts to the patriotic sentiments of one of his comrades:

> I was always embarrassed by the words *sacred, glorious,* and *sacrifice* and the expression *in vain.* We had heard them, sometimes standing in the rain, almost out of earshot, so that only the shouted words came through, and had read them, on proclamations that were slapped up by billposters over

other proclamations, now for a long time, and I had seen nothing sacred, and the things that were glorious had no glory and the sacrifices were like the stockyards at Chicago if nothing was done with the meat except to bury it. There were many words that you could not stand to hear and finally only the names of places had dignity. Certain numbers were the same way and certain dates and these with the names of the places were all you could say and have them mean anything. Abstract words such as *glory, honor, courage,* or *hallow* were obscene beside the concrete names of villages, the numbers of roads, the names of rivers, the numbers of regiments and the dates. (chap. XXVII)

While the cataloging may seem simple enough as a technique, O'Brien's narrative is anything but simple. This can best be illustrated by the way Lavendar's death outside the village of Than Khe becomes the focal point for a narrative that keeps turning back on itself. Lavendar's death is alluded to but not explained in the second paragraph, referred to periodically, and then finally described in paragraph 24, and discussed again in paragraph 32, where its connection to the destruction of Than Khe is implied. The final section of the story (paras. 56–73) returns appropriately to an earlier consequence of Lavendar's death: Lieutenant Cross's resolution of his "romance" with Martha. He burns her letters and resolves to be a better officer. The story ends on the eve of the move "out toward the village of Than Khe," which, as we already know, his men will destroy in a horrifying rampage.

Flannery O'Connor   Good Country People   (p. 120)

A useful way to begin to think about this story is to explore the irony contained in the title. "Good Country People" suggests a cluster of values traditionally associated with the pastoral (as opposed to urban) life: simplicity, openness, physical and mental good health, kindness, neighborliness, and so forth. Gerásim in Tolstoy's "The Death of Iván Ilých" embodies those positive traits evoked by the title of O'Connor's story. But in Mrs. Freeman and Mrs. Hopewell and, above all, in Hulga and Manley Pointer, we are shown the blind ignorance, the psychic deformities, and the terror that dominate the lives of these good country people.

Each of them is locked into a set of illusions or pathologies that renders communication, much less communion, impossible. Mrs. Hopewell insulates herself from reality by reducing everything to a comfortable cliché. "Everybody is different," she remarks and thereby protects herself from recognition of the fact that her daughter is an embittered thirty-two-year-old woman with a wooden leg, a weak heart, and no future. If Mrs. Hopewell (as her name suggests) is compulsively driven to deny the ugly and the unpleasant, her dear friend Mrs. Freeman is just as compulsively preoccupied with "the details of secret infections, hidden deformities, assaults upon children." Superficially opposites, Mrs. Hopewell and Mrs. Freeman exist in a symbiotic relationship that feeds each other's blindness: Mrs. Freeman is as ignorant of the reality of her daughters' lives as Mrs. Hopewell is of the truth about Hulga.

While the two mothers are not developed beyond the level of "humors" characters, Hulga is given a fuller and more complex development. Deformed in body, Hulga devotes herself to the life of the mind. With a Ph.D. in philosophy, she has presumably equipped herself to rise above the ordinary human illusions that bodily health and beauty are important. Confident that she is acting on an impersonal and philosophical truth rather than a deep need arising out of her bodily deformity, she does everything she can to enhance her ugliness, notably by adopting the ugliest name she can find. All that matters, Hulga believes, is the mind, the educated and philosophical mind that has penetrated beyond the illusions of body and emotions and seen that in reality there is nothing.

Her encounter with Manley Pointer reveals how futile is her philosophy, how defensive are her arrogance and contempt for the good country people she is condemned to live with. Her immediate and excited responsiveness to Manley's romantic, sexual advances suggests quite clearly that she has by no means transcended the needs of the body, the dreams of romantic love. While Hulga clings to her philosophy by directing to her brain the "surge of adrenalin" released by the first kiss and by patronizing Manley as an innocent child, she succumbs utterly in the hayloft when he asks her to remove her wooden leg. After Manley removes the leg himself, Hulga in a rising panic asks him to put it back on. But Manley is now in control and begins kissing her instead. This time, "Her brain seemed to have stopped thinking altogether." Then, in a kind of ultimate horror, Manley opens his valise and reveals himself as a lecherous and obscene psychopath.

The central and devastating irony of the story is embodied in Hulga's pathetic murmur, "Aren't you just good country people?" It is she who is revealed as ignorant and childlike, astonished by her confrontation with the profound moral void represented by Manley, compared to which her philosophy is superficial.

Amos Oz   If There Is Justice   (p. 675)

The historical situation of "If There Is Justice" may be unfamiliar to students, but the familiarity and intimacy of the narration should draw them into the story (and there is much to discuss about how Oz pulls the reader into his narrator's thoughts). This is a story set in the middle of the long-running conflict of a nation struggling to define its place in the world, debating the way in which it will relate to its neighbors, and the main character deals with similar issues of self-definition and place in the world. Rami's struggle to determine his place in his society, in relation to friends and family and community, is intertwined with his relation to his nation and by extension with its relation to it neighbors.

Starting discussion with Rami's personal conflicts, then, can lead naturally (with the supplying of a little background) to discussion of the larger national conflict and to the parallels between the personal and political in this story—particularly concerning notions of violence, manhood, and identity. Connecting the importance of these notions to the story may help students think about Rami's near suicide, which they should see is about more than his feelings for Noga, and may help them recognize the story's attitude about the effects of aggression on the aggressor.

Edgar Allan Poe   The Cask of Amontillado   (p. 1298)

Students will understand that Montresor plays on Fortunato's vanity to entice him to the vaults. But some questions remain unanswered. What insufferable insult (added to "the thousand injuries") caused Montresor to plot his terrible vengeance? And to whom, fifty years later, is Montresor telling his story? These questions might lead to a discussion of the artful uses of the tacit. Ask the students to specify an insult awful enough to justify Montresor's revenge. The question will produce a lively debate, even though specifying the insult is likely to diminish it as a motive for the horrible murder. In fact, by not specifying the source of Montresor's rage, Poe allows each reader to conjure his or her own uniquely unbearable insult. Had Poe revealed the insult, he would have jeopardized the power of his tale, and readers would find Montresor's vengeance unreasonably harsh.

Next, consider the listener described in the second sentence—"You, who so well know the nature of my soul." We would argue that Montresor, fifty years later, is speaking to a priest, pursuing salvation by making a deathbed confession. Can students suggest some other viable listener? This discussion ought to attend to the strange comment in the last paragraph. Montresor reveals that when he placed the last brick in the wall of Fortunato's tomb his "heart grew sick." Not, he adds after a momentary pause, at the enormity of his crime, but rather because "of the dampness of the catacombs." One might reasonably argue that Montresor attempts to stifle his humanity, surely the source of that heartsickness, in order to complete his single-minded vengeance. Thus, he proclaims that dampness, not conscience, is responsible for his feelings.

You might, finally, encourage a discussion of Montresor's thoughtful two-part definition of *vengeance*: (1) the avenger must punish with impunity and (2) the victim must recognize that he is being punished. Thus Montresor's vengeance cannot be simply to murder Fortunato—he has to evade punishment for the crime and enjoy Fortunato's desperate recognition of his plight.

Katherine Anne Porter   The Jilting of Granny Weatherall

(p. 1346)

The story opens in the morning with Granny on her deathbed in the home of her daughter Cornelia, who hovers solicitously over her mother throughout. In the morning she is looked at by the doctor, who returns in the evening after her condition worsens. A priest is then summoned to administer the last rites, and shortly thereafter Granny dies. While the line between past and present, reality and recollection, blurs in Granny's mind, the reader is constantly aware that two interrelated narratives are underway—Granny's final hours as seen by her family and friends, and Granny's recollections during those final hours.

What emerges is the portrait of a sturdy, self-reliant southern Catholic lady who, despite her advanced age, is not quite prepared to die. There are, after all, so many things yet to take care of, so many loose ends of her long life to attend to before dying. A woman who has raised her children alone, doing both a man's and a woman's work ("She had fenced in a hundred acres once"), knows the value of planning and efficiency and the need for "a little margin over for peace" so that "a person could spread out the plan of life and tuck in the edges orderly." "Tomorrow," she repeatedly says in the first part of the story, "tomorrow" there will be time to take care of the loose ends.

But Granny knows that there will be no tomorrow. In the face of death, her mind travels over the years, seeking some answer, some key that will tuck in the edges of her life and give it order. Recollections flash through her mind, but the answer eludes her. "What was it I set out to do?" she vainly wonders, her mind providing not an answer but the image of a rising fog.

When the fog dissipates, her mind comes to rest on the crucial event of her youth: the day sixty years before when her fiancé, George, left her jilted at the church. After six decades that have included a husband (John, now dead), children, grandchildren, work, and struggle, her mind fastens on the jilting as somehow embodying the answer she seeks. Her recollections suggest that after the jilting she married John though she did not love him, but that over the years of their marriage, she truly came to love him. Hapsy (who had apparently died) was born out of this love and is, therefore, "the one she had truly wanted." She desperately wishes to find George, to tell him that despite his cruel jilting of her she went on to live a happy, successful life. "Tell him," she says, "I was given back everything he took away and more." But Granny is suddenly aware that the loss she suffered in the jilting goes much deeper. For she immediately cries: "Oh no, oh, God, no, there was something else besides the house and the man and the children. Oh, surely they were not all? What was it? Something not given back."

As death approaches, confused thoughts and images out of the past mingle indistinguishably in Granny's mind with events in the present. The recollection of the jilting, when "the whole bottom dropped out of the world," recurs sharply; and, as she receives the last rites, she reaffirms that her loss of George meant nothing, since "I found another a whole world better."

Now Granny yields herself to imminent death, shutting everything out of her mind and concentrating upon the diminishing point of light that is her life. A pious and good woman, she awaits the revelation of Christ that will herald her resurrection into eternal life. But the greatest pain of her life, its deepest sorrow, occurs at the very moment of her death when "For the second time there was no sign. Again no bridegroom and the priest in the house." For the second time in Granny's well-ordered and controlled life, she suffers the unendurable pain of a jilting that robs her life of its meaning. And now we understand why Granny, who has "weathered all," broods over the jilting in her final hours. Somehow, that jilting robbed her of her youth and passion, the fervor of bright expectation with which a twenty-year-old girl faced the future. And now, with her life ending after years of successful struggle, she looks back upon it with the painful if dim sense that something was irretrievably lost when she was left waiting at the church, and she turns once again to await a bridegroom who does not appear.

There is, of course, great dignity and strength in Granny, but it emerges most movingly during the final hours of her life that there is, tragically, not "always a little margin over for peace" and that one cannot, finally, "tuck in the edges orderly."

Nahid Rachlin   Departures   (p. 1282)

While there are many departures in this story, the most important one may be one that doesn't happen. Farogh, who feels trapped in a number of ways in her life, doesn't leave it. While Rachlin never makes this idea explicit, the departures of Karim and Ahmad lead one to think of the departures Farogh might wish to make—from her marriage, from cultural and religious tradition, from her community's attitudes toward the war—but seems unable to. Asking students to think about the departures named in the title more broadly, by including those that do not happen, could help them appreciate Rachlin's interest in Farogh's historical situation.

Aspects of that situation include the attitudes toward the war with Iraq, the denial of its danger, and the attraction to martyrdom and traditional beliefs about the role of women in society and about marriage. These are highlighted by Farogh's deviation from them, at least in her thoughts, and by the return of Karim from America. They are also emphasized by the ways in which the romantic hopefulness of youth is replaced by the resigned bitterness of experience; in a way, the sense of possibility found in youth is another thing that has departed in this story.

Leslie Marmon Silko   The Man to Send Rain Clouds   (p. 1372)

Understated to the point of terseness, this account of the death and burial of an old Indian (unaccountably named Teofilo—Beloved of God) describes the meeting point of two traditions that would seem to be vastly different. The Native Americans' response to death is ritualistic. When the young men find Leon's grandfather dead under the cottonwood tree, they treat the body formally. It is necessary to wrap him in a red blanket, but before wrapping him, Leon ties a feather in the old man's hair, and paints the dead man's face with lines of white, yellow, blue, and green. Further, Ken throws pinches of cornmeal and pollen (suggestive of fertility in an agricultural community) into the air over the corpse. Presumably, these ritual acts will benefit the community—the men address the corpse with a request: "Send us rain clouds, Grandfather." Later, at a Native American funeral conducted by tribal elders equipped with candles and medicine bags, more cornmeal had been thrown over the body.

But Catholics have established themselves in the community as well. Father Paul knows Ken and Leon, knows they have been looking for Teofilo, and expects them to attend mass (as they must have in the recent past) along with Teofilo. Curiously, Ken and Leon do not tell the priest that Teofilo is dead—surely they are trying to avoid a conflict. The Church has its own formal rituals for dealing with death, and though the men, presumably, are members of the Church, death is too important to be left to priests. They want a funeral conducted by tribal elders—not the priest.

But Louise would like to do right by Teofilo and the rest of the community. On the one hand, the Catholic view of death envisions a soul released from the clay of its body, purified by confession and the sacrament of the last rites, and cleansed with holy water. On the other hand, as Father Paul's ruminations at the grave make clear, the Native Americans perform complex rituals to ensure good harvests—and the priest wonders whether he is being perversely manipulated by a congregation that remains deeply pagan. He goes so far as to doubt whether Teofilo is even really dead. But he is a wise priest after all, and knows which battles to avoid. He chides Leon for not calling the priest in to give last rites and conduct a funeral mass. Leon responds simply, "It wasn't necessary father." From the priest's point of view, this is heresy. From Leon's point of view, the feather, the lines of paint, the pollen, and the cornmeal were necessary, and the proper rituals had been performed.—Now it would be nice to have some holy water sprinkled on the corpse—not to cleanse it and protect it from diabolical intrusion, but so that grandpa would not be thirsty, so that, through some form of sympathetic magic, the old man "could send them big thunderclouds for sure." And the priest cooperates, despite his theological misgivings. Note that as the burial ends, we see in the distance a highway lane full of headlights. This nice detail insists on all the technology, all the skeptical complexity of the modern world, in order to deny any primacy to that skepticism and science. Survival depends on rain, and rain depends on proper ritual and pious forms—Native American forms, together with whatever useful ritual the Christians might have figured out.

34

Amy Tan Two Kinds (p. 464)

This episode from Tan's first novel, *The Joy Luck Club* (1989), contains extraordinary comic sparks struck off the flinty encounter between an ambitious mother and her recalcitrant daughter. The climactic argument in the piece occurs when the mother angrily asserts: "Only two kinds of daughters. Those who are obedient and those who follow their own mind! Only one kind of daughter can live in this house. Obedient daughter!" The daughter/narrator's hideous response alluding to her half-sisters who had died in infancy—"I wish I were dead! Like them"—works much too well. The mother is defeated, but the daughter fantasizes "worms and toads and slimy things crawling out of" her chest.

Doubtless, most students will understand this struggle, having experienced it themselves in various forms. An exploration of the differences between parents' aspirations for their children and the children's personal dreams could animate some lively classroom discussion.

But the story also displays the foibles of expatriate Chinese families—and those foibles can be hilariously funny. Read some passages aloud to savor the story's richly comedic tone, particularly the bragging disguised as complaining when Lindo Jong and Jing-mei's mother exhibit despair at their daughters' supposed failings.

At the outset of the story, Jing-mei's mother decides that her daughter should be a Chinese Shirley Temple, and they dutifully watch old movies to learn the tricks of the trade. This leads to a visit to a beauty training school for a (cut-rate) Shirley Temple haircut, which ends in disaster. At this point, the daughter, gaining enthusiasm for the prodigy game, begins to fantasize, seeing herself as a dainty ballerina, even as the Christ child "crying with holy indignity." Since the mother's notion of prodigious comes from the many out-of-date magazines she picks up as a house cleaner, the tasks she imposes on the narrator become increasingly bizarre. Jing-mei cannot learn the capitals of nations, she cannot recall the contents of lengthy Bible passages; she cannot stand on her head without using her hands. She learns to defeat her mother's constant attempts to discover some special talent, and is well on her way to freedom when they happen to see a nine-year-old Chinese girl prodigy play the piano on the Ed Sullivan show. Hilariously, the quest for the prodigious is reborn when the mother arranges lessons for Jing-mei with a deaf piano teacher. That quest doesn't end until the disastrous recital, and the bitter fight that devastates the mother.

But finally, Jing-mei softens toward her mother. After her mother's death, she learns that the "Pleading Child" and the "Perfectly Contented" child were "two halves of the same song." Without prompting, you might ask how many in the class sympathized with and understood the mother's point of view. Was the mother a monster manipulator trying to gain status through her daughter's achievements or was she simply trying to get her daughter to do her best?

Leo Tolstoy The Death of Iván Ilých (p. 1304)

The richly evoked world of Iván Ilých—a world of concrete physical detail inhabited by an assortment of largely petty, ambitious, and selfish people—is integral to this story's theme. A stable, affluent, middle-class world is Iván's by birth. He was not required to struggle for it. He questions neither his right to that world nor the values by which it is defined. He is, we are told, "a capable, cheerful, good-natured, and sociable man, though strict in the fulfillment of what he considered to be his duty: and he considered his duty to be what was so considered by those in authority." "Those in authority" are not only his official superiors who control his career but, more generally, the complex attitudes that govern middle-class life and impel him to conduct every detail of his life—from dancing to selecting a wife—so as to advance his career.

This context animates the startling sentence that begins chapter II: "Iván Ilých's life had been most simple and most ordinary and therefore most terrible." It is the ordinariness and simplicity, as we come to see, of a comfortable, secure, and tightly regulated society. Unquestioningly, Iván Ilých conducts every detail of his life with an eye to his social and professional success. And while he suffers minor disappointments and setbacks (his depression over not receiving the judgeship in a university town, the difficulties with his wife), his life is solidly successful. At the very moment in his life when he is flushed with success and happiness, Iván Ilých ironically sustains the trivial injury that leads to his long and painful final illness. He has taken everything into account in his well-regulated life except death. And it is only as he faces death that the full terror of his life is revealed to him.

His understanding of that life is embodied in the texture and details of the entire story. From the outset of the story, a nonhuman or antihuman quality is apparent in the mode of life Iván and his society live. In order to establish the nature of that society, Tolstoy begins the story immediately after Iván's death. For his friends, his death means the possibility of promotion, a card game missed; for his wife, his death means a grant of money from the government. Until he faces death, Iván Ilých's life is perfectly adumbrated by the opening section. He is actuated by the same superficial, calculating concerns and is incapable of establishing a vital and meaningful relationship with others. In a profession that brings him into daily contact with the real problems and passions of others, he remains cool and aloof. He successfully manages "to exclude everything fresh and vital, which always disturbs the regular course of official business, and to admit only official relations with people, and then only on official grounds."

As he approaches death, he comes to realize that his wife and friends are incapable of understanding the terror, the anguish, the anger he feels; unsurprisingly, he is merely a burden and an embarrassment to them. Significantly, the person who responds instinctively and sympathetically to Iván Ilých in his plight is the "clean, fresh peasant lad" Gerásim. Gerásim is the very antithesis of everything Iván's society represents. A simple peasant, close to the earth, he brings to his master what no members of the artificial, bureaucratic, selfish society can: an unquestioning and instinctive acceptance of and compassion for a fellow human being who is suffering. Notably, the only other person who responds to Ivan with the same warmth is a child, his own son.

This contrast between the dehumanizing, artificial society that has defined Iván's social and psychological life and the more human life represented by Gerásim (and the son) was central to Tolstoy's own life when he wrote this story. Eight years earlier, he had experienced a profound spiritual crisis that brought into question the very meaning of his life as a writer and as a wealthy member of Russia's hereditary aristocracy. As a result, Tolstoy renounced his earlier life (and writings) and lived thereafter as a simple peasant dedicated to serving his fellow man. Only such a primitive life, Tolstoy felt, informed by a few simple Christian precepts, could redeem man and save him from the spiritual death of modern civilization.

And in the final section of the story, after the physical suffering and the even more terrible mental anguish of Iván, Tolstoy brings his hero through the "black hole" of utter despair and terror into "light." This symbolic rebirth is sudden, mystical, and Christian, and releases Iván from terror and doubt. Freed from the prison of his selfish and artificial life, he is flooded with feelings of pity and forgiveness for those around him. But even more significantly, he accepts total responsibility for his own life, thus recognizing that it is he who must ask forgiveness of others. This fundamentally religious insight "rectifies" Iván's life and defeats death.

Alice Walker Everyday Use (p. 742)

The opening paragraphs of this story, describing the cleanly swept yard and Maggie's nervousness at the impending visit of her sister, effectively set the tone and suggest the tension of the narrative. The yard as an extension of the living room suggests a rural world, a closeness to the earth and a simplicity of life, that Maggie and her mother know the educated Dee will disdain. The narrator's own apprehensions as well as her tough-minded good sense emerge in the following section, as she dreams of being joined with Dee on the TV show. Like Maggie, the narrator stands in some awe of her educated daughter and so sees herself on the imaginary TV program reshaped exactly as Dee would like her to be: lighter of skin and weight, hair glistening, tongue sharp and defiant. But the narrator knows that her vision is only a dream, and in some ways an unworthy one, as her description of who and what she is indicates.

In the narrator's reminiscences and ruminations that follow, she recalls the fire that burned Maggie (and gave such pleasure to Dee), and Dee's attempts to educate a benighted mother and sister. Those reminiscences develop and heighten the dramatic tension between two ways of loving and feeling. Up to this point in the narrative we might say that, while the story is obviously about a black family, blackness is subordinate to the more general theme of family conflict arising out of a child's sense of shame about and rejection of her family's way of life.

But the arrival of Dee and her friend makes immediately clear that blackness is in fact an important part of the story's theme. Dee's childhood hostility toward her family and her African American heritage have now, presumably as a result of a university education, culminated in her adoption of some sort of black nationalism. Paradoxically, her new views embody a more profound rejection of her heritage that takes the form of a supercilious and cold interest in African American culture. Though she had hated the house as a child, now she wishes to photograph it—with a cow, whenever possible! What she is photographing is not the home that was once hers and is still her mother's and sister's; it is a curiosity, an artifact. Dee returns to her home not with love and care and understanding; she descends upon it like some insensitive anthropologist eager to examine the native ways and carry off as many decorative artifacts as possible.

That is the shameful and finally ignorant attitude expressed by Dee in her exasperated comment that gives the story its title. Maggie, Dee says about the quilts she covets, would "probably be backward enough to put them to everyday use." And indeed she would, for the quilts symbolize the living and vital continuity of a family and culture that Dee has rejected as dead. Intimidated as she is by her educated and forceful daughter, the narrator recognizes the profound significance of the fight over the quilts and, calling upon that very considerable strength we have seen she possesses, she insists that Maggie have them.

Dee is, in a sense, admirable for her defiance of white racism and in her inability to submit to an inferior role, while her mother is something of an Uncle Tom (see, for example, the final paragraph of the second section). Yet the moral weight is all with the narrator and Maggie. Thus, the story deals with the danger of allowing abstract ideas and ideology, however philosophically attractive, to take precedence over human beings and family and compassion.

Richard Wright   The Man Who Was Almost a Man   (p. 406)

While this work stands on its own as a powerful and ironic version of the universal theme of coming of age, students should be urged to read the paragraph on Wright in the "Biographical Notes on the Authors" at the end of the book. There they will learn that Wright himself grew up in the deep South at a time when total separation of the races, the system known as Jim Crow, kept African Americans in a state of perpetual subordination and oppression. At about age seventeen, Wright realized that he could not play the part of the ignorant, shuffling black that a racist society demanded and went north to Chicago, where he began his writing career.

One way to explain the paradox of the story's title is to remind ourselves that while the passage from childhood to manhood is signaled in very different ways in different cultures and at different times, it always involves two distinct but inseparably linked perspectives: the feelings of the young boy about himself (subjective), and the attitudes his society holds about him (objective). Many cultures define the precise age when the transition from boyhood to manhood occurs and celebrate the passage with a formal ceremony.

At the other extreme are the large, industrialized societies where for many young men the markers of manhood exist only in vague, attenuated forms.

While Dave has grown up in the rural South, he lives in a community that is dominated by the larger industrialized society, powerfully symbolized by the gun he covets. Dave feels strongly the stirrings of manhood in himself. But manhood is more than biology; it is also a social construct. Until society, family, and friends acknowledge Dave's manhood, he remains "almost a man." It is no accident that Dave, an American, feels that owning a gun is the simplest and most dramatic way to get that validation.

However, Dave is also black, which makes all the difference and gives Wright's narrative a specific historical and social meaning beyond most coming of age stories. Dave and his family essentially live in a state of peonage, heirs to the legacy of slavery and the system of sharecropping that succeeded it following the Civil War and emancipation. Dave spends his young life plowing for Hawkins for wages (in classic sharecropping, a tenant farmer paid as rent a share of the crop). It's obvious the wages are minimal, certainly not enough to build any kind of future. When Dave accidentally kills Hawkins's mule and realizes that it will take him two years of plowing to repay his debt (surely an indication that Hawkins has grossly inflated the mule's market value), he decides to make his escape.

That escape, we can be certain, is to the north, the direction that has historically meant freedom and opportunity for southern blacks. And yet, as Dave retrieves the gun in the moonlight and thrills to the sound as he squeezes the trigger, then jumps the train as he heads into his uncertain future, "somewhere where he could be a man . . . ," his expectations evoke sadness and irony. He is too innocent to fully understand that the gun on which his hopes rest represents violence, and that the ghettos of the north, where he will no doubt end up, will be plagued by the many kinds of violence racism spawns. Wright's story seems eerily prescient in its implication, faint though it is, that the frustration that propels Dave northward may very well turn into the black rage that will erupt later in northern ghettos.

Dave and his family exist in extraordinary isolation. There is no suggestion of any network of friends or extended family to give Dave and his family emotional or other support. For Dave, his mother represents nurturing and love, while his father is a stern and unsympathetic presence. In fact, Dave's resolve to leave is strengthened by his recollections of severe beatings at his father's hands. Perhaps saddest of all, Dave is a totally alienated protagonist. Except for the beatings and his regret at not having had the chance to scare Hawkins by shooting into his house, Dave has nothing to say, much less regret, about the life he is leaving.

Can Xue   Hut on the Mountain   (p. 359)

Students will undoubtedly find "Hut on the Mountain" tough sledding. One way to smooth their path to understanding this story is to discuss it in generic terms. While representative of the tradition of allegorical critiques of repressive states found not just in China but in Eastern Europe, other parts of Asia, and Latin America, "Hut on the Mountain" can also become more familiar to students if parallels are drawn to the genres of horror and absurdist, Kafkaesque narrative. Paying close attention to tone, mood, language, and the question of plausibility will help students see these parallels and understand what Can Xue is up to here.

The allegorical dimension will be the hardest to talk about, and the discussion may be just as good without the instructor providing very much background to Chinese history and politics. It is more important that students see the general idea — that the narrator of "Hut on the Mountain" is living with a family that is not functioning correctly, whose members are working against each other rather than together, and that this family lives on an inhospitable "bleak and barren mountain" populated by rats, wolves, cold winds, and perhaps a prisoner in a hut. It pays off when pursuing this angle to keep an eye on the physical state of the characters: their blood vessels throb, they have cold sweats, and their eyes hurt from the light. These symptoms, like the strange aspects of the mountain and the confusing failures of communication and perception exhibited by the characters (who repeatedly speak at cross purposes and have trouble hearing and seeing), can be understood as physical manifestations of whatever is out of whack in this family and the larger world or nation for which it stands.

The question of the fantastic, of what is "real" in this story and what is not, will trouble students. This reaction can be an opportunity not just to discuss our expectations of realism in fiction but also to think about the possibilities of intentionally subverting those expectations both for creating literary effect and for expressing something about the experience of people in certain kinds of situations — in this case, the experience of feeling that life is not as it should be under certain kind of governments or in certain kinds of societies. Drawing attention to the fact that the family relationships that seem to be going wrong here are between parents and children—that the parents do not seem to be fulfilling their responsibilities as parents—can help students see that just as we have expectations of fiction and of parents, we have expectations of states and societies, and when these expectations are not met, the effects are alienating and sometimes terrifying.

Poetry

Anonymous Bonny Barbara Allan (p. 1083)

There are many versions of this ballad of the cruel Barbara Allan, including some American versions. The English ballad is severely elliptical; things of crucial importance happen, but we learn only the consequences and frequently have to infer as best we can what occasioned them. The first stanza fixes an event in time—John Graeme fell in love with Barbara Allan in November. Clearly some time passes between the first stanza and the second (another version sets the death in May). Sir John is apparently dying of unrequited love, and presumably the proper response from Barbara will save him. But she replies to his implied request (ll. 13–14) with scorn (ll. 15–20). Because of his insulting refusal to toast her at the tavern, he shall never have her, though he were bleeding before her. He turns his face to the wall and dies, and his death does touch her. Her pitiless vengeance recoils upon herself, and she too dies, presumably for love. Or, is it possible that Barbara actively caused her lover's death, perhaps with poison, and expects to die herself, either by suicide or on the gallows?

Anonymous Edward (p. 1376)

Two matters might be emphasized in teaching this ballad: the mother's motive and the form of the poem. As is often the case in medieval ballads, we are provided with an event of profound psychological implications. Here Edward's mother uses her son as the executioner of her husband. We are never told why. Further, the relationship between Edward and his mother prior to the events must be inferred. What circumstances would make it supportable for Edward to murder his father on behalf of his mother? The great strength of this ballad derives largely from the complex, ghostly psychological presences that are generated from the artfully simple diction of the poem.

The form, somewhat modified from basic ballad meter, employs the typical repetitive refrains of the ballad form as well as incremental repetition as Edward alters only the last element in his first three answers ("O I ha'e killed my hawk sae guid, my reid-roan steed, my fader dear"). Lines 3 and 7 in each stanza are exact repetitions of lines 1 and 5, respectively. One explanation for such repetition is the musical character of ballads: they were sung, and such structure is common in songs. But, again, if the poem is read without the repetition (by skipping lines 3 and 7), a marked loss in the ominous tone and movement of the poem occurs. The repeated lines, in any case, demand an ironic tone, tinged with despair, while the initial statements may be read straightforwardly as exposition.

Note also the narrative structure of the poem as it builds to its horrid climax. Edward is a nobleman—he has a gaming hawk, many horses, towers and halls. Guilty of patricide, he must go into exile, giving up all the wealth and privilege of his position. His wealth is likely to be forfeit, for his wife and children must become beggars—that is his gift to them. But his gift to his mother is the worst of all—the curse of hell. That curse results in great tension, since readers do not understand Edward's bitterness. Not until the last line of the poem does the tension snap, as we discover that his mother was the principal mover of the tragedy.

Matthew Arnold Dover Beach (p. 1106)

We provide here an extended treatment of "Dover Beach" for those instructors who may wish to explore diverse critical approaches to the same literary text. The following is an in-depth look at "Dover Beach" from formalist, sociological, and psychoanalytic approaches.

A Formalist View

From the perspective of the formalist critic, the fact that Matthew Arnold was deeply concerned with how to enjoy a civilized life under the pressures of modern industrialization or that Arnold appears to have suffered in his youth an intense conflict between sexual and spiritual love may be interesting but ought not to be the focal point in an analysis of his poetry. After all, the historian is best equipped to reconstruct and illuminate Matthew Arnold's Victorian England, and it is the biographer's and psychologist's job to tell us about his personal life. A critic of "Dover Beach" who speculates on these matters is doing many things, perhaps quite interesting things, but he or she is not giving us a description of the work itself.

"Dover Beach" is a dramatic monologue, a poem in which a speaker addresses another person at a particular time and place. In the opening lines, Arnold skillfully sets the scene, introduces the image of the sea that is to dominate the poem, and establishes a moment of tranquillity and moon-bathed loveliness appropriate to a poem in which a man addresses his beloved. The beauty of the scene is established through visual images that give way, beginning with line 9, to a series of auditory images that undermine or bring into serious question the atmosphere established by the opening eight lines. In this contrast between visual and auditory imagery, a contrast developed through the entire poem, Arnold embodies one of the poem's major themes: appearance differs from reality.

In the second stanza, the "eternal note of sadness" struck in the final line of the first stanza is given a historical and universal dimension by the allusion to Sophocles, the Greek tragedian of fifth-century B.C. Athens. We become aware that the sadness and misery the speaker refers to are not the consequences of some momentary despair or particular historical event but are rather perennial, universal human conditions of mortal life. Indeed, the allusion to Sophocles and the Aegean extends the feeling not only over centuries of time but over an immense geographical area, from the Aegean to the English Channel.

The third stanza develops further the dominant sea imagery. But the literal seas of the earlier stanzas now become a metaphor for faith, perhaps religious faith, which once gave unity and meaning to life but now has ebbed away and left humankind stranded, bereft of virtually any defenses against sadness and misery. The "bright girdle furled," suggesting a happy and universal state, turns into a "roar" down the "naked shingles [i.e., pebble beaches] of the world."

The poet, therefore, turns, in the final stanza, to his beloved, to their love for each other as the only possible hope, meaning, and happiness in such a world. And his words to her echo the imagery of the opening lines with the important difference that the controlling verb *is* of the opening lines, denoting the actual and the real, is now replaced by the verb *seems*. The beautiful world is an illusion concealing the bleak truth that the world provides no relief for human misery. This grim realization leads to the powerful final image, which compares life to a battle of armies at night. We have moved from the calm, serene, moon-bathed loveliness of the opening scene to an image of violence in a dark world, where it is impossible to distinguish friend from foe or indeed even to understand what is happening.

"Dover Beach," then, is a meditation upon the irremediable pain and anguish of human existence, in the face of which the only possibility for joy and love and beauty is to be found in an intimate relationship between two human beings. The depth of the speaker's sadness is emphasized by his powerful evocation in the opening lines of the beauty of the scene. The first eight lines move with a quiet ease and flow with liquids and nasals, a movement enhanced by the balancing effect of the caesuras. In lines 9 to 14 the sounds also echo the sense, for now the sounds are much harsher as the plosive *b*'s intrude, and most of the lines are irregular, broken up by more than one caesura.

We have already noted that the dominant image of the poem, the key to the poem's structure, is the sea. It is the real sea the speaker describes in the opening stanza, but when it sounds the "eternal note of sadness," the sea becomes symbolic. In the second stanza, the speaker is reminded of another real sea, the Aegean, which he associates with Sophocles, and the developing unity is achieved, not only at the literal level (Sophocles listening to the Aegean parallels the speaker's listening to the northern sea) but at the symbolic level (Sophocles perceived the ebb and flow of human misery as the speaker perceives the eternal note of sadness). The third stanza further develops the sea image but presents something of a problem, for it is not altogether clear what the speaker means by "Faith." If he means religious faith, and that seems most likely, we face the problem of determining what period of history Arnold is alluding to. "Dover Beach" establishes two reference points in time—the present (1867) and fifth-century B.C. Athens—that are related to each other by unpleasant auditory images. Since the function of the lines about the Sea of Faith is to provide a sharp contrast between the poem's present and fifth-century B.C. Athens (the visual image of "a bright girdle furled" associates the Sea of Faith with the opening eight lines), the time when the Sea of Faith was full must lie somewhere between these two points or earlier than the fifth century. Since a formalist critic deals only with the work itself and since there appears to be nothing else wherein the poem that will allow us to make a choice, we might conclude that these lines weaken the poem.

For the formalist critic, however, the final stanza presents the most serious problem. Most critics of whatever persuasion agree that they are moving and memorable lines, poignant in the speaker's desperate turning to his beloved in the face of a world whose beauty is a deception, and powerful in their description of that world, especially in the final image. But what, the formalist critic will ask, has become of the sea image? Is it not strange that the image that had dominated the poem throughout, has given it its unity, is in the climactic stanza simply dropped? On the face of it, at least, a formalist critic would have to conclude that the abandonment of the unifying image in the concluding stanza is a serious structural weakness—lessened perhaps by the power of the images that replace it, but a structural weakness nonetheless. On the other hand, a formalist critic might commend Arnold for his effective alternation of visual and auditory imagery throughout the poem. The first four lines of the final stanza return to visual images of an illusory "good" world (controlled by *seems*, as we have already noted) and concludes with a simile that fuses a somber vision of darkness and night, with the harsh auditory images of alarms and clashes.

A Sociological View

To understand "Dover Beach," we must, according to the sociological critic, know something about the major intellectual and social currents of Victorian England and the way in which Arnold responded to them. By the time Arnold was born in 1822, the rapid advances in technology that had begun with the Industrial Revolution of the eighteenth century were producing severe strains on the social and intellectual fabric of society. An agrarian economy was giving way to an industrial economy, and the transition was long and painful. The new economy was creating a merchant middle class whose growing wealth and power made it increasingly difficult for the upper classes to maintain exclusive political power. The passage of the celebrated Reform Bill of 1832, extending suffrage to any man (women were not enfranchised until 1928) who owned property worth at least ten pounds in annual rent, shifted political power to the middle class and gave cities a greater political voice. It was not until 1867 that the franchise was extended to men of the lower classes. The intervening years were marked by severe social crises: depression, unemployment, rioting. Indeed, during these critical years, when England was attempting to cope with the new problems of urban industrialism, the agitation and rioting of the lower classes created genuine fears of revolution (many remembered very clearly the French Revolution of 1789).

The ferment was no less intense and disruptive in the more rarefied world of intellectual and theoretical debate. While it would be erroneous to assume that preindustrial England was a world of idyllic stability, there can be little doubt that the pace of change had been much slower than during the nineteenth century. Despite sectarian strife, perhaps the greatest stabilizing force in preindustrial England was religion. It offered answers to the ultimate questions of human existence and, on the basis of those answers, justification and authority for the temporal order—monarchy (or political control by a small aristocracy), sharp class distinctions, and the like. The technology that made industrialism possible grew out of the scientific discoveries and methodologies that challenged some fundamental assumptions and articles of faith. Scientific discoveries seemed to undermine the old religious faith (for example, Darwin's *Origin of Species,* published in 1859); the scientific approach of skepticism and empirical investigation, in addition to critical scholarship, led to numerous studies of the Bible not as a sacred text of infallible truth but as a historical text that arose out of a particular historical time and place. Close examination of the Bible itself resulted in discoveries of inconsistencies and contradictions as well as demonstrable evidence of its temporal rather than supernatural origin.

Matthew Arnold, born into a substantial middle-class family and educated at England's finest schools, established himself early as an important poet and as one of the leading social critics of the period. In much of his poetry and his voluminous prose writings, Arnold addressed critical questions of his time. The old values, particularly religious, were crumbling under the onslaught of new ideas; Arnold recognized that a simple reactionary defense of the old values was not possible (even if one still believed in them). Unless some new system of values could be formulated, society was likely to, at worst, fall into anarchy or, at best, offer the prospect of an arid and narrow life to individuals. And since the destiny of the nation was clearly devolving into the hands of the middle class, Arnold spent much of his career attempting to show the middle class the way to a richer and fuller life.

For an understanding of "Dover Beach," however, Arnold's attempt to define and advance cultural values is less important than his confrontation with the pain and dilemma of his age. Caught in what he called in one of his poems "this strange disease of modern life," Arnold found that modern discoveries made religious faith impossible, and yet he yearned for the security and certainty of his childhood faith. In his darker and more despairing moments, it seemed to him that with the destruction of old values the world was dissolving into chaos and meaninglessness. In these moments, he saw himself as "wandering between two worlds, one dead, / The other powerless to be born."

"Dover Beach" expresses one of those dark moments in Arnold's life — a moment shared by many of Arnold's contemporaries and modern readers as well, who, in many ways, instinctively understand the mood and meaning of the poem because the realities to which it responds are still very much with us. Simply stated, it is a poem in which the speaker declares that even in a setting of the utmost loveliness and tranquillity (a sociological critic might very well here discuss the opening lines in much the same way a formalist critic does), the uncertainty and chaos of modern life cannot for long be forgotten or ignored. For uncertainty and chaos so permeate the life and consciousness of the speaker that everything he sees, everything he meditates upon, is infected. The scene of silent loveliness described in the opening lines turns into a grating roar that sounds the eternal note of sadness.

In the second stanza, the speaker turns to ancient Greece and its greatest tragic playwright in an effort to generalize and thereby lessen and defend against the overwhelming despair he feels. If the confusion and chaos of modern life are part of the eternal human condition, then perhaps it can be borne with resignation. Yet the third stanza seems to deny this possibility, for it suggests that at some other time in Western history, Christian faith gave meaning and direction to life, but now that faith is no longer available.

Trapped in a world where faith is no longer possible, the speaker turns in the final stanza — turns with a kind of desperation because no other possibilities seem to exist — to his beloved and their relationship as the only chance of securing from a meaningless and grim life some fragment of meaning and joy. Everything else, he tells her, everything positive in which humans might place their faith, is a mere "seeming." The real world, he concludes, in a powerful and strikingly modern image, is like two armies battling in darkness. Whether or not the final image is an allusion to a particular historical battle (as many critics have suggested), it is a graphic image to describe what modern life seemed to a sensitive Victorian who could see no way out of the dilemma.

A Psychoanalytic View

"Dover Beach" is richly suggestive of the fundamental psychic dilemma of people in civilization. And since people in civilization are, by definition, discontented because social duties require them to repress their primal urges, it is not surprising that the opening visual images that create a lovely and tranquil scene—calm sea, glimmering cliffs, a tranquil bay, sweet night air—are quickly modified by the ominous "only" that begins the seventh line of the poem. That *only*, in the sense of "in contrast," is addressed to a woman who has been called to the window to see the quiet and reassuring scene. No reassurance, finally, remains, as the images shift to an auditory mode:

> Listen! you hear the grating roar
> Of pebbles which the waves draw back, and fling

The tone is strangely changed, the emotional impact of "roar" suggesting something quite different from the serenity of the opening image, and the first stanza closes with the sounds of the surf bringing "the eternal note of sadness in."

Why should sadness be an *eternal* note? And why is the visual imagery largely pleasing while the auditory imagery is largely ominous? The answers to these two questions provide the focus for a psychoanalytic reading of the poem.

The "eternal note of sadness" (an auditory image) represents Arnold's recognition that, however sweet the night air and calm the sea, the central human experience is sadness. At the point in the poem where that sadness is recognized, the poet recalls the Greek tragedian Sophocles, who heard that same note of sadness over two thousand years ago. (It is, after all, an eternal sadness.) For Sophocles, the sadness brings to mind the "turbid ebb and flow of human misery." Now Sophocles' *Oedipus Rex* ends with the chorus pointing out that no one should count himself or herself happy until at the moment of death he or she can look back over a life without pain. Fate, as it afflicted Oedipus, afflicts us all. As we mentioned, the fate of Oedipus provided Freud with the name of that psychic mode through which we all pass. We might all be guilty of parental murder and incest were it not necessary to repress those urges in order to construct a viable society. The unacceptable passions are controlled by guilt. We may not commit murder or incest on pain of punishment. We may not ever desire to commit murder or incest on pain of possible psychic punishment. The dilemma, the guarantee of guilt or the guarantee of discontent, defines the eternal note of sadness that the poet hears.

We might go further. In infancy and very early childhood, the tactile and the visual senses are most important. Somewhat later the auditory sense increases in importance. Consequently, the child recognizes security—certitude, peace, help for pain—tactilely and visually, in the warmth and the form of the omnipresent and succoring parent. Later, through the child's ears comes the angry "no!" When discipline and painful interaction with others begin, the child experiences the auditory admonition that frustrates his or her desires. It is significant to the psychoanalytic critic that in "Dover Beach" the tranquillities are visual but the ominous sadness is auditory—the "roar" that brings in the "note" of sadness, the "roar" of the sea of faith retreating to the breath of the night-wind, the "alarms," and the "clash" of ignorant armies by night.

We need to look at the opening lines of the final stanza. Certainly the principal agency developed by society to enforce the morality it required was religion. Ancient religious teaching recognized those primal urges that Freud systematically described and made them offenses against God. Faith, then, became the condition that made society possible; religious injunction and religious duty served as a sort of cultural superego, a mass conscience, that not only controlled human aggression but substituted for it a set of ideal behavior patterns that could guarantee a set of gratifying rewards. Hence the poet recalls:

> The Sea of Faith
> Was once, too, at the full, and round earth's shore
> Lay like the folds of a bright girdle furled.

This is a strange image. Surely the emotional tone of "the folds of a bright girdle furled" is positive—that bright girdle is a "good" thing, not an ominous thing. Yet, that girdle (i.e., a sash or belt worn round the waist) is restrictive. It is furled (i.e., rolled up, bound) around the land. In short, the Sea of Faith contains, limits, strictly

44

controls the land. In the context of the poem, that containment is a good thing, for without the restricting Sea of Faith the world, despite appearances,

> Hath really neither joy; nor love, nor light,
> Nor certitude, nor peace, nor help for pain.

Without strong religious faith, acting as a cultural superego, the primal aspects of the psyche are released—aggression comes to dominate human activity:

> And we are here as on a darkling plain
> Swept with confused alarms of struggle and flight,
> Where ignorant armies clash by night.

A certain confusion persists. On the one hand, the Sea of Faith serves a useful function as an emblem of the *superego* (loosely, the conscience), the name Freud gives to the guilt-inducing mechanism that incessantly "watches" the *ego*, or self, to punish it for certain kinds of behavior. When it is at the full, ignorant armies, presumably, do not clash by night. On the other hand, the superego as associated with auditory imagery is ominous. It reverberates with the painful experience of frustration. Finally, however, the usefulness of the Sea of Faith is illusory. The note of sadness is eternal. Sophocles, long before the foundation of Christianity, heard it. What emerges from the poem's images, understood psychoanalytically, is a progression from a mild note of sadness (frustrated desires) to alarms and clashes (threatening, uncontrolled, aggressive desires). The calm sea and the fair moon suggest a land of dreams—illusory and without substance. Sadness, struggle, and flight are real.

We need to deal with the woman to whom the poet speaks; we need to understand his relationship to her. The quest for that understanding involves another psychoanalytic principle, another set of images, and a reconsideration of the image of the Sea of Faith.

In earliest infancy, the *ego* (the sense of self) is not yet formed. The infant child considers the mother, particularly the mother's breast, as part of himself or herself. A gradual and painful recognition must occur in which the child is dissociated from the mother. The process begins with the birth trauma. In the womb, the child is utterly safe, never hungry, never cold. Although there are discomforts for a time after birth, the mother and her nourishing breast are so much present that the infant does not distinguish where he or she ends and the other, the mother, begins. But this state of affairs does not continue, and the infant becomes increasingly dissociated. Slowly the infant learns what is "him" or "her" and what is not, what he or she can control by will (moving an arm, say) and what he or she cannot (the mother's availability). In short, the infant learns the borders of his or her being, the edges of his or her existence.

Images of borders and edges constantly recur in the poem. Such images may be taken as emblems of dissociation—that is, symbols of the separation between the warm, nourishing mother and the child. Consequently, they are symbols of painful dissatisfaction. The Sea of Faith that

> . . . round earth's shore
> Lay like the folds of a bright girdle furled

seems, on the other hand, much like that warm, encompassing mother who, to the infant, was a part of the infant. But dissociation occurs, and the distressed speaker perceives that comforting entity withdrawing, retreating "down the vast edges drear / And naked shingles of the world." He has an edge and can no longer reside safely in close association with the source of comfort and security.

Instantly the speaker turns to the woman and says

> Ah, love, let us be true
> To one another!

He perceives his companion not erotically but as the source of security, as a replacement for the withdrawing emblematic mother. He offers his "love" a mutual fidelity not to reassure her of his commitment but to assure himself of hers. He wishes to dissolve the edges of his ego and associate, as in infancy, with his "mother." Such an association will protect him from a world in which "ignorant armies clash by night."

Matthew Arnold Growing Old (p. 1385)

The first two stanzas describe the normal physical decay that comes with advancing age—the loss of beauty and strength. But there is more to growing old, and that additional aspect is psychological rather than physical. In stanzas 3 and 4, the speaker declares what growing old is not. Age does not create a mellowed recollection of a fully lived life. Rather, to grow old is to be imprisoned, to forget that one was ever young. It is to lose the ability even to feel and to remember change, not "profoundly stirred," but with no emotion at all (heavily emphasized by the last "none" of stanza 6). Growing old, finally, is to perceive that the same "world" that had attacked him when he was a "living man" is now honoring a powerless, frozen phantom—a "hollow ghost." Note the difference in the imagery of stanzas 3 and 4 from that of the last three stanzas. Rejecting the euphemisms commonly associated with age— "mellowed," "softened," "sunset glow," "golden," "stirred," "fullness"—the speaker insists in the final three stanzas on a bleak reality: "immured," "prison," "weary pain," "feebly," "dull," "frozen," "phantom," "hollow ghost."

Hanan Mikha'il 'Ashrawi From the Diary of an Almost-Four-Year-Old (p. 182)

'Ashrawi, who earned a Ph.D. in the United States, writes in English. Though she has served as an eloquent spokesman for the Palestinian Authority, her public pronouncements, like her poetry, have a measured tone despite the exasperation she endures over the plight of her people. This straightforward first-person narrative describing a terrible injury to a girl child is remarkable for its bemused tone. The poem does not succumb to the hatred and rage that such an event usually engenders. Rather, the child wonders about her own world—how will the loss of an eye affect her perceptions? And she remembers the soldier who wounded her with "a look in / his eyes / I could not understand." Ask the class to comment on that "look." The poet parleys the trope in the final stanza, where our young narrator comments on a nine-month-old baby who also lost an eye because a soldier seems to be "looking for little girls who / look him in the eye." Why, you might ask, does the soldier, given the complex nature of the Israeli/Palestinian conflict, find it so difficult to deal with children who (too young and inexperienced to be fearful) look him in the eye? What is it about being looked in the eye that is so disturbing? Surely the poem's power depends upon its understated pathos—quite different from the bravado and passion of Tawfiq Zayyad's "Here We Shall Stay" (p. 495) and "A Million Suns in my Blood" (p. 497).

Hanan Mikha'il 'Ashrawi Night Patrol (p. 509)

In this poem, 'Ashrawi again assumes a persona—this time, an Israeli soldier on night patrol. And the poet infuses the narrator with an empathy rarely granted to adversaries. She perceives the soldier (though an enemy) as humane—one who recognizes the humanity of others—a recognition that remains, perhaps, the only hope when rage and violence dominate the passing days. Here, as in "From the Diary of an Almost-Four-Year-Old," children provide the understated emotional power that drives the poem. The narrator is confronting jeering, stone-throwing children—but it is "this deliberate / quiet in their eyes that / threatens to wrap itself / around my well-armed uniformed / presence. . . ." Even as he fires tear gas at them, he is troubled by "glimpsing / glimpsing the child I / was in one of them. . . ." You might ask for comments on the rhetorical effect generated by the repetition of "glimpsing." In the second half of the long second stanza, the narrator perceives, perhaps, that the children attacking him mirror the struggle for the establishment of Israel—that he discovers in his tormenters an image of himself. Might the allusion to the "organism on its evolutionary trek" relate to the evolutionary maturity of Israel colliding with the evolutionary beginnings of Palestine?

The narrator wishes to but cannot "grasp" the thread that ties him to his adversaries (consider again, the rhetorical energy lodged in the repetition "If I should once, just / once, grasp . . ."). And, finally, the narrator descends from his heightened awareness into a mundane world "clutching my / cocoon of army issue blankets." Firing on children who seek the same consideration that Israelis sought and now possess is too much for the narrator—the problem beyond his power to resolve. His only desire is for "a different posting / in the morning."

Again, 'Ashrawi, by granting her adversary a thoughtful humanity, by characterizing the children as having "this deliberate quiet in their eyes," compels a far more powerful response from her readers than would a jingoistic rant against foreign oppression.

W. H. Auden   Musée des Beaux Arts   (p. 1399)

The Musées Royaux des Beaux Arts in Brussels houses Pieter Brueghel the Elder's painting *Landscape with the Fall of Icarus,* which appears following Auden's poem on p. 1399. Auden also refers to two other paintings by Brueghel—*The Census* ("The Numbering at Bethlehem"), in lines 5–8, and *The Massacre of the Innocents,* in lines 10–13. Auden is responsive to Brueghel's vision that another's suffering is of little concern to those who must continue with their lives and labors. Further, there is a mundane banality about even great tragedy, contrary to the frequent historical and artistic celebration of transcendent tragic events. The fall of Icarus, whatever it might abstractly suggest about the failure of human aspiration and the failure of Daedalus as an artist-craftsman, does not generate in Brueghel or in Auden the pity and terror that are supposed to cause an emotional purging. Nothing of importance to the onlookers changes—the sun continues to shine, the ship sails on.

Robert Frost's "'Out, Out—'" can be usefully compared to this poem.

W. H. Auden   The Unknown Citizen   (p. 489)

As the parenthetical and rhymed subtitle suggests, the Unknown Citizen (with its echo of the Unknown Soldier) represents the perfect product of a mass, industrialized society; his life has been lived exactly as the experts who control society want it to be lived. He is the citizen whom Creon (in *Antigonê*) and the Ticktockman (in Ellison's story) wish to create: a man without an inner life, without a mind of his own that might question and create trouble. The state honors the Unknown Citizen as its supreme product precisely because every important fact about his life is capable of being measured. The satire is driven home in the last two lines, for in the society that honors the Unknown Citizen, freedom and happiness are irrelevant.

Bruce Bennett   The True Story of Snow White   (p. 178)

This Petrarchan sonnet does not celebrate love; it firmly sets the record straight on the foolishness of some fairy tales and folk literature. Poetic justice, alas, is more apparent in such fiction than in life. Hence, this "true" story of Snow White. As we compose this essay (Jan. 30, 2001), the morning newspaper reports the disappearance of a Ukrainian journalist who had the temerity to bluntly criticize his country's president. He disappeared some time ago, and recently his headless corpse turned up. Similar events crowd modern history. Snow White didn't criticize anyone; she became the victim of her own beauty. But this cruel queen left nothing to chance—she had the dwarfs terminated and demonstrated a relentless power so fierce that even the magic mirror "learned to lie." The sestet demonstrates the chilling quality of a power that extends even to children who do not weep at the whispered story (lest some of the queen's devices overhear) of a beautiful child harried to a "sleep" no "prince on earth has power to break." Most students will know the story of Snow White—likely they saw the film when they were young. But you may, perhaps, have some foreign or exchange students from a culture that does not include this tale in its folklore.

Can the poem (depending on explanatory footnotes) forcefully affect such students? Does the sonnet form, usually devoted to a lover's praise, add an ironic dimension to this celebration of hatred?

Elizabeth Bishop   One Art   (p. 1115)

Somewhat like Edna St. Vincent Millay's sonnet "Love is not all: it is not meat nor drink," this tightly constructed villanelle surrounds the idea of love without ever attempting to define it. Beginning innocently as a dissertation on the management of loss, the poem moves relentlessly through a sequence of more and more formidable losses, the last of which, of course, is the speaker's beloved, at which point, with just two parenthetical words—"(*Write* it!)"—she reveals both the motivation for her argument and its futility. In short, the art of losing "you" is quite impossible to master.

Note that the first losses—door keys, hours, her mother's watch—are all particularized. As Bishop builds her case, she moves to increasingly figurative language that culminates in the loss of two cities, realms, a continent. What do the students make of these metonyms? In the culminating stanza, quite deliberately, she returns to the modest particulars that invest the "you" of the poem with warmth and immediacy: "(the joking voice, a gesture / I love)." The logic of the climactic progression, thus, invests those humble humanities with more force than any of the preceding losses the speaker suffered.

William Blake   The Chimney Sweeper   (p. 152)

"The Chimney Sweeper" offers a good example of dramatic irony. The speaker is the young, innocent chimney sweep who comforts himself and Tom Dacre with the lessons of conventional Christian piety. The speaker himself believes that if he and others do their duty (and remain dutiful), no harm will come to them. But the cruelty of a social and religious system that (apparently) forces fathers to sell their young sons into such horrible lives, and the realization that those children dream of death as an escape, lead the reader to reject the very faith the young speaker has. We are compelled to ask what "duty" is and, whatever it is, whether it is defensible if it justifies the kind of inhumanity the poem describes.

William Blake   The Garden of Love   (p. 153)

"The Garden of Love" is yet another of Blake's many attacks upon the constricting and antihuman effects of conventional Christian morality. The speaker, in his innocent childhood, played on a green—The Garden of Love (much like the Garden of Eden before the fall)—where sin and guilt were unknown, and love (of nature as well as the body) was natural. When he returns as an adult, however, the speaker discovers that a chapel has been built on the green—an institutional structure, consecrated not to freedom and joy and affirmation but to a dour negation. Instead of the open green (the symbolism of the color is obvious), there is denial and death, and priests are binding the spontaneous "joys & desires" of innocent childhood with the "briars," the pain of "Thou shalt not." Those "briars," suggesting Christ's crown of thorns, relate these priests to those original crucifiers who rejected the message of love and joy that Jesus brought into the world. The Garden, then, is Blake's objective, summary rendering of the psychic process whereby the joyful innocence of childhood is transformed by a conventional Christianity into joyless, guilt-ridden adulthood.

William Blake   London   (p. 154)

The poem is an attack on the established order that makes life burdensome and crushes the men and women it was established to succor. The word "chartered" emphasizes the responsibility of government for the hopelessness of the people of London. The "mind-forged manacles" suggest that the people themselves participate in their own misery—they accept the mind-created social system that imprisons and oppresses them.

48

The chimney sweepers (cf. "The Chimney Sweeper") were practically slaves—sold to a master by their impoverished parents and made to labor in horrible circumstances. The very possibility of such child labor speaks worlds about the difference between the ideals of Christian institutions and the realities they preside over. The church is literally "blackening" in the dirty air of London, but it is also figuratively blackening in the face of a fundamental inhumanity that it either cannot or will not correct. The cries of the child-slaves "appall" the church; that is, they turn it "white" with fear, in an ironic interplay of black and white, both indicative of evil and horror.

The "palace walls," a metonym for government that should provide the wisdom and leadership required for a peaceful and prosperous society, are stained with the blood of the government's soldiers, just as the church is blackened by the cries of chimney sweeps. The government, established to care for the needs of its citizens, sends them off instead to kill and be killed. Most horrible of all, however, is the "curse" of the "youthful harlots." They curse a society that forces them into prostitution to survive economically, a society that through the repression of normal sexuality creates harlots. Further, the harlot's curse is venereal disease that often results in infant blindness and death. And the tears of fearful infants are appropriate, given the fate that awaits them; the very procreative urge of the society is destined to produce only more weak and woeful men and women; the wedding carriage is at the same time a funeral carriage.

William Blake A Poison Tree (p. 1104)

After stating the psychological principle in the first stanza, the speaker uses rather terse figures of speech to establish, with remarkable economy, the growth of wrath. The third stanza introduces the idea of a sort of inverted Garden of Eden. The poisonous tree of the poet's wrath is paralleled by another poisoned tree—the tree of the knowledge of good and evil that led to the expulsion from paradise and human mortality. The foe, like Adam and Eve, secretly steals and eats the fruit. But a tension develops in the final couplet. Presumably God was not gladdened by man's sinfulness; the speaker, revenged, is. Is the reader also gladdened by the death of the speaker's foe? The speaker admits that he cultivated that poisoned tree with fears, (false) smiles, and deceitful wiles—not particularly admirable behavior. The foe, on the other hand, is a thief. Perhaps the important didactic element in the poem is contained in the opening couplet: a proper and compassionate humanity tells its wrath and thereby ends it.

William Blake The Tyger (p. 152)

Many interpreters of this poem see it as a fairly straightforward statement of an ancient theological question: How can we account for the presence of evil in a world created by an all-knowing, beneficent God? The tiger—fearful, ominous, and threatening—burns brightly in the dark forests of primeval creation. Contrasted with the tiger is the lamb, which is meek, gentle, and associated with Christ. In fact, the lamb is introduced in a stanza (5) that apparently alludes to Lucifer's expulsion from heaven in Milton's *Paradise Lost*. The angels weep not only over the tragedy of Lucifer's doomed rebellion but also over the introduction of evil into the world, which will be one of the rebellion's consequences.

When this poem is read in the context of Blake's other works, however, this apparently clear-cut analysis does not fare so well. For one thing, Blake did not believe in the reality of evil in a metaphysical sense (evil is created by humans, as "London" powerfully shows). For another, he felt that Milton was wrong in *Paradise Lost* in making the rigid distinction between good (God) and evil (Satan). In *The Marriage of Heaven and Hell*, Blake declared, "The reason Milton wrote in fetters when he wrote of Angels & God, and at liberty when of Devils & Hell, is because he was a true Poet and of the Devil's party without knowing it." More to the point, he also asserted in the same work, "Without Contraries is no progression. Attraction and Repulsion, Reason and Energy, Love and Hate, are necessary to Human existence." The tiger represents repulsion and hate but, above all, energy; the tiger is, therefore, as important to humans as the gentle lamb.

Anne Bradstreet   The Prologue   (p. 149)

This poem introduced *The Tenth Muse Lately Sprung Up in America * * * By a Gentlewoman of Those Parts,* published in London in 1650, and surely one of the most delicious titles in American literature.

Our students are probably not aware of how firmly gender roles were defined in Europe and colonial America in 1650. Poets were men. Nervous about her bold, possibly inappropriate incursion into that male domain, Bradstreet timidly proposes no great ambition—no epics from this pen; I know my place as a woman, and certainly represent no threat to the male establishment. The third stanza reinforces this supposed inferiority of women with a peculiarly comic rhyme in the closing couplet. But the verses Bradstreet composed reveal that she had benefited from an education that included areas usually reserved for men. Women, generally, needed to learn practical homemaking arts—not classical literature.

But having properly denigrated her talent, having recognized her inferiority to Bartas, a popular contemporary author of religiously themed epics, and Demosthenes, who overcame a speech defect to become the paradigmatic classical orator, Bradstreet, finally, allows herself a little testiness. In stanza 5, she begins to exhibit a bit of feminist feeling. Why am I criticized for writing poetry instead of doing needlework? Why do men assume that women are witless? And in stanza 6, she steps out! The Muses, themselves, were women! In the last two stanzas, Bradstreet reaffirms her opening gambit: women, she supposes, will never write with the power that men exhibit, but grant me a little acknowledgement for what skills I display. She brings her plea home with a nice pair of images. I may not merit a laurel (i.e., "bay") wreath, but surely you might award a wreath of thyme or parsley (particularly suitable, perhaps, for a lady who ought to be in the kitchen). And if my work is like unrefined ore, it will serve nicely to enhance the "glistering gold" of poems written by men.

Bertolt Brecht   War Has Been Given a Bad Name   (p. 487)

Anyone who knows even a little about Brecht's life and writings will understand that this poem is saturated in irony. The very title suggests, ironically, that war always had a good name, so to speak, until that "natural and necessary" activity (l. 13) was discredited by the bestial excesses of the German government's attempt to exterminate the Jews and other "undesirables" during World War II. But irony is a tricky literary device: if a reader does not pick up on it, then he or she will not just misinterpret a work but rather receive a message that is precisely the opposite of the intended one. Such was the case of the eighteenth-century peer who rose in the English House of Lords to denounce the barbarity of "A Modest Proposal" (p. 625), Jonathan Swift's savage satire that recommended the slaughter of infants and the sale of their meat for food as a way of improving the miserable conditions of the Irish poor. An interesting exercise might be to ask students how both authors ensure that readers will recognize the tone of irony.

The ironic tone—and indeed the poem's theme—is introduced in the opening lines that deplore World War II because its barbarities have clouded the future of war. By the end, the speaker is registering irritation and regret that those responsible for the cruelties of World War II (the SS, the industrialists, the bishops) have made future wars harder to justify.

Brecht's irony is deepened by the contrast between the fastidious detachment of the prosaic language and what is being described. The agentless passives of "I am told" and "Are said," the faceless "people," the "Ruhr industrialists," above all the exquisite delicacy of "The extermination of certain peoples" give an antiseptic, bureaucratic cast to the unimaginable barbarity of Nazi Germany during World War II.

John Brehm   At the Poetry Reading   (p. 189)

The Iowa Writers Workshop ought to be identified as one prestigious womb of young writers in America, and students who have been to some poetry readings will have no difficulty in empathizing with the speaker. Not much needs to be explained here. On the one hand, you might attend to the speaker's easy distinction between a kind of barren and boring "art" and the intoxicating "life" represented by the poet's wife. On the other, point out that the two merge again in the last two lines—that luscious wife is, after all, a poem—presumably a much better poem than all that claptrap about loss of innocence and hydrogen.

What (in the absence of rhyme or repetitive meter) makes this a poem rather than prose set down in unequal lines? The work provides a nice insight into the "line" as a fundamental formal unit in poetry. You might have the students consider each line separately, then discuss the effect of either ending the line with the penultimate word, or adding the first word of the following line to the previous line. Which is better?

> I can't keep my eyes off the poet's
> I can't keep my eyes off the poet's wife's
> I can't keep my eyes off the

Or,

> Now he's on to science, a poem
> Now he's on to science, a
> Now he's on to science, a poem about

The exercise might produce a nice feel for the "poetic line" that, though firmly tied to the preceding and following lines, is, nonetheless, in some sense, an entity as well.

Joseph Brodsky   A Tale   (p. 504)

This whimsical, but underneath deadly serious, ballad on the generic connections among nationalistic empire-building, wealth, military adventurism, art, and history itself, is breath-taking in its relevance to the world we perceive as we write these notes (November 2004). The sixth stanza of the second section is, perhaps, a bit obscure, but it likely alludes to the visual aspect of the art that will display the consequences (for history) once we "push the button." "And lo, the world turns topsy-turvy, / in other words, goes bust." The ballad seems to chronicle war through the ages by incorporating horses and swords, by alluding to Carthage and to history, and to the art that renders history (not necessarily truthfully). But this war includes nuclear weapons—and, at its conclusion, the Emperor confronts mutants, falling temperature, and a motionless world—the consequences of nuclear explosions that utterly destroy the enemy. "'Hey enemy!' the Emperor shouts. 'Are you / there?'—There's no response." And we are left with a physical and moral emptiness that induces a bit of melancholy, but, finally, we still can enjoy the pleasure of a victor's cigar. We have, after all, by destroying all enemies, threatening to extinguish all life forms, finally put an end to war.

Gwendolyn Brooks   *from* The Children of the Poor   (p. 492)

Although *The Children of the Poor* appeared in 1949, most black Americans would argue that, despite the passage of over half a century, the issues Brooks raises, though somewhat mitigated, are still with us. In this sonnet, Brooks urges her fellow blacks to struggle for freedom, for only after that struggle has been won can the grace and beauty of her people flower. The first part of line 1 establishes the order in which the events must occur. Fiddling will express the soul of beautiful black people; but fiddling will not be possible, paradoxically, until black people, armed with hate and impervious to music and beauty, "Rise bloody" against their oppressors and win a space in which to be civilized, in which to pursue all the lovely arts represented by the fiddle.

Robert Browning   My Last Duchess   (p. 155)

This poem is a splendid example of dramatic irony, for as we listen to the Duke of Ferrara describe his last Duchess, and thus, obliquely, what he expects in his future Duchess, his cold arrogance emerges. From the outset he reveals the selfish pride that controls his human relationships. The Duchess is not a human being but the subject of a fine painting by a celebrated artist. Yet, even as he describes her failings, she emerges as a warm and attractive woman whose joyful pleasure in life was an affront

51

to the haughty Duke. He found it intolerable that she ranked his "favor at her breast" and his "gift of a nine-hundred-years-old name" with "anybody's gift." Of course, the Duke explains, he might have discussed his feelings with his wife, but that would have required more skill in speech than he commanded. Even if he had had the skill, he declares, it would have been demeaning to discuss the matter, "and I," he ominously continues, "choose / Never to stoop." He therefore "gave commands" that ended her smiles. What those commands were the Duke does not explain; but they have removed his last Duchess from the scene, leaving him free to remarry.

The following lines make clear that the Duke has been addressing the emissary of the Count whose daughter he hopes to marry. Having made clear what he will expect of his new Duchess (with a skill in using words that belies his earlier disclaimer), the Duke explains that while it is the woman herself he is most interested in, he is confident that the Count will not reject a reasonable demand for dowry (in lines that further reveal his considerable skill in speech as well as his overriding preoccupation with power and possession). As he leads the emissary downstairs, he proudly points out another fine art object, and we feel the full impact of the ironic distance between the Duke's fine aesthetic sensibility and pride of possession on the one hand and his moral insensitivity on the other. What he is bargaining for is not a wife but an ornament and a possession.

Robert Burns   A Red, Red Rose   (p. 1105)

The beginning of this lyric is so well known that the instructor will have to make some effort to penetrate its meaning. Why is the speaker's love like a red—rather than a pink, yellow, or white—rose? Why is "red" repeated—how does a red rose differ from a red, red rose? Is "sweetly" an appropriate modifier for "played in tune"? The first half of the poem owes much of its charm to the word play on "love." In the first stanza, "love" is a noun standing for his lady; in line 6 it is a noun standing for his condition, really a modifier; and in line 7 it is a verb. It might be argued that the poem flags in intensity toward its conclusion, since the hyperboles of the center of the poem are certainly more striking than the poem's conclusion.

Thomas Campion   I Care Not for These Ladies   (p. 1097)

This poem draws upon two ancient traditions: one associating the city with artificiality and game-playing sophistication; the other, by contrast, associating rural life with honest and open simplicity. The speaker rejects the painted ladies of the city whose love must be purchased with elegant fineries. He prefers the straightforward simplicity of the "nut-brown" Amaryllis (a conventional name for the country lass in pastoral poetry), who, after a brief struggle, is always willing.

Rosemary Catacalos   David Talamántez on the Last Day of Second Grade   (p. 179)

This poem celebrates the life-affirming exuberance of an irrepressible seven-year-old child while, at the same time, suggesting that the pedagogic principles that teachers routinely apply may tend to stifle creative energy The teachers apparently propose that "rules," not creative impulse or the emotional energy of a child's observations of the world around him, dominate one's early education.

David lives in an Hispanic community (note the names of the house and businesses in the concluding stanzas). His mother, we are told in the first line, is at work. We may surmise that David's family is not wealthy, and David himself is probably not subject to a great deal of parental control during the day. His difficulty with spelling, and English in general (see lines 22–23), indicate that English is not his native tongue. We may reasonably surmise that David does not always listen, does not stay in his seat, is not quiet. Furthermore, his work is constantly "marked down" (l. 9)—not necessarily because he is wrong, but because he doesn't follow the "rules." Critical red marks afflict him because he doesn't put his name in the right place, because he didn't skip a line between the heading and the answers, because he is messy, because (worst critical affliction of all) he adds ("freehand" — a telling word here) a bird, clouds, a butterfly to his artwork. Surely the poet has stacked the rhetorical deck in David's favor. And, surely, we sympathize with the child as he crosses out the "teacher's red numbers" and replaces them with giant affirmations of his own existence: "Yes! David, yes!"

You might generate a lively debate about how schools work. After all, rules are necessary, and the value of teaching is likely to be diminished in a lawless classroom. Furthermore, exuberance doesn't compensate for the absence of skills and the discipline to apply them. Our students can, surely, provide their own anecdotes of deadly repressive teachers; perhaps, as well, they will remember the exciting teachers who rewarded exuberance, and encouraged them to create outside the lines. In any case, the language of this poem is clearly designed to defend David's position. Ask the students to demonstrate how the poem's language functions to that end.

Victoria Chang Morning Ritual (p. 1421)

We don't know how old the speaker is, and, doubtless, will be shocked at the implication of the last two lines. Traditionally, poems like this lean toward a sentimental reflection on family ties. Memories of grandmother, dying in the upstairs bedroom, lovingly cared for by her children and her children's children — such ageless celebrations of traditional family life appear in the literature of most cultures. But here we have a different sort of response. The speaker wants that bed, and, obviously, wishes her grandmother would just push off — the sooner the better. Though her father superstitiously rubs the Buddha's head to prolong his mother's life, the speaker defiantly wears white (the color of death in Chinese culture) and sticks her chopsticks vertically in her rice bowl — presumably another invitation to bad luck. Prevented from any but symbolic actions to hurry the death of her grandmother, the speaker takes particular pleasure in maliciously stealing her grandmother's raisins. It might be interesting to ask the students to reflect, first, on the nature of their own households, and then on the nature of this household. What are the grandmother, the father, and the child like? Do any of them merit the reader's sympathy? Disapproval? Is the child's malice purely a function of her reprehensible greed to acquire the bed the dying grandmother occupies?

Sandra Cisneros My Wicked Wicked Ways (p. 188)

Students should be clear at the outset that the speaker is describing an old photograph of her father and mother and herself as an infant. The speaker describes her father in the first stanza — a handsome man, presumably dressed in fashionable clothes of the 1950s, with a hat rakishly tilted over one eye and wearing two-toned shoes. In the last line of this stanza, the focus shifts to the mother, who is then described in the first half of the following stanza.

The four lines devoted to the mother describe her expression, which might be mistaken for crying but in fact was caused by the sun's glare. The relevance of this explanation is immediately apparent in the following four lines about "the woman," who "does not come till later." With the reference to this woman, the short, declarative, mostly simple sentences begin to take on an emotional freight and significance all the more powerful because the staccato style at first seems to be devoid of passion. The description of the father in the opening lines — the man who looks like Errol Flynn (who was not only a famous actor but also a notorious womanizer) — now takes on more significance; so does the mother's hatred of the two-toned shoes, as part of the portrait of a handsome philanderer.

The third stanza quickly sketches in the aftermath: the angry scene over the other woman, then the emotions ebbing into forgetfulness as the years go by. Throughout the poem, the iceberg of rage and unhappiness concealed beneath the surface is implied by the dry and rapid details. Consider, for example, "After a while everyone / will forget it" (ll. 24–25). Everyone seems to suggest that the scandal was widely known within the family and over the years took its toll.

The concluding lines effectively return to the photograph and focus on the infant speaker in the arms of her mother. In the final line, the speaker seems to identify with her errant, "bad" father, not in defiance of her mother but in the sad (and now retrospective) realization that the path of goodness is difficult to stay on. The title of this poem is the title of Cisneros's third volume of verse, which contains other poems suggesting the sexual guilt of a writer brought up in a strict Catholic environment.

Lucille Clifton   There Is a Girl Inside   (p. 1127)

We had a difficult time deciding which thematic section this poem belongs in. We decided to leave it in "Love and Hate" even though good arguments could be made for including it in other sections. The writing topic in the text asking students to compare it with Helen Sorrells's "From a Correct Address in a Suburb of a Major City" explains why it might be included in "Conformity and Rebellion." The speaker's struggle against old age and its stereotypes makes the poem appropriate for inclusion in "The Presence of Death." We mention all this not because students should be concerned with our thematic divisions as abstract categories but because a lively, illuminating discussion about this poem could be generated by asking students just what it is about.

Is it about love? It is, in the sense that the speaker protests against the decay of her body, the "old woman" with "gray hairs," inside of which is a vital, young girl who, in the controlling metaphor of the poem, is like a green tree in the woods, ready to burst into a blossom that her lovers will harvest in wild wonder. If we make a distinction (not necessarily an invidious one) between love and lust, however, we are surely dealing with lust in this poem. This woman is not caught up in the throes of a romantic dream (though there is tenderness enough implied by the "honey and thyme" of line 16). She is "randy as a wolf," she is a "green tree/ in a forest of kindling" (ll. 6–7), ready to take fire and amaze everyone "with the damn wonder" (l. 18) of her sexuality.

But if the poem is about love (or lovemaking) and presents a speaker who rebels against stereotypes imposed on the elderly, it is also about decay and death. The speaker's declaration that she will not "leave these bones / to an old woman" (ll. 4–5) signifies her determination to rage against the dying of the light. From this point of view, the poem bears comparing with Matthew Arnold's "Growing Old," W. B. Yeats's "Sailing to Byzantium," and Dylan Thomas's "Do Not Go Gentle into That Good Night."

Judith Ortiz Cofer   Latin Women Pray   (p. 810)

Since the poem's twenty lines of free verse are clear, the most interesting approach is to ask students to characterize its tone—that is, the relationship between the poet and the women she is describing. It is a safe bet that the women themselves would not (could not?) describe their situation in the same way. Clearly, the description of God's lineage and the contrast between His skin color and that of the praying women is ironic. The poet further assumes a kind of omniscience in presuming to know God's feelings (another irony?) and the content of the women's prayers. But the last six lines indicate that the poet is distilling her knowledge of Latin women—the names in line 12 suggest a composite portrait—into the generalizations she makes about them. As befits a poem that is light rather than heavy-handed, amused rather than angry, the poem comes to a witty conclusion: however alienated the poet thinks these women should be from this God who has been "[u]nmoved by their persistent prayers," she understands that if He could at least speak Spanish, they would accept the oxymoron of a powerless God.

Billy Collins   Sonnet   (p. 1128)

After dealing with typical love sonnets, let students enjoy this clever takeoff on the Petrarchan form. Though none of the lines exhibit end-rhyme, the poem is loaded with alliteration, assonance, and occasional internal rhyme. Note the assonant sequence in the first four lines: *we/need/...teen/seas/beans*—no wonder the poem seems to rhyme. The next quatrain delivers *easily/Elizabethan* and *iambic/rhymes/lines*. Further, note the alliteration of lines 3 and 4: *launch, little, love, left*. This sonnet turns out to be an example of what it is attempting to accomplish—like many sonnets, it is a seduction poem. And the final sestet, in typical sonnet fashion, resolves the issue. Laura, somewhat randy, no doubt, pleads with her would-be lover to stop wasting time by trying to seduce her with windy poems, get out of those ridiculous costume-drama clothes, snuff the candles, and come to bed.

Victor Hernandez Cruz   Problems with Hurricanes   (p. 1419)

Students won't have trouble with this poem. The philosophical field worker has a refined sense of the sublime and the ridiculous. If you must be killed by a hurricane, there is a certain honor in being drowned or slammed by that furious wind into a mountain boulder. But one needs to exercise some caution in order to die with dignity. The trouble is that, in a hurricane, you are more likely to be killed by a flying fruit. How could your family bear to explain that a mango smashed your skull, or that you "got killed by a flying / banana"?

   Well, we suppose you can turn even this lighthearted reflection into something serious after all. You might ask the class to consider (absent that hurricane) what sort of death robs the victim of dignity; what sorts of death remain a celebration of the ended life. One soldier dies by hurling his body on a grenade to save his buddies; another drowns in a rice paddy by accidentally driving off the road. But to defend one's honor in a hurricane it is necessary to "beware of mangoes / And all such beautiful / sweet things."

Countee Cullen   Incident   (p. 169)

One needn't belabor this simple and moving poem beyond pointing out the effective irony of the title. In a literal sense, the episode the speaker describes is an "incident"— a minor, casual event. Yet the title also suggests that the violation of the child's innocence by racial bigotry is a common, ordinary event.

e. e. cummings   the Cambridge ladies who live in furnished souls   (p. 797)

Cambridge, Massachusetts, is the home of Harvard University, where the nineteenth-century poet Henry Wadsworth Longfellow taught (it was also the alma mater of e. e. cummings). Cummings views the Cambridge ladies (perhaps in contrast to their pioneer ancestors) as upper class but spiritually empty. Their lifelessness is immediately apparent, for their minds and souls are described as one might describe a house or apartment: "furnished" and "comfortable." We are not surprised to learn, therefore, that for these superficial ladies, the pleasant poet Longfellow is as believable as Christ. Nor are we surprised to discover that their lives are spent idly in charitable activities for the poor (the "is it" in line 8 wonderfully suggesting the ladies' indifference to the objects of their charity). The hollowness of their lives is underscored by "permanent [i.e., expressionless] faces" that delight in gossip. In the final lines, it is the moon—suggestive of the vast, real world these ladies do not acknowledge that angrily protests against their narrow lives. The final line seems to suggest that the ladies have reduced the moon—like Christ, the suffering poor, and everything else— to the passionless, flat scale of their lives, symbolized by the brittle candy.

e. e. cummings   if everything happens that can't be done
(p. 1111)

Love is better than learning, says cummings, in this modern treatment of a familiar theme that celebrates the heart (as emblemized by nature) above the intellect (as emblemized by books and teachers). The central statement on the condition of the lovers is the word "one," with which the poem paradoxically ends—the merging of two into one being a traditional figure for lovers.

Cummings's syntax often defies the rules of ordinary discourse. Sometimes he changes the parts of speech of words; thus, in "one hasn't a why or because or although," words never so used are made nouns; and in "so world is a leaf so tree is a bough," nouns (*leaf* and *tree*) are made to function like modifiers. Sometimes he telescopes separate clauses so that the object in the first clause becomes the subject in the second clause, as in "and anything's righter / than books / could plan" and "buds know better / than books / don't grow." That telescoping of clauses is featured in lines 2–4 of each stanza. The stanzas are actually fairly regular, and printing lines 2–4 and 6–8 of each stanza as single lines would reveal a regular rhyme scheme of *aaba* (the consonantal off-rhymes in the first and last stanzas being the only deviations from regularity). The poem is further cemented by the repetition of the last word in each stanza as the first word in the succeeding stanza. The poem is, in short, quite formal.

e. e. cummings nobody loses all the time (p. 1395)

Poets writing about death rarely see it as the occasion for starting a worm farm. Poets writing about erotic love, on the other hand, often see death this way (cf. Marvell, "To His Coy Mistress"). Poe's poem "The Conqueror Worm" also celebrates the worm, but with a tone that distinguishes it utterly from this poem.

The first line of this poem is presumably justified by the last line—finally, Uncle Sol will not fail. But his success simply underlines the despair of a man who can escape failure only through suicide. The poem might provide the opportunity for a discussion of the line as the basic poetic unit. Most of the lines are not end-stopped, yet frequently they end at a happy syntactic moment. Further, the poem is marked by considerable assonance, alliteration, and consonance, all of which provide an elusive melody behind the prosaic lyric. Consider, for example, "my Uncle Sol's farm / failed." The vowels of *Uncle Sol* come close to assonance; *Sol* and *farm* are assonantal; the *m* of *my* is picked up in the *m* of *farm*. The alliteration of the last two words is melodically reinforced by the closeness of their vowel sounds; the sibilance of *Sol's* is reinforced by the hissing of the following *f* sound. The sequence of three stressed syllables, with the third occurring in a new line, provides a sort of funereal tolling to accompany the message.

e. e. cummings O sweet spontaneous (p. 1397)

This poem, like many others of cummings (particularly "if everything happens that can't be done"), expresses the poet's anger at those who attempt to reduce the spontaneous beauty of the earth to the Procrustean formulas of philosophical systems, the cold rationality of scientific theory, or the arrogant certainties of religious dogma. He compares such people to dirty old men—they are prurient and naughty, they prod and squeeze and buffet—bent upon violating a lovely and innocent beauty. But these blandishments are pathetic and futile, for the earth remains true to its only and eternal lover, death, in a union that creates spring. This last idea is strikingly similar to the statement in Wallace Stevens's "Sunday Morning" that "death is the mother of beauty."

While it may be difficult to account for all the idiosyncrasies of cummings's punctuation and line arrangement, this poem does offer an opportunity for students to deal with some of the more elusive elements and effects of poetry. Single-word lines tend to slow down the movement and give prominence to words. Likewise, cummings's unconventional punctuation controls the end-stops and caesuras perhaps more decisively than conventional punctuation. In a poem that has none of the elements of conventional form, cummings achieves cohesion through the use of alliteration, assonance, and consonance. Finally, students might profitably speculate on why cummings, a modern poet, uses obsolete forms ("thee," "thy," "thou," and "answerest") to apostrophize the earth. Perhaps such biblical-sounding forms help reinforce the speaker's conviction that the "spontaneous earth" has a divine validity superior to the systems that attempt to define and limit it.

e. e. cummings   when serpents bargain for the right to squirm
(p. 1112)

Have students compare this (relatively) plain old-fashioned Shakespearean sonnet to other older sonnets they have read. The fun is in the sequence of compelling and unusual images—much in the spirit of Donne's famous "Song" (p. 1099). Donne satirizes court society while he writes of his despair at ever finding "a woman true, and fair." Cummings describes a nature gone awry as the condition required for finding an "unanimal mankind." We are, after all, animals—a part of nature in which serpents unconditionally squirm, thrushes sing, and oaks bear acorns. Mankind, by implication, is a creature adorned (and, presumably, sullied) by animal characteristics.

Mahmoud Darwish   Identity Card   (p. 688)

As in the other works in this casebook, the voice of the speaker is important to "Identity Card." Comparing the three would be a good way both to help students focus on form—on how Darwish creates the voice of his speaker—and also to help them think about what is influencing the emotional tenor of that voice. Identifying the causes of the poem's tone—the answer to the repeated rhetorical question, "what's there to be angry about"—requires a little background, but the poem makes plain, from its title to its historical and contemporary grievances, what the causes are. Recognizing one of the most important causes, stated in the poem's title, can lead to a discussion of the ways the situation affects identity—a phenomenon of a different order from the equally devastating effects of displacement and hunger.

Another useful angle of approach could begin with making sure that students understand that Amos Oz ("If There Is Justice," p. 675) and Darwish are on opposite sides of this conflict. By exploring the ways in which the two works do not express entirely different opinions about the conflict, students not only can understand the works more fully but also might think in more complicated ways about that conflict and other, similar situations. Darwish, as a member of a displaced people, expresses an anger felt by all in his situation; in contrast, Oz more subtly reflects on the self-doubt of the aggressor, who, even if he believes he is using force for the purpose of self-defense, must deal with the consequences of aggression not just on its target but on himself.

Catherine Davis   After a Time   (p. 1410)

This poem is a reply to Dylan Thomas's "Do Not Go Gentle into That Good Night." In precisely the same villanelle form, and stanza by stanza, Catherine Davis reasserts literature's more dominant attitude toward death in a rebuttal to Thomas's urge to rage. We are born "stripped," and we die stripped of physical and mental qualities by age. In the second stanza, here, Thomas's wise men have not the wit left to understand their probing and do not regret their failure, since, finally, all losses are the same. In the third stanza, the "frail deeds" of Thomas's good men are judged "a losing game." In the fourth stanza, the wild poets are subdued by the "bare thought" of mortality. In the fifth stanza, Thomas's grave men do not regret the "treachery" (of a life that hid gaiety from them)—"the want, the blame" through which they lived—for those too are stripped at death. Finally, age and infirmity so deplete us that we go to death not raging but tame, stripped the way we came.

C. Day-Lewis   Song   (p. 1088)

See the entry for Christopher Marlowe, "The Passionate Shepherd to His Love."

Emily Dickinson   After great pain, a formal feeling comes
(p. 1386)

The poem throughout attempts to illustrate and define its first line. What associations with the word "formal" make it an appropriate adjective for "feeling"? What might an "informal feeling" be like? Note that the images evoke the tension and rigidity that follow "great pain." Words like "ceremonious," "Tombs," "stiff," "mechanical," "Wooden," "Quartz," "stone," "Lead," "Freezing," and "Stupor" all serve to define the "formality" of the first line. The last four words of the poem reveal the powerful possibilities of almost inarticulate diction. Practically a cliché, the words nevertheless remarkably release the tension built up in the poem. Lines 3–4 of the first stanza introduce the timeless quality of great pain through the allusion to Christ's pain—the redemptive pain upon which the salvation of all depends—and the confused question implies that a day of great pain is like two thousand years of great pain, and allows us to infer that the speaker's pain, like Christ's, is redemptive.

Emily Dickinson   Apparently with no surprise   (p. 1387)

The relatively light tone of this piece provides a counterpoint to its chilling and ominous point. The happy flowers, apparently, are not surprised by their fate—the sun takes no notice of the blond assassin—and, presumably, God is pleased. Is the speaker purely objective in her report of the inevitability of death? Is she resigned? Or is there, in the final three lines, a hint of distaste at the divine order? The regular ballad rhyme of the first four lines is not continued in the last four; the final word, God, is thrown into relief because it violates the expected rhyme, but it is incorporated into an assonantal sound pattern: *unmoved-off-another-approving-God.*

Emily Dickinson   I felt a Funeral, in my Brain   (p. 157)

Because this poem dramatizes a funeral, most students assume it is about physical death. They tend to overlook the fact that the opening stanza announces a funeral "in my Brain" that leaves the speaker with the feeling "Sense was breaking through." In stanza 2, the mind grows numb; in stanza 3, the soul creaks; and, in the climactic final stanza, reason collapses. This poem is one ("After great pain, . . ." is another) of Dickinson's great poems describing the ravages of intolerable pain, of grief that finally becomes unbearable.

The "Mourners" of the first stanza appear to be personifications of the grief and pain. The funeral service is dominated by lugubrious and insistent sounds: treading, beating, and, as tension mounts, the ominous creaking of the heavy "Boots of Lead." These discrete sounds finally blend into a great tolling of space as the speaker, like some solitary ship sailing a surreal sea, approaches a catastrophe. The speaker's world, under pressure, inexorably contracts. She becomes merely "an Ear." Now the sounds that have dominated give way to an ominous silence, a kind of calm before the storm.

The storm breaks in the final stanza when the "Plank in Reason" breaks and the speaker plunges through worlds of nothingness into oblivion. Whatever other meanings the "knowing" of the final line may have, it signals the end of even that narrowly focused self-awareness that allowed the speaker to describe the process of spiritual death.

Emily Dickinson   I heard a Fly buzz—when I died   (p. 1386)

Inevitably, the fly in this poem has been the object of numerous symbolic readings. Is it life being rejected by the speaker? Is it symbolic of carrion nature? Is it somehow demonic? We think not. It is a remarkably appropriate, minuscule fact of experience to perceive at death; its carrion nature and its buzz serve well as harbingers of death, but it is principally a real fly—the last point of life the shrunken perceptions of the dying speaker can identify.

The metaphorical language of the first two stanzas is notable. The atmosphere in the room where watchers await the certain death of the speaker is like the calm between "Heaves of Storm." The stormlike pain and agony of the dying speaker are stilled, and the friends and relations are past tears, bracing themselves for the return of the storm, the death agony itself, figured as the appearance of God. Meanwhile, in the understated language of the law courts ("willed," "assignable"), the speaker has divested herself of all earthly possessions. The fly is reinvoked as the final point of experience, the last sensory experience before the "Windows failed." Windows, of course, cannot fail—the senses of the speaker, her windows to the world, fail. The failing windows and the last paradoxical line, "I could not see to see," objectify death, placing it, somehow, outside the speaker, who reports that death is simply darkness.

Emily Dickinson Much Madness is divinest Sense— (p. 477)

The particular strength (or weakness) of this poem is that it states what most people will consider a general truth but leaves the matter at the level of generalization. It is not a political poem, although it is reasonable to suppose on the basis of the disparaging reference to "the Majority" that Emily Dickinson is thinking of a society that rules by majority vote. Without becoming too heavy-handed about the poem, it is worth noting that many ancient and primitive societies connect madness with divinity and special insight, an idea that one finds embodied in the Shakespearean fool. And in an extraordinary number of heroes of modern fiction—Richard Wright's Fred Daniels, Joseph Heller's Yossarian—madness is a form of sanity.

Emily Dickinson She rose to His Requirement (p. 477)

Much has been written about Emily Dickinson's many so-called "bridal poems," which deal with the tension she herself felt between earthly and heavenly love. One critic, in discussing these poems, writes that Dickinson, "like Edward Taylor and other religious poets, . . . dramatically merges the sacred and the profane aspects of human passion, transforming her desire for human marriage into a Bride of Christ vision." While one might argue that "She rose to His Requirement" belongs to this group, it seems to strain the poem's plain earthly meaning to try to read into it a heavenly theme. Perhaps, more simply, it expresses a feminist perspective on the spiritual price a woman (certainly a nineteenth-century woman) must pay for respectability. To the extent that the poem is autobiographical, it explains why Dickinson chose spinsterhood (and poetry) rather than marriage.

That price is succinctly suggested in the first stanza. The spatial metaphor locates "His Requirement" above and thus superior to the speaker's life. What he (or marriage) will demand of her is serious. In exchange for "The Playthings of Her Life" she will assume "honorable Work," that is to say, a role that is socially recognized and approved. The role is a consuming one, admitting no distinction between "Woman" (private and introspective) and "Wife" (public and social). At the general level, Dickinson is saying that a woman remains a trivial creature until marriage confers on her seriousness, honor, and dignity. The autobiographical subtext is that for a person like Dickinson, marriage constitutes spiritual entombment.

But the poem uses the past tense, describing a woman who has already married. The second and third stanzas describe the process by which the woman is entombed in the wife. The syntax of both is gnarled. It would seem that "Amplitude," "Awe," and "Prospective" are the object of the preposition "Of" in the dependent clause that begins the second stanza, but that "Or" in the phrase "Or the Gold" begins a parallel dependent clause, and should be read, "Or if the Gold. . . ." In any event, we can paraphrase the second stanza as follows: if the woman lost in marriage the awareness of life's scope, mystery, breadth ("first Prospective" perhaps alludes to youth's sense of limitless possibilities), or if the frictions of married life erode the most valuable part of her being ("Gold"), we can never know.

The final stanza is dominated by the simile of the sea. In the darkness of the sea's depth, the true spirit of the woman, entombed but not dead, abides. Perhaps the sea is an image of the woman's inner, buried life, and the meaning of the penultimate line is that we can never know whether her true self has transmuted into pearl or weed.

The density of the poem's language is matched by a complexity of form. The rhyme scheme is *abcb, cdec, fghi*. The meter is alternately iambic tetrameter and iambic trimeter (with variations such as the extra beat of the first line and the anapest of line 3). It was this kind of disregard for the poetic conventions of her day that made Dickinson realize early on that she would never be recognized in her lifetime. In fact, the few poems published during her lifetime were done by well-meaning friends who changed parts of the poems to eliminate what one of her friends referred to as "her fractured grammar" and otherwise make them more conventional.

Emily Dickinson   What Soft—Cherubic Creatures—   (p. 787)

Emily Dickinson begins her scathing satire on fashionable ladies with a stanza that seemingly praises them for those genteel qualities much prized in her day. They are gentlewomen, soft and utterly feminine. But the compliment here is ambiguous, for lines 3 and 4 suggest that the women are superficial and decorative, as well as coldly remote in an explicitly sexual sense.

Indeed, so rarefied are these ladies that they are horrified by ordinary human nature, "freckled" suggesting both a healthy outdoor quality (in contrast to the images of decorative fabrics the ladies are associated with) as well as the imperfections of humankind. Such attitudes are tantamount to being ashamed of Christ, who befriended thieves and whores and died on the cross to redeem them and all of "freckled" humankind. These ladies will never understand that the "Glory" of salvation is "common," not just for the wealthy and well placed and sophisticated but for everyone, and especially the lowly, like those "Fishermen" (not gentlemen) who became Christ's apostles. Such "Brittle," supercilious ignorance makes "Redemption" ashamed of them.

Moyra Donaldson   Infidelities   (p. 1142)

This wicked and deliciously ironic account of a married couple's mutual infidelities will not be difficult for students. Surely they will understand why he couldn't make this call from the house. As well, they will respond to the "guilt" the pile of coins gathers along with dust; they might wonder whether the wife's guilt was justified, given the husband's use of the coins. You might consider this poem in tandem with Mary Karr's "Revenge of the Ex-Mistress," another wicked insight into the perils of adultery.

John Donne   Death, Be Not Proud   (p. 1382)

This sonnet is an intense and mocking (though not comic) apostrophe to death, based on the Christian belief in resurrection. The mode throughout is paradoxical, depending on two different understandings of the word *death*. It signifies the end of life, and it also signifies the entry into an eternal life. For the nonbeliever, death, as the end of life, signifies oblivion, and this meaning is brought into the wordplay, especially in the final couplet.

The poet chides Death for his arrogance. Death is not final, says the Anglican priest; therefore, Death is neither "mighty" nor "dreadful" nor even competent— "nor yet canst thou kill me." Actually, Death is rather pitiful—"poor Death"—and, far from being terrifying, is really to be welcomed like "rest" and "sleep." Donne then uses the clichéd notion that the good die young to point out that Death is nothing more than a transition to heavenly reward. But at the end of the octave of this mixed-form sonnet, the mood changes. There are other reasons to deprecate Death. In this third quatrain, Death is characterized as a slave to human will and fate who dwells in poison, war, and sickness. The implications are clear—Death is not mighty (it is a slave), and Death is ignoble (keeps bad company). Sedatives are just as effective, even more effective, in producing sleep. Why then, Death, do you swell with pride, take yourself so seriously? The concluding couplet allows us to transcend death by passing through it to eternal life, thus killing Death by robbing it of its dominion.

The poem begins as a Petrarchan sonnet, and it does turn at the beginning of the sestet. But the final couplet, carrying the burden of resolution, is a Shakespearean device. Analysis of the meter in line 9 might generate an interesting discussion. It contains at least one extra syllable, and provides three stressed syllables in a row, making the sequence "fate, chance, kings" rather portentous. Further, lines 9 and 10 hiss with sibilance, perhaps reinforcing the poet's contempt for Death.

John Donne   The Flea   (p. 1098)

This poem, as well as "A Valediction: Forbidding Mourning," may be used to illustrate poetic conceit. The poem might also be contrasted with other carpe diem poems in the "Love and Hate" section of the anthology to highlight the boldness of Donne's outrageous image.

The event described by the poet—a flea sucking the blood of his beloved after having bitten him—becomes the emblem of a sexual union between them. The lady, reluctant to surrender to the speaker, is admonished by the example of the flea, who by mingling their blood within its body is metaphorically pregnant with their child ("swells with one blood made of two"). The poet refutes her arguments against sleeping with him: the flea's act is not a sin, a shame, or a loss of maidenhood (understood as a moral consequence more than as a physical consequence for the purpose of the argument). In the second stanza, the lady moves to kill the flea by crushing it with her fingernail. The poet, resorting to clerical language, protests that the act would be thrice sinful. Since he and the lady are "cloistered" within the flea, which is their marriage "temple," killing the flea would be to kill the poet, to commit suicide, and to kill the new entity formed of their mingled blood. But she does kill the flea, purpling her nail with their blended blood, the blood of innocence. She presumably argues that the poet's earlier view of the flea's symbolic value must be wrong, because neither he nor she is the weaker for the flea's death. The poet then attempts to convert her logic to his own ends: since the flea's death took no life from the lady, neither will a sexual encounter take any honor from her.

John Donne Song (p. 1099)

A lively discussion might begin by asking students to defend or attack the proposition that the poem is a libel on women and that the speaker is suffering from unrequited love if not misogyny. Since we learn nothing specific about the speaker, we cannot say for sure that he is reacting to a broken love affair, though that assumption is not unreasonable. Given the poem's sweeping generalizations, we could argue with more plausibility that it is misogynistic. The speaker is a bitter, angry man. Although we don't know the source of his anger, we might indulge in a bit of Freudian analysis and speculate that his early childhood experiences with women, chiefly his mother, have left him with a terror and hatred that explain his libelous generalizations. We could argue along these lines, but we would be wrong. Such an analysis would betray a tone deafness, a literalness that fails to hear the poem's music, so to speak.

First, the poem should be located in the context and tradition of the love poetry of Donne's era. By his time, English love poetry, written almost exclusively by men, had developed a rather elaborate set of conventions to describe a woman's beauty and character traits (on this subject, students should be directed to Shakespeare's "Sonnet 130" [p. 1096] and Thomas Campion's "I Care Not for These Ladies" [p. 1097]). These conventions grew out of the medieval tradition of courtly love and the celebrated love poems of the Italian poet Petrarch (1304–1374) to his idealized love—the exquisitely beautiful and unattainable Laura. This is not to deny that the tradition grew out of a patriarchal society that, certainly from our perspective, demeaned women as it celebrated them; it is merely to remember that retroactively applying modern standards to an earlier society always runs the risk of distorting the past.

Second, a reading that focuses on its content and ignores its form distorts the poem. It overlooks the crucial aspect of tone—the humor that emerges from the pervasive and insistent hyperbole. The speaker seems to be young, but experienced enough to pronounce on female inconstancy and betrayals. It would be easier, the speaker declares, to perform the impossible feats listed in the first stanza or to have the supernatural powers alluded to in the second than to find "a woman true, and fair" (l. 18), with a pun on "fair." His is the voice of a man weary of a world where "an honest mind" (l. 9) is as difficult to find as an honest woman. Both have proven unworthy of this honest and fair man. Indeed, he has been the exemplary courtly lover, ready to make "a pilgrimage" to the shrine of a faithful woman, though he knows there will never be occasion to make that journey.

John Donne A Valediction: Forbidding Mourning (p. 1100)

Because of the poem's title, students often fail to recognize the simile in the first two stanzas. The point is that virtuous people can accept death easily, being assured of paradise. Let the mildness of the death of a virtuous person be a simile for the tone of the separation we must experience. That separation is characterized metaphorically as melting, another quiet physical event. Donne pokes fun at some of the poetic fustian associated with separation—"sigh-tempests," "tear-floods." He employs the clerical note, suggested by the first stanza, to argue that a noisy separation would be a "profanation" because it would be widely known by the "laity"; the suggestion is that our love is sacred and that we are the exalted priests of the mysteries of that spiritual love. The next three stanzas define the difference between the common love of the laity and our spiritual love. Stanza 3 points out that while earthquakes are harmful and fearful, they can be accounted for—humans understanding the consequences. The "trepidation of the spheres" is a technical feature (having to do with the observation of erratic orbital movements) in the earth-centered Ptolemaic cosmology; here it is parallel with earthquakes—hence, sphere-quakes. Those sphere-quakes are much more significant cosmologically than are earthquakes, but they do no damage. Metaphorically, the earthquakes describe the laity's emotional pain at separation; the trepidation of the spheres describes our pain. The cosmological notion is continued in the fourth stanza with the reference to sublunary lovers, and a set of metallurgical images is introduced. Earthbound lovers depend on physical contact that "elemented" their love; our love, however, is "refined." And our two souls, when the speaker leaves, are not separated but fill the space between like gold foil. The final three stanzas develop the famous conceit in which the souls of the lovers are compared to a drawing compass. There may be a few students who visualize a directional compass on first reading.

Rita Dove Daystar (p. 811)

For this frazzled mother of children in diapers, wife of a somewhat insensitive husband who is content to lurch "into her," an hour stolen during the children's nap is the best part of her existence. There, behind the garage, she finds "a little room for thinking," she finds "things to watch." And, while "a floating maple leaf" might generate some pleasant emotional response, what can we make of that "pinched armor of a vanished cricket" (perhaps the pleasant memory of cricket noises in the night)? And on other days, she strove to see "only her own vivid blood." That image powerfully suggests a rare, critical insight: at the center of her being she exists independently of the mundane duties that define her life. Most important of all, she creates a moment in which she is not a harassed mother, not a put-upon wife, not a laundress; she is "nothing, / pure nothing." For that hour, responsible to no person and burdened with no work, she is magically free of all earthly demands and constraints—a daystar.

Will the students find the poet's exceedingly modest requirement a reasonable escape from tedium? Perhaps the speaker should find more pleasure in her children, and conspire for a better sex life with Thomas. But that's a different poem.

Rita Dove Lamentations (p. 186)

The poem is addressed to lamenters, mourners, deniers of life. We don't know what the troubles are of the collective "you" of the poem. But the speaker wishes to shake those people out of a life-denying despair. "Throw open the shutters," she cries— emerge from the darkness. The life-affirming music of the "pipes" represents, perhaps, all the sounds that enliven an inviting world, including the hungry wind that shakes those branches. The light, the pipe music, the sighing of the olive branches, the "hunger" itself, must imbue "you" with life! To deny the pleasurable experiences they promise is to deny the world, to "descend rung / by rung into no loss and no desire." That is, to embrace a nihilistic anomie. The speaker demands a response to vibrant life—and, in a kind of down-home conclusion, chides her depressed listeners: you can't return to the womb; you're here—deal with it! "Stop crying / and suck the good milk in." That "good milk," doubtless, stands for all the good and tasty things the world can offer—light, music, soughing olive trees.

Paul Laurence Dunbar We Wear the Mask (p. 787)

If one did not know that Dunbar was black, the poem would still be effective as the lyric cry of a person belonging to a group (not precisely identifiable) that is downtrodden (for reasons not explained). But knowing that Dunbar was an African American makes clear both the group Dunbar is writing about and the historical reality of its plight. The mask does not suggest hypocrisy but survival. African American literature is replete with treatments of the protective mask blacks have had to assume in a white world. That theme is reflected in the title essay of James Baldwin's *Nobody Knows My Name* as well as Ralph Ellison's *Invisible Man*.

Stephen Dunn   Bourgeois   (p. 502)

The unspoken first words of this prose poem are surely "We have become . . ." The "tra la" that follows, nonsense syllables often associated with lighthearted songs (as in "The flowers that bloom in the spring, tra la"), establishes the tone of bantering self-mockery. As the older speaker looks back on his young self, he is startled to realize how the years have stealthily tamed "it" (l. 4), the brash, high-minded idealism of youth, into a toothless and tepid middle age. In the only metaphor of the poem, the speaker personifies capitalism as "that fat boy with quick feet" (l. 7) who, impervious to the youthful radical rantings of the speaker and his peers, dodges their blows and ends up a friend. They retain some of those earlier beliefs, but their present rebelliousness (described in ll. 14–18) has become a pathetic simulacrum of their fiery youth. By an inexorable declension, they have begun to succumb to the raptures of the mall, the convenience of "remotes," and thence to stasis. Thus, the speaker might have said, doth affluence make conservatives of us all.

Steve Earle   Rich Man's War   (p. 512)

Music and political commentary come together in this popular song. Play the song for the class (you can probably borrow the CD from your students—or you may own it yourself—and, of course, there is always the Web). The edgy populist message is clear: wars benefit the rich and kill or ruin the poor, despite the moral imperatives created by each side to justify conflict. The three victims differ. The first is a drifter who can't find a job (due to certain deleterious effects of globalization that often escape discussion in the legislative chambers); the second is a true patriot—hot to serve and protect the country, but economically ruined by the cold-eyed corporate forces that sent him; the third, a Palestinian schooled by a curriculum of religion and hatred, faced with hopeless oppression and poverty, becomes the agent of the Mercedes Benz–owning rich on the Islamic side of the conflict who also profit from the continued instability and terror.

   Compare this lyric with J. D. McClatchy's "Jihad," where we find the predecessor of Earle's Ali, practicing stone-throwing outside the mosque, and ending as a martyr who kills thirty-four innocents in the name of Allah and a cause. His reward, of course, is the promise of divine salvation—always a useful tool in the hands of the rich and powerful. Might the emotional energy that McClatchy and Earle project alter the views of their readers? If so, which would be more effective—the rock and roll song lyric or the somber poem? Perhaps the McClatchy poem could be set to music; challenge the musicians in the class to accept the task and perform the result.

T. S. Eliot   The Love Song of J. Alfred Prufrock   (p. 793)

This poem provides the opportunity for a discussion of the relationship between meaning and understanding in poetry. Without help, most students will not recognize the literary allusions in the poem and will be baffled by the many lines that elude crisp and pointed paraphrase. Yet the dominant tone of the poem, the images Prufrock uses, and the climax of the poem project unmistakable feelings about Prufrock and the social world he inhabits.

   Many commentators explain the "you and I" of the first line as two aspects of Prufrock's being. The "I" who speaks the poem in a sort of stream-of-consciousness monologue represents the passive, defeated Prufrock; the "you," presumably, represents the active and erotic principle. But this widely held view presents difficulties. After the first line, the "you" disappears—the other aspect of Prufrock plays no role—and the "I" switches to "we" in the final tercet of the poem in a context that doesn't support the view that the plural includes opposite types. The epigraph from Dante suggests an alternate view that has the advantage of being less subtle. Guido da Montefeltro, when asked how he came to hell, replies that he would not tell if he thought his listeners would return to the world—but since none ever return from hell, he answers without fear of infamy. Immediately, then, we read, "Let us go then, you and I." The blending of the epigraph and the opening of the poem lends support to the view that the "you" of line 1 is Prufrock's listener—in this case, the reader. Prufrock takes the reader on a revealing tour of his own personal hell.

The simile describing the evening introduces the note of unhealth that dominates the poem. The "sawdust restaurants with oyster shells" are mean fish-and-chips places that often display oyster shells in the window. The "half-deserted streets" follow aimlessly like a "tedious argument" to lead you (no longer the "you" of line 1, but the indefinite "you" of line 27) to an "overwhelming question." And Prufrock tells his listener that he will not state the question but rather will reveal it to him by taking him subjectively through a day in his own personal hell. The bleak tone of the first stanza is reinforced by the yellow fog of stanza 3. And in the fourth stanza, Prufrock reveals his spineless nature: the social games he plays, the uses to which he puts time, and, finally, the absurd climax of the day's activities—"the taking of a toast and tea." The Michelangelo refrain illuminates the social games in Prufrock's set. The women are dilettantes engaged in endless small talk about the great. In the next stanza (beginning with line 37), Prufrock reveals the inner turmoil he suffers as he prepares to call on a lady. He wishes to make love to her, but he torments himself with the question "Do I dare / Disturb the universe?" and ends again with indecision; And that indecision is justified by the reminiscences of the next three stanzas that move from a sense of his own insignificance ("I have measured out my life with coffee spoons"), his vulnerability ("When I am pinned and wriggling on the wall"), back to his erotic desires suggested by his remembrance of the arms. But the section ends with an indecisive question.

He proposes—as an answer to the question "And how should I begin?"—that he might speak of his perception of the lonely men leaning out of windows along narrow streets. Is this to be his future? And the anguish of his situation causes him to regret his existence—he wishes he had been some lobster or crab exempt from a uniquely human self-consciousness.

In the next three stanzas, he imagines himself in the woman's apartment, wondering whether he would have the "strength to force the moment to its crisis." He is no John the Baptist, strong in his zeal despite the cost; he is no Lazarus returned to tell mysteries. He is not likely, we feel, to squeeze the universe into a ball, as Marvell proposes to his coy mistress, and enjoy an erotic encounter with the lady. He will not act because he is terrified by the possible response of the lady—"that is not what I meant at all." Would it have been worthwhile, he asks, to attempt to make love to the lady even if she rebuffed him?

And his answer is "No!" He is not Prince Hamlet, who finally moves from thought to action. He is a minor player—a Polonius, a Horatio, almost a Fool—not the central figure in a Shakespearean tragedy. And his final self-analysis is deprecatory. He is growing old; he is consumed with trivial worries about his appearance; he will join with other lonely and ineffectual men walking along the beach. The emotional pain of his perception of his own ineffectuality is thrust into high relief by the conclusion of the poem. In two of the saddest lines in English verse, he recognizes the distance between himself and all the romance and excitement that life might hold. "I have heard the mermaids singing, each to each," Prufrock says, recalling the legendary sirens who sang to passing sailors an invitation to all their fondest desires. But, acutely aware of his own desperate failure, he immediately adds, "I do not think that they will sing to me." The five lines following suggest that Prufrock has had his dream fantasies, has lingered with the sea-girls in the gorgeous chambers of the sea "Till human voices wake us, and we drown." But strangely, the last tercet is introduced by "we," though the pronoun "I" dominates the poem. Perhaps the poet here suggests that Prufrock's world of cakes and ices, novels and coffee spoons, is "drowned" by the stultifying social conventions in which it is immersed.

James Fenton God, A Poem (p. 1420)

This whimsical spoof of soteriology—that is, spiritual salvation accomplished through Jesus Christ—might offend some students. But it provides a nice opportunity to talk about commonplace things and events as emblems of terribly serious considerations. After all, the poet compares the cosmic disappointment of ultimate death with "a nasty surprise in a sandwich." (For me, that sandwich was the soggy mess my mother used to pack for my lunch back in elementary school: lettuce and tomato on a kaiser roll—made at 7 A.M., consumed at noon.) A limp handshake, a sexual indiscretion (that "mistake in a nightie")—these come to symbolize the difference between one's vast expectations and an ugly reality: "you are a diet of worms." Someone is bound to point out that supposedly nonexistent God speaks the last six stanzas, but note that He (paradoxically, to be sure) defines Himself as "a crude existential malpractice." Consider the powerful resonance of that characterization—"malpractice." Do the students know what a crumpet is? Ask them to list the things "crumpet" symbolizes in the third stanza. Consider the comic effect of such polysyllabic rhymes as *nightie—Almighty; fact is—malpractice*. Ask them, as well, to discuss the differences between the last two stanzas and the first two—the movement from the speaker's condemnation of an indifferent and unsatisfactory God to God's condemnation of unsatisfactory humans.

Lawrence Ferlinghetti Constantly Risking Absurdity (p. 172)

Seeking metaphors for the poet and poetry seems an idle enough trade, and a number of modern poets have wrought such metaphors cunningly. Robert Francis compares the poet to a baseball pitcher who outwits the batter; here, Ferlinghetti likens the poet to a wire-walking acrobat at the circus—plying his dangerous art. One misstep and the poem falls. This makes the poet, since his life is at stake, "the super realist"—a view likely to contradict most easy notions of poets.

The second controlling image of the poet is "a little charleychaplin man," the tragicomic figure circling desperately below the fair eternal form of Beauty, which he must catch to preserve.

This poem might make a nice occasion to talk about the line as a unit of poetry. Although the lines are constantly enjambed, each line, however short, has an integrity of its own.

Lawrence Ferlinghetti In Goya's Greatest Scenes (p. 1401)

The force of this poem lies in the parallel the poet draws between the almost unbearably real scenes of "suffering humanity" captured by the great eighteenth-century artist Goya and the pictures presented by modern America. Goya's scenes, drawn from the horrors of war, convey to the poet the quintessence of human brutality and pain. Ironically, modern America presents a strikingly similar picture. While the landscape may be different—while the people may be sitting comfortably in painted cars rather than writhing at the end of a bayonet—modern Americans are maimed as surely as Goya's people by a meretricious, vulgar society that is indifferent to human and humane values.

Donald Finkel The Great Wave: Hokusai (p. 1405)

Katsushika Hokusai (1760–1849) was one of the most creative Japanese printmakers of the early nineteenth century. Departing from the eighteenth-century tradition of figure painting, Hokusai made his reputation as a landscape artist. The famous woodblock print of *The Great Wave off Kanagawa*, part of his "Thirty-six Views of Mount Fuji," manifests, in some respects, the spirit of a contemporaneous western romanticism in that nature overwhelms tiny humans and their boats.

Finkel plays with the idea suggested by the epigrammatic excerpt from Herbert Read's *The Meaning of Art*. In the poem, an average Englishman "Walks round a corner, thinking of nothing" and comes suddenly upon this painting. Read (and Finkel) imagine "us" hidden behind a screen as observers. We hear the Englishman grunt, we hear his cry, as he becomes, in some sense, the men in Hokusai's boats as well as the dangerous, clawing wave. The first stanza of Finkel's poem describes the print, but concludes that the persons in the picture are safe—"the wave is still." The dramatic tension projected by the engulfing wave is harmless—the picture represents a stasis. Consequently, "In the painter's sea / All fishermen are safe." But the "innocent bystander" is not an art critic, and ". . . He is / Not safe, not even from himself." The sea he travels is full of serpents, and he, like the biblical Noah, is blindly driven. His salvation, like Noah's, depends on arriving at his own Ararat—the dry land that will save him from the great waves that threaten him in his own world.

Carolyn Forché The Colonel (p. 511)

Although the colonel is surely from Central America, probably El Salvador, his nationality is deliberately and quite properly not specified. He might be any powerful agent of oppressive government. Students will have no trouble understanding this poem. One question you might ask is: What distinguishes this work from a prosaic newspaper feature story? Like Mezey's "My Mother," Sexton's "Cinderella," and, most of all, like Rukeyser's "Myth," this poem seems to be prose. What, then, makes it a poem? And, do the things that make it a poem make it more effective as a political statement?

To begin with, the writer establishes with remarkable economy in just five lines (counting prosaically) the nature of this household. It is recognizable and ordinary except, of course, for the pistol on the cushion. And the evocation of the household depends on concrete things. One might ask, in response to the opening comment of the poem, What has one heard that is true? The answer is likely to be that this colonel lives an ordinary life in the midst of an ordinary household with children and pet dogs and even a talking parrot. The one ominous difference from our lives is, perhaps, that gun on the cushion (that cushion seems a peculiarly unlikely place for a gun in any case, but soon we will understand why it is there).

The next three lines reinforce the ominous differences between this household and all the others it so much resembles. And the "poetic" images that describe the security precautions begin to operate on the reader. The broken glass designed to "scoop" (like ice cream?) intruders' knees or cut their hands to "lace" is juxtaposed against the ordinary, even elegant, motions that seem to inform this household.

The horror increases and culminates with the dried human ears kept in a paper grocery sack. This paterfamilias, stomach filled with rack of lamb and good wine, spills a sackful of dried human ears before the poet whose liberal ideas he detests. And with a terse obscenity, the colonel sums up his attitude toward civil rights, political reform, and all the rest of it. The last two sentences of the poem suggest a small measure of hopefulness—surely that is what the poet means to convey with the words "some of the ears on the floor were pressed to the ground." They, emblematically, hear the distant future approaching.

As an exercise in the nature of poetic form, particularly the role of the line in poetry, have the students rearrange this work into "poetic lines" (even on the left and jagged on the right, or jagged on the left and right). Then have them defend their choices for line breaks and physical arrangement on the page.

As another exercise in the way artists work, ask the students where their sympathies lie, and why. That is, how does the poet generate the attitude toward this man that the reader finally adopts?

Alan Fox Return Address (p. 179)

The poem won't trouble students. You might point out that the father's comments come after they see a performance of *Death of a Salesman*. The father resolves never to suffer the deprivation and misery of Willie Loman. By god, he will purchase whatever he wants. But perhaps it was the frugality—the careful husbanding of resources exemplified by the hand-altered return address labels—that placed him in that happy position.

Robert Frost After Apple-Picking (p. 1391)

Frost often uses rural images as symbols for the most consequential human activity. While this poem is about picking apples, it is also about how life is lived, and it wonders what death is like. The ladder stretching toward heaven provides an early suggestion that the ladder is symbolic, and it seems reasonable to read apples as the fruit of experience. The speaker is old; winter is approaching, and along with it, drowsiness and sleep—all suggestive of mortality. As death approaches, the speaker considers his life of apple-picking; he has missed some apples and has left some barrels unfilled—he has, in short, not grasped every possible experience. But he has cherished many experiences, lived them carefully, saved those apples from the cider-apple heap. And in retrospect he perceives, in a daydream, the distorted face of the world as through a pane of ice. He assumes that the approaching sleep will bring him clear images detailing the rich experiences that he lived through and the labor (the ache on his instep arch, the pressure of the ladder rung) underlying them.

At its conclusion, the poem raises some problems. His sleep (which some critics insist is only sleep) will be troubled. Earlier (ll. 16–17) he asserts that he knows what form his dreaming will take; it will recapitulate his experiences. Here (ll. 37–38) those dreams will trouble his sleep, and he wonders whether that sleep is like the woodchuck's hibernation or just some human sleep. Two possibilities suggest themselves. The woodchuck, being nonhuman, is without dreams, and its sleep is a kind of oblivion—presumably untroubled. On the other hand, the woodchuck is a hibernator and will reawaken to a new life in the spring. Will the speaker enjoy a new life, a resurrection (like the woodchuck), after his sleep, or is the sleep of death no different from the sleep of life with its troubled dreams?

Robert Frost Birches (p. 164)

The speaker's voice in "Birches" is informal and conversational, and the structure of the poem contributes to this tone, for the poet seems to wander, as one does in idle conversation. He begins with boys and birches, but in line 5 he begins a long apparent digression on how birches look in winter, then catches himself in line 21 and returns to the matter he set out to discuss. In lines 22–40 he explains that he would prefer to have the birches bent by a young boy living far from the city where the typical sport is baseball. In lines 41–42, the speaker connects himself and the young boy he imagined and devotes the rest of the poem to a meditation upon life, in which he establishes the symbolic meaning of swinging on birches. The apparent digression is not a digression at all, for lines 5–20 establish a reality (of how birches are bent) that contrasts with the poet's wish. Birches bent by an ice storm, however beautifully, are less desirable than birches bent by a young boy because the world of *human* distress and joy, sadness and elation, is the speakers theme. Taming birches becomes one of those joyful human acts that allow us to escape momentarily the weariness of life by climbing *"Toward"* heaven" (l. 56). But the poet insists on "toward" because the perfection that heaven represents is not allowed to humans. And earth is, finally, the best place for love.

Robert Frost Departmental (p. 788)

In "Departmental," which expresses his disapproval of modern, bureaucratized society, Frost gives us a genially comic description of a totally mechanical and efficient society. The light, comic tone is made possible through Frost's use of the beast fable—an ancient device for commenting on and satirizing the foibles of humankind and since an ant colony is an efficiently organized society that subordinates the individual to the group, it serves Frost's purposes well. The ants are marked by a mechanical, unquestioning efficiency. Although the first one comes upon an enormous and presumably mysterious object (the moth), he is neither surprised nor deflected from his "duty," because it is the job of others to look into the mysteries of God, time, and space. Even the death of a fellow ant does not interrupt the routine but once again results in a report to a "higher up." And as the mortician disposes of the body, he creates no disturbance, for in this society, even death does not interfere with duty or become the concern of any other "department."

Robert Frost   Design   (p. 1394)

The argument that God's existence is proved by the discernible design in nature is here confronted with the knotty theological problem of natural evil. The argument from design, of course, *must* account for "a thing so small." Therefore, God is accountable for the predation here used as an emblem of horror. Or, God does not exist.

The perverse use of "white," usually associated in literature with innocence and purity, together with such words as "dimpled," "satin," "snowdrop," "froth," and "kite"—all of which connote a different sort of experience than is described here—intensifies the horror and the paradox that the sonnet confronts.

Robert Frost   Fire and Ice   (p. 1109)

Characteristically, Frost uses natural phenomena as figures for human behavior. A sort of Sunday-supplement debate addresses the question of how the world shall end. Some argue that the sun will cool; some argue that it will grow hotter. Frost's equating of fire with desire and ice with hatred embodies the ominous suggestion that both human attitudes have significant capacity for destructiveness.

Robert Frost   Nothing Gold Can Stay   (p. 1392)

One interesting way to approach this poem would be to compare it to a poem that postulates a realm of absolute being and perfection—one of the Keats odes, for example (or the yearnings of the lady in Wallace Stevens's "Sunday Morning")—and to any of the carpe diem poems, with which it bears a certain similarity of theme. In the odes, Keats, overwhelmed by the sense of his own mortality, yearns to escape the common fate and so imagines an ideal and timeless world. In contrast, the carpe diem poems, accepting rather than protesting or lamenting the transitoriness of things, urge us to enjoy the brief time we are given.

Frost's poem implicitly rejects the possibility of a world beyond time and mortality. Existence does not unfold in some linear fashion that permits us to speak of birth and death as discrete events (culminating, perhaps as the lady hopes in "Sunday Morning," in the timelessness of eternity). In Frost's poem, birth and death are so inseparably linked that at the very moment of its appearance, green is already gold, the leaf is a flower. While we may want to see "gold" and "flower" as somehow special and culminating, in the world of Nature they are merely part of the ceaseless cycle of birth, death, and rebirth.

In the last lines, Frost underscores his theme by using a series of verbs that reverse the common metaphor of growing up: "subsides," "sank," and "goes down." The natural world cannot hold its gold; nor can we, who are part of that natural world, hold our golden, Edenic innocence.

Robert Frost   'Out, Out—'   (p. 1392)

In this poem Frost illustrates Macbeth's gloomy conception of life with a senseless accident in the ordinary day of a Vermont farm boy. The poem is insistently understated, and the understatement culminates in the final two lines—not as an expression of indifference but as the need, finally, to go on living and to meet the present demands of life.

Robert Frost   The Road Not Taken   (p. 165)

This well-known poem is often interpreted as a symbolic representation of the poet's decision to become a poet—to take the road "less traveled by." But you might have a good time challenging the deep-reading students on their understanding of figurative language. Surely the road is a metaphor for a life-determining choice, and clearly the speaker (presumably the poet, but not necessarily) describes a fundamental choice that narrowed his options. And his choice "made all the difference." But did the speaker make the right choice? If so, then why does he tell his story "with a sigh"? Was it a bad choice? Would the other road have led to even better experiences?

We may understand the speaker's wishful notion that he might return to this fork in the road and try the other branch someday—but he recognizes the impossibility of such an opportunity, "knowing how way leads on to way." The speaker's choice of the less traveled road is a bit suspect, since he tells us that "the passing there / Had worn them really about the same." We can confidently say the poem is about choosing one path in life rather than another, but to go much further is to burden the poem with a reader's emotional baggage—not necessarily a bad thing, but a weight that the poem might not support. The life lying before students is funnel-shaped, and they are at the wide end. With every choice, they, like the speaker of this poem, move to a narrower set of possibilities.

Robert Frost   A Semi-Revolution   (p. 482)

This poem is discussed on p. 111 of this manual.

Robert Frost   Stopping by Woods on a Snowy Evening   (p. 1393)

This is one of Frost's—and modern poetry's—most justly celebrated lyrics. It is one of the most eminently teachable as well. It allows the instructor to deal effectively with a number of axioms students often come to formulate in introductory literature courses:

1. If I understand the poem on first reading (or at least am not confused by it), either there is something wrong with the poem (it's too simple and the instructor will probably trash it) or I really didn't understand it at all—I just thought I did.
2. Most poems employ symbolism and (even when I recognize that something is probably a symbol) I don't know what it means.
3. Do writers really put as much conscious effort into their writings as the instructor says they do? How do we know that what we find in a work is really there?

Because Frost's poem is dense and consciously formal, it is worth beginning with these elements. Students are often surprised to discover (because the poem reads so smoothly) that its rhythm is rigidly regular (iambic tetrameter), its rhyme scheme a complex pattern of interlocking stanzas (*aaba, bbcb, ccdc, dddd*). But the meter and rhyme are only part of the poem's formal achievement. Each stanza is a complete sentence, and each sentence follows the structure of colloquial English (with the possible exception of the inversion of subject and object in the first line).

Since the poem narrates an episode in simple language, students will have little problem paraphrasing it. They also generally respond to the tone, and sense that the episode means more than itself, that something symbolic is happening. The lonely winter bleakness of the setting (the "frozen lake," "the gently falling snow," the "lovely, dark and deep" woods), read along with line 8, establish the tone, the symbolic weight of this brief moment when the speaker is drawn to what the woods represent—death, perhaps, or at least a temporary release from life's wearying round of duties and obligations. The speaker's weariness is wonderfully underscored by "downy flake" (l. 12), a phrase that sets vividly before us the image of snowflakes wafting downward and that also evokes the idea of pillows and sleep.

In fact, we might say that the double meaning of "downy" reflects in miniature the way the entire poem works. The speaker straightforwardly and literally describes a setting and some of his thoughts about it. He does it with such skill, however, we sense that the literal embodies something symbolic. In addition to the ways we've already indicated, Frost invests the experience with significance by having the speaker in the opening stanza contrast the village (civilization and ownership) with the elemental world of the winter woods. The next stanza and a half (ll. 5–10) are devoted to the speaker's horse, brilliantly keeping the poem focused on the scene itself while making it clear that the speaker is breaking a habitual routine, that something unusual is happening. (Ask students who the speaker is. They will often try to guess his profession—country doctor, for example. Such a discussion gives the instructor the opportunity to make a point about what is and what is not legitimate inference. We can say that the speaker is someone who habitually takes a particular kind of route and never stops "without a farmhouse near." But the poem will not support anything more specific than that.)

We can now turn to the last two lines. One might argue that Frost was compelled to make the lines identical in order to escape from the pattern of interlocking stanzas, to bring his poem to an end. Yet since the poem's narrative carries a symbolic meaning, the repetition is not a mere redundancy. It is a brilliant joining together of literal and symbolic. The speaker literally has miles to travel before he reaches his bed. The "miles" and the "sleep" of the final line suggest perhaps the future (with all its travails) the speaker must live through before he will be able to rest (in death, perhaps).

In his essay "The Figure a Poem Makes," Frost declared that a successful poem "ends in a clarification of life—not necessarily a great clarification, such as sects and cults are founded on, but in a momentary stay against confusion." This is a wonderfully accurate phrase to describe "Stopping by Woods." The common interpretation of this poem as expressing a death wish (first proposed by John Ciardi in "Robert Frost: The Way to a Poem," *Saturday Review* XLI, April 12, 1958) is attractive and plausible. However, such an interpretation is misleading if we fail to note that, finally, the poem affirms life. The experience of breaking his routine and gazing into the woods is one of those "momentary stay[s] against confusion" that sends the speaker back to life with a sense of renewal.

Shirley Geok-lin Lim Father from Asia (p. 363)

As is the case in the analysis of most poetry, close attention to the form of "Father from Asia" will be rewarded. Reading the poem with an eye toward its use of repetition, address, image, and tone will help the class see the ways in which the poet uses the resources of poetry, especially for expressing her ideas. This close attention to the form of the poem will allow students to appreciate the subtlety of these ideas, which are more complicated and ambivalent than they might at first glance appear.

The key ambivalence, of course, is in the speaker's attitude toward the father. Asking students to track these feelings throughout the poem can provide the thread that will run through discussion. Each image and form of address by speaker to father can be evaluated as positive or negative, and as the class does this, the discussion can also tackle the larger question of what situations are to blame for the father's failures: whether the poem blames the father or the larger context—or continent, even—for which he stands. Raising this last question can also direct our attention to the speaker's relation to Asia not just geographically but also in terms of time and history, and so help students integrate the references to ghosts and memory into their understanding of the poem.

W. S. Gilbert To Phoebe (p. 1092)

See "Looking Deeper: From Poetry to Song" on p. 1085 of the anthology.

Dana Gioia Unsaid (p. 186)

The Gioias tragically lost an infant child—one possible impetus for this work. The poem quietly recognizes that what we find most moving, our most intense responses to experience, are often left unsaid. But our failure to overtly share those intense feelings—of grief, of love—makes them no less an important, perhaps the most important, aspect of our lives. Because decorum so constrains behavior, we live the most telling, the most emotional part of our lives "inside." We "conceal" partly to protect ourselves, partly to deceive others, because confiding leaves one terribly vulnerable. Only the "letters that we write our dead" are safe communications, since that therapeutic cleansing remains private.

Nikki Giovanni Dreams (p. 507)

This poem does not offer much material for traditional literary analysis since its language is direct and prosaic, devoid of imagery, symbolic language, and complex musical effects. The free verse is patterned, particularly in the repetition of "i used" and the movement from "militant" to "radical" to the thrice-repeated "natural" of the final lines. It is fascinating as the summary autobiography of a contemporary African American woman who moves from black militancy with its emphasis on a leftist political ideology (suggested by the adjective "correct") to a women's liberationist view. Interestingly, the awakening releases her from the earlier world of radical militancy that demanded theory and action and ushers her into a world that requires, apparently, only the cultivation of her inner self. One might reasonably ask, however (from the perspective of the world she's abandoned), what a "natural woman" is or, more to the point, whether "natural" in this sense can have any meaning at all.

Kate Gleason   After Fighting for Hours   (p. 1143)

John Donne's poem "The Flea" is a celebrated example of a "conceit," an image that works out an elaborate and even jarring parallel between two dissimilar things or situations. Gleason's poem is a modern example of the same poetic strategy. In the first two lines, the couple fall desperately to making love in an attempt to overcome intractable anger. The word *fall* is somewhat weighty. For centuries, we have been falling into each other's arms, but here the word generates a mildly ominous resonance. The extraordinary image characterizing this carnal encounter does not radiate sensual overtones but rather a desperate toiling.

The rest of the poem is devoted to a simile that gives the poem's first two lines meaning. The comparison to the tribulations of the pioneers heading west over the Rockies into unknown territory and an uncertain future has obvious relevance to the lovers who have gone from fighting to making love. Line 10 clearly echoes the act of making love with which the poem begins. But how do other details of the pioneers' struggles relate to the lovers? Is the strain of the pioneers' journey a metaphor for the lovers' relationship? Does the pioneers' determination to survive the journey stand for the lovers' determination to survive the fighting? Do the unyoked oxen suggest, perhaps, that only the lovers, unaided, can save their love and get their earthly goods—their love—over the divide? The word divide is also a peculiarly judicious word. Does the notion of the divide indicate that just enough abatement of anger can keep the couple from both the emotional and economic expense of "dividing"?

Robert Graves   The Naked and the Nude   (p. 166)

A good deal of the fun in this rhetorical tour de force derives from the Greek and Latinate vocabulary that may well delay students' delight while they look up the meanings of the words. Some—*deficiency, synonyms, anatomy*—will slide right by, but *lexicographers, construed, hippocratic, dishabille, rhetoric*, and those whip-equipped *Gorgons* may slow them down. Further, the poem tweaks the standard cultural take on the difference between *naked* and *nude*. Generally, in the West, *nakedness* is somewhat shameful, even wicked, and certainly low class, while *nude* suggests a culturally acceptable exhibition of the unclothed, but beautiful, human form—distinctly high class. Surely, all those paintings and statues in our museums support such a view. But Graves's malicious pen will not have it! He wants to highlight the class warfare that is ever with us—perhaps more so in Great Britain than in the United States. Those upper-class nudes are bold, sly, mock-religious—in short, artful tricksters. As surely as their rich and powerful social kin—leaders of industry, bankers, government ministers—they dominate. The lower-class naked have no chance to compete against the money and political power of those nudes. But justice (alas, in the next world—thus was it always for the disfranchised) will come. And, in a clever bit of wordplay, Graves provides a special hell for the "sometime nude," pursued by vengeful Gorgons and stripped naked, finally, of the art and power that protected them.

Thomas Hardy   Hap   (p. 158)

Hardy's sonnet can usefully be compared to Matthew Arnold's "Dover Beach." Both describe a universe incomprehensible in human terms, and both see it as hostile to human beings. But whereas Arnold glances yearningly back to a time when man's place was more secure and clings to his love as offering some present hope, Hardy finds nothing but indifference. If he knew that some "vengeful god" derived pleasure from tormenting him, then at least he would have the solace of knowing that his undeserved pain had a purpose (giving pleasure to "a Powerfuller"). But, as he says in the final stanza, that is "not so." A life of pain and a life of bliss are equally accidental.

Stanza 1 offers a hypothetical explanation of the speaker's pain; stanza 2 states the grim resignation he could achieve if the hypothesis were true. But stanza 3 rejects the hypothesis, leaving the speaker only with questions and no comfort. In the first two stanzas, Hardy conditionally describes whatever force rules the universe as a "vengeful god" and "a Powerfuller than I," thus suggesting a force comprehensible in human terms. But in the final stanza, the force becomes "Crass Casualty," then "dicing Time," and finally "These purblind Doomsters," all suggesting accidental forces that humans can neither control nor understand.

Thomas Hardy   The Ruined Maid   (p. 158)

The skill and humor of "The Ruined Maid" result largely from the comment-and-response structure of each stanza. 'Melia's response in each stanza develops a comic definition of "ruined." In the first stanza, she uses the word simply to describe herself; in the succeeding stanzas, she associates it with elegant dress, polish, leisure, and liveliness. Further, 'Melia's language is polished and proper until, in the final stanza, she reverts, with obvious relish, to the vernacular "ain't" of the country life she led before she was "ruined."

Robert Hayden   Those Winter Sundays   (p. 1115)

This tribute to the poet's father is the more powerful for its refusal to indulge in the kind of sentimentalism one often finds in such poems. The father is evidently a manual laborer (ll. 3 and 4), and the family harbors such intense angers that the poet recollects being afraid to face each morning. The child fears this stern father, who rose early to warm the house, to polish his shoes, before awakening him. Manifesting that fear, the child spoke to him "indifferently." Only now does the poet realize what the child could not (the repetition in the next-to-last line appropriately releases the intense emotion): that what his father did he did out of love.

Students may find it useful to consider the final line, especially the connotations of "austere" and "offices" — words that fittingly characterize the love of this (seemingly) demanding and perhaps taciturn father whose love the child could not recognize. They might also consider how the second word of the poem, the adverb "too," quietly and concisely sketches the character of the father, who arose early during the week to the aching work that supported the family and on Sundays too, the day of rest, to discharge the "offices" of love.

Seamus Heaney   Mid-term Break   (p. 1415)

The first consideration would be to place this poem in the elegiac tradition—to compare it with Housman's "To an Athlete Dying Young" and Roethke's "Elegy, for Jane." You might also read David's lament over Jonathan (II Samuel 1:19–27—How the mighty have fallen) to the class. The more recent elegies project a more profound grief—the dead are ordinary people, not heroes or political icons. Thus the details surrounding death in modern poems tend to be humble and graphic rather than ceremonial and heroic. And Big Jim Evans (l. 6) is clearly a friend or neighbor—not the mythical or heroic figure an earlier elegy might embody. The experience of this poem is heightened by a misleading title—usually, a mid-term break is a pleasant holiday.

You might be able to stir up a lively debate and provide some insight into the mysterious workings of poetry by challenging the class to decide whether this piece is poetry or just prose with the lines broken up. Scansion reveals that the poem is largely pentameter, though some lines have 11 or 12 syllables. The final two lines provide the only decisive rhyme, yet the poem is full of music—note particularly "Counting bells knelling classes to a close" (l. 2) and "He lay in the four foot box as in his cot" (l. 20). You might challenge students to consider the assonance and consonance throughout the poem that distinguish it from most prose (prose that is not, itself, "poetic").

Finally, you might focus on the poem's ending. Were students surprised to discover that the subject of the poem is a four-year-old child? Would that knowledge diminish the emotional experience of rereading the poem? That is, does this poem depend on surprise for its success?

Seamus Heaney Valediction (p. 1128)

In an old-fashioned poem of four quatrains rhymed *abab*, the poet uses an extended marine metaphor to lament the departure of his "lady." Characterized as a boat, time and the days have become unmoored and tossed violently on an angry sea. Worse, the vessel's crew (the speaker) is in mutiny. Nothing will be serene and controlled until the lady returns to resume command.

Some interesting prosody enlivens the poem and might provide an opportunity to discuss the relationship between sound patterns and emotional energy. For instance, the second quatrain rhymes *presence* with *absence* and *anchored* with *unmoored*. These weak rhymes depend on unstressed syllables—they lack the decisive force of such rhymes as *skirt–hurt* and *bound–sound*. Might the weak rhymes color the reader's understanding of the situation before the lady left? Were things too soft, too undefined—pleasant without purpose? It is perilous to attribute morphemic quality to phonemic events, but it might be interesting to stir students up by suggesting possibilities.

As well, ask students to characterize the lady. What does a "frilled blouse" and a "simple tartan skirt" suggest about the lady? Challenge students to defend their answers by examining their own experience. Why *Lady* rather than *woman, girl,* or a name? Have some fun, finally, by asking students to suggest why the woman left. Is she likely to return?

Anthony Hecht The Dover Bitch (p. 1116)

This poem depends on a familiarity with Matthew Arnold's "Dover Beach." Hecht's speaker sees the woman in Arnold's poem as a flesh-and-blood woman, more interested in the carnal than the ideal. Disappointed by finding her presence the occasion for a philosophical discourse about the fragmentation of values in nineteenth-century society, she insults Arnold brutally. The speaker understands her outburst, exhibits some compassion for her, and supplies for her (and himself) some of the carnal gratification that Arnold does not. The tone of the poem is richly comic, but there are finally some dark overtones. The relationship between the speaker and the woman is certainly not vital, and the existence she leads as a good-natured bedmate, running a little to fat, is hardly an attractive one. In place of Arnold's ignorant armies clashing by night, this poem concludes with the speaker's gift of a cheap perfume called "Night of Love." Perhaps the speaker and the woman represent the sort of social decadence that Arnold speaks of in "Dover Beach."

Robert Herrick To the Virgins, to Make Much of Time (p. 1091)

See "Looking Deeper: From Poetry to Song" on p. 1085 of the anthology.

Jane Hirshfield Salt Heart (p. 1140)

The poem is a reflection on mortality—particularly the imminent death of the speaker's suffering "friend" (l. 25). But the first half of the poem is not at all ominous. Through line 20, the speaker creates a quiet, refulgent summer scene. The bee delves the lavender. The distant sounds of a mason building, of a neighbor raking, of the bee's droning, of the lavender's fragrance—all establish a pleasant reality in which the tired speaker, reclines, "half-sleeping in the sun." The fretful question of line 12, "'What about joy?'" begins to suggest a reality darker than the quiet summer scene. What a curious question. We soon discover the reason for the question as the speaker's mood swings from her contemplation of the pleasant summer scene (one reasonably likely to generate "joy" in its perceiver) to a world that "turned back to heart-salt / of wanting, heart-salts of will and grief." Presumably, there is no place for "joy" in that world.

You might engage the class in a discussion of the title. What emotional quality does "salt heart" project? Something good (like sweetheart, or the pleasure of a salty hot pastrami sandwich, for example)? More likely, the students will suggest the salt of grieving tears; the heart-salt within crystallized by her dying friend. That river, named Suffering, will finally kill her friend, and go. But what remains for her? First, she complains that the dreadful river swallows everything, signified by the elements of the bucolic scene that open the poem. But, finally, despite the tendency toward emotional paralysis that the inevitability of suffering and mortality seem to engender, the speaker asserts "the only sin is distance, refusal. . . ." Finally, the poem seems to project a therapeutic catharsis for the speaker. Though her inability to save her friend's life or soften his pain destroys the possibility of present "joy," she opts for a future regardless of what it brings. Ultimately she, like him, will vanish in pain and suffering, but before vanishing, she chooses not distance and refusal, but an invitation to experience: "Come even joy. / Even now, even here. . . ."

Tony Hoagland The Dog Years (p. 1139)

This good-natured account of the rivalry between the lover and his lady friends' dogs will not puzzle its readers. The speaker, at the outset, laments the privileged position of each girlfriend's pet. The dog is more important and more permanent in their lives than he—a mere boyfriend destined to become "another / anecdotal mugshot / in the history book of non-commitment." But sometimes he triumphs. The description of his pleasure—"the warm, aromatic dark / full of animal mysteries / and spiritual facts" evokes a variety of sensuous and sensual responses. Why is the dark (a matter of sight) "warm" (a matter of touch), and what makes it "aromatic" (a matter of smell)? (You might want to use this opportunity to introduce students to synesthesia in the "Glossary of Literary Terms.") What is an animal mystery, and what, precisely, is a spiritual fact, and how are the two related? Further, he wonders at his luck. He sees himself as a sinner, unaccountably admitted to heaven, while the saintly dog "who had lived by all the rules / howled and scratched at the shut door" like some tormented soul unjustly condemned to hell.

Though written in quatrains, the verse is free, without end-rhyme, and with lines ranging from 3 to 13 syllables. But alliteration and assonance provide a nice melody throughout. Have the students locate the sound patterns that make the verse musical. Call their attention to the *p* alliteration in the fifth stanza. Consider the short *a* assonance in lines 29–35: *admitted–aromatic–animal–facts–baffled.* Does the short *a* sound seem harsh? Does such a pattern of sounds work against the mood of the sexual encounter described? Dangerous as it is to attach morphemic value to isolated phonemes, it can be instructive to get the class thinking about such issues. Have them look at Pope's lines from "An Essay on Criticism" in the definition of *onomatopoeia* in the "Glossary of Literary Terms."

M. Carl Holman Mr. Z (p. 799)

M. Carl Holman might very well have been the Mr. Z of this poem—he earned an M.A. from the University of Chicago and an M.F.A. from Yale, and taught in the English departments of a number of universities—but he wasn't. He became involved in racial politics, and from 1971 until his death in 1988 he served as director of the Urban Coalition, an organization promoting inner-city development. Doubtless, he met the sort of black people satirized in this bitter poem—those who loathed their blackness and sought to distance themselves from any identification with racial considerations.

The poem describes a black man who disassociates himself from all things black—music, food, neighborhood, even black women. Consequently, he becomes "An airborne plant, flourishing without roots" (l. 22). And his white widow suffers from the insistence of the obituary writers that he was "One of the most distinguished members of his race" (l. 26)—the race he spent his life denying.

The poem's form provides an opportunity to discuss the relationship between form and substance. The line lengths vary—does that variation subtly suggest some weakness, some disorder in the foundations of Mr. Z's life? Perhaps that argument can be extended to the curious end-rhymed couplets. Those rhymes are either feminine, depending on an unstressed syllable (*error–honor; salads–collards*), or off-rhymes (*died–flayed; phrase–race*). The resulting uneasiness, the reader's sense of not-quite-right, might serve to reinforce the poet's feelings about Mr. Z. And the characterization of this eminent but deluded man as Mr. Z (as opposed to A-1, signifying the best) marks him still further as an object of the poet's contempt.

Gerard Manley Hopkins   Pied Beauty   (p. 1108)

This paean depends for its success on its unusual images and the unusual syntax in which they are rendered. It moves finally to the observation that multicolored, multi-faceted, and changing nature is fathered by a changeless God. Hopkins called this poem a "curtal" sonnet—except for the last, each line has five stressed syllables, and the poem consists of a six-line section followed by a section of four and one-half lines—proportionally similar to the standard sonnet with an octave followed by a sestet.

Gerard Manley Hopkins   Spring and Fall   (p. 159)

Margaret, the speaker observes, is grieved that the trees' golden leaves are beginning to fall. In lines 3 and 4, with the syntax distorted to achieve emphasis, the speaker asks Margaret (silently, we assume) how it is that she can care about leaves "like the things of man." As she grows older, he points out, she will be able to see whole worlds of moldering leaves without emotion, but she will weep nevertheless and know that her sorrow is over age and death. She grieves, now, the speaker concludes, not for the leaves, the passing of spring into fall, but for herself. Her heart knows what her intellect does not express: the dying leaves portend "the blight man was born for."

A. E. Housman   Terence, This Is Stupid Stuff   (p. 161)

The question asked of Terence in the first fourteen lines of this poem is one that students often ask about much of the great and serious literature they are required to read. Terence's response, which constitutes the rest of the poem, provides one kind of answer. If, Terence says, you want something to set you dancing (that is, to make you feel unalloyed happiness), you should take to drinking liquor. A good drunk, Terence knows from personal experience, can cast a rosy glow over the world and do wonders for one's self-satisfaction. However, in a sober state, the world and the self return with their same, prealcoholic imperfections.

The absurdity, the evil, the irrationality of human fate cannot be justified (even by the great poet John Milton); they can only be drowned in the temporary bliss of an alcoholic haze. And since the world has "less good than ill" and "Luck's a chance, but trouble's sure," it behooves a thinking person to learn how to soberly face those facts without being overwhelmed (driven to suicide?). That is what Terence has learned in his periods of deepest despair and what his poetry can teach his friend. Lines 51 and 52 are troublesome. Terence brews or ferments the stuff he brings for sale, not from grain or grapes, but from the harsh stems that cut his hands as he pressed them to extract the bitter liquor they contain. Like the increasing doses of poison Mithridates took to immunize himself, Terence's poetry can function as a kind of spiritual homeopathy against the tragic conditions of human existence.

It ought to be pointed out that while Terence is a cynical and largely pessimistic man, he is not unrelievedly gloomy. As the opening lines indicate, he eats and drinks with great gusto and does declare that there is "Much good" in the world. And an important point of the story of Mithridates is that "he died old."

A. E. Housman   To an Athlete Dying Young   (p. 1387)

Though this poem is transparently clear, it provides good opportunities for a discussion of irony, paradox, and metonymy. The meaning of "shoulder-high" ironically and obviously changes between the first and second stanzas; the cheering town of life becomes the "stiller town" of death. The third stanza is the densest. In its mildly sardonic suggestion (in the curious address "Smart lad") that an early death at the height of achievement has its compensations, it raises questions about the value of a life in which, inevitably, pain and infirmity outweigh joy and gratification. The final couplet employs traditional symbols—the laurel for victory and the rose for youth and beauty. The poet calls on a long history of poetic associations with the rose as ephemeral to argue that the laurel—glory—is even more ephemeral. The word "shady" in line 13 evokes the "shades" in Hades, and the final stanza suggests a crowd of shades—"the strengthless dead"—that reminds readers of the "strength" required for athletic success and its futility in the face of mortality. Paradoxically, among the dead the garland of laurel does not wither, even though it is "briefer" than the garland of roses.

A. E. Housman When I Was One-and-Twenty (p. 160)

Is the poem literal or ironic? That is, may we accept the speaker's statement that in one year he has truly learned the lesson of the wise man, or is the speaker's judgment, based on so little experience, finally ironic? Is there nothing left for him to learn about painful human relationships?

Langston Hughes Harlem (p. 489)

This simple but powerful poem can best be discussed from the point of view of the similes Hughes employs. Each of them—the raisin, the sore, the rotten meat, the syrupy sweet, and the heavy load—suggests different possibilities, all of them quiet and undramatic. The question of the final line, in dramatic contrast, poses the possibility of violent reaction. In light of the final, italicized line, is the poem a meditation or a threat?

Major Jackson Euphoria (p. 190)

Poetry has always given us demon lovers, ill-fated destinies, ugly war, tyrannical rulers, the horror of injustice. But rarely has poetry examined a dysfunctional society in such terms as Jackson uses here. This devastating examination of one modern form of "euphoria" pointedly reveals the ubiquitous nature of addiction. While his mother smokes crack cocaine in the house across the street, the high-school-aged speaker pays a sixteen-year-old hooker five dollars to pleasure him. The scene is set in a miserable, impoverished neighborhood: street loungers swill malt liquor as addicts, "eyes spread thin as egg whites," roam the sidewalks. But the speaker comes from a different social class altogether. He wears a school tie, suggesting that he attends an expensive private school. He guards his mother's Mercedes-Benz while she nourishes her euphoria in the crack house. All the advantages of wealth and privilege are threatened by addiction to cocaine and sex, which the speaker understands. In the throes of sexual excitement, he mishears the Luther Vandross lyrics—not "creep" but "Weep." His joy—satisfaction of his lust—is "incomprehensible." And his addled mother, as though returning "from the ride of her life," reveals in her bearing a yearning for dope-induced highs, which diminish everything else in her life, including her family. Clearly, this family is headed for collapse, but that will be another poem.

Ben Jonson Song, To Celia (p. 1090)

See "Looking Deeper: From Poetry to Song" on p. 1085 of the anthology.

June Jordan Memo: (p. 177)

This poem requires little in the way of explication. The language is flat and colloquial; the imagery, what little there is, easy to comprehend. One of the best ways to approach it is by focusing on tone. The instructor might begin by asking the class to define the tone. If, as will probably happen, most students perceive it as ironic, the instructor might challenge them to convince her or him that their analysis is correct. What is the evidence that we are dealing with irony? The internal evidence is the speaker's use of hyperbole in such statements as "I've always despised my women friends" (l. 5) and "They must be morons: women!" (l. 19); the reference to "orgasm after death" (l. 16); the use of opposite statement in a phrase like "the weaker sex" (l. 14); and, in the list of men's powers, the juxtaposition of "babies" and "war" (l. 13). Finally, there is the speaker's comparison of herself to "That Cosmopolitan Girl" (l. 24), an allusion to *Cosmopolitan* magazine's ideal girl, who strives to achieve the perfect body and studies how to attract and keep her man. The external evidence is also worthy of note. The date of the poem, 1980, might alert a reader that the tone is ironic. The fact that the author is a woman might do the same. The fact that the author is June Jordan, an African American feminist, removes any doubt.

Note one thing about the first three lines. Students may miss the allusion to a comment that has become something of a cliché among many people involved in modern liberation, therapy, and twelve-step programs. One often hears them saying that having broken free from old fears and constraints, they have "decided" or "given themselves permission" to do something they previously would have shunned.

Jenny Joseph   Warning   (p. 495)

The enormous popularity of this poem can be gauged by the number of Web sites that reprint it. One site bills it as "[t]he nation's favourite post war poem" (the nation is England, the war is World War II). It has inspired a Red Hat Society (http://www .redhatsociety.org) which came into being—as its statement of purpose explains— "as a result of a few women deciding to greet middle age with verve, humor, and elan. We believe silliness is the comedy relief of life, and, since we are all in it together, we might as well join red-gloved hands and go for the gusto together. Underneath the frivolity, we share a bond of affection, forged by common life experiences and a genuine enthusiasm for wherever life takes us next."

One can understand the poem's popular appeal. It expresses the yearning for rebellion from the constraints of polite society while comfortably putting off the rebellion to the vague future. The contemplated acts are small indeed, daring in a genteel sort of way and certainly not likely to cause much of a stir. But perhaps this is unfair since, as the final three lines make clear, the acts the speaker contemplates will shock and surprise only "the people who know me." Helen Sorrells writes about the same subject in her poem "From a Correct Address in a Suburb of a Major City" (p. 490), but her treatment of it is dramatically different. Also, compare Joseph's poem to Robert Pinsky's poem on old age, "An Old Man" (p. 503).

Mary Karr   Revenge of the Ex-Mistress   (p. 1142)

This straightforward rendering of poetic justice is likely to delight its readers. But how will it affect the philanderer to whom it is addressed? The short piece projects considerable music, supplied by the internal rhymes as well as insistent assonance of the short *e* throughout, echoing the sound of *x: ex-mistress / x / let / guessed / address / best / regrets / x*. The long *e* assonance provides another pretty good melody: *the / beef / beer / me / ear / me / we / please*. When the students are through smiling, raise the question of how the mistress must have felt when she was abandoned. How did the perceptive wife feel about her husband's unfaithfulness? This question is partly answered in the poem. And how does the abandoned husband feel, now that he is the one betrayed?

John Keats   Ode on a Grecian Urn   (p. 1383)

The painted urn causes the poet to muse upon the relationship between the timeless representation of life provided by art and the feverish mortality that all humans share. In the first stanza, the urn is addressed as a "bride," a "foster child," a "sylvan historian," and the poet sketches a montage of the pictures that cover it. In the second stanza, we move closer, and consider a piper and a lover. These particular figures are used to animate the central notion of the poem: though music may be beautiful, some ideal music, unheard, is even more beautiful; that is, the realization of an aesthetic ideal is inferior to the ideal itself—or, put another way, artists always fail to render into concrete existence the abstract visions that motivate them. This idea is further illustrated by a series of poetic observations. Although the painted world of the urn is static—the lover cannot kiss his beloved; she cannot fade; the boughs cannot shed their leaves; the melodist, who never tires, forever pipes new songs; the very love remains forever happy and warm, still to be enjoyed, young—the paintings represent a condition that, in its ideality, is superior to the human condition. The passion depicted on the urn is far above human passion, which inevitably results in a cloyed and sorrowful heart, a burning forehead, and a parching tongue.

In the fourth stanza, the poet embellishes the world depicted on the urn by imagining parts of it that are not represented. Since the urn pictures a religious procession, there must, somewhere, be a town forever emptied of its people.

The last, much-debated stanza reflects on the conclusions to be drawn from the graceful ancient shape. The pictures of life that cover it "tease us out of thought / As doth eternity." The urn compels the poet to reflect on the difference between his own suffering mortality and the unchanging loveliness of the urn. Yet the pastoral scene there presented is but a scene—and Keats's ambivalence is suggested by his strange judgment: "Cold Pastoral!" Yet, however cold the representation of some ideal pastoral existence might be in relation to the poet's mortality, he still responds with considerable awe to the overwhelming fact of the urn's eternal existence, and concludes with the famous lines that have provoked so much dispute. Despite its coldness, the urn will remain, through all the woeful human history to come, a friend to humans to whom it reveals the relationship between beauty and truth. From one point of view, "Beauty is truth, truth beauty" is simply nonsense. But if understood as a comment that defines art, the observation points out that the successful realization of an aesthetic ideal is, as well, the successful realization of the truth in one's art. To extend this notion into more concrete terms: the message of the urn, finally, is a statement about all great art. Great art crystallizes the truth; it conveys to those who experience it an insight into their own human possibilities in the most effective way. That's why beauty is truth.

The poem provides the opportunity to discuss paradox and the uses of punning and ambiguity in such words as "still" (l. 1), "haunts" (l. 5), "brede" (l. 41), and "overwrought" (l. 42). We accept the view that the urn speaks the last two lines.

John Keats On First Looking into Chapman's Homer (p. 155)

The controlling metaphor of this sonnet, the equation of reading with travel and exploration, gives it an extraordinary compression and resonance. Keats is able, in the octave, to tell us a great deal about himself and his attitude toward literature. He has read widely ("traveled much") in the great literature ("realms of gold") of western civilization ("western islands"). Line 5 might be read to mean that Keats had not read Homer before discovering Chapman's translation, though it is more likely that he had, in the pale closed couplets of Pope's translations. The travel and movement end climactically with the discovery of the Chapman translation that closes the octave.

His lengthy travels having ended with this exhilarating discovery, Keats maintains the basic metaphor in the sestet, but from a different perspective. He compares his feelings to those of explorers who find themselves gazing at something never before seen. Such rare experiences are so awesome, indeed shocking, that they leave the discoverer in stillness and silence.

This brilliant sonnet is a particularly good one for demonstrating to students how the language of metaphor is no mere ornament in poetry. It is only through metaphor that Keats is able to objectify, concretize, and thus communicate what was an intensely private experience. Students might also be interested to know that Keats wrote this poem immediately after he and a friend excitedly spent an entire night reading through Chapman's translation.

Jane Kenyon Surprise (p. 1131)

He (probably Kenyon's husband, her former teacher, the poet Donald Hall) has arranged a surprise party for her, and gets her out of the way by suggesting a meal at the local diner and a walk through the countryside (Hall and Kenyon lived on a farm). Meanwhile, friends are bringing party food to the house. The conundrum here, perhaps, is the loving detail with which the poet describes the rebirth of plant life that pushes aside "last year's spectral leaves," and seems to have nothing to do with the central events of the poem. Kenyon's final years (she died at the age of forty-eight, and this is a late poem) were troubled by profound depression and devastating illness. Surely those "spectral leaves" evoke thoughts of mortality. And though we are not told the occasion for this party, we can imagine, perhaps, her depressing reflections on the arrival of another birthday. "Last year's spectral leaves" are pushed aside by this year's budding growth—but for the (doomed?) poet, the future holds no budding growth.

Freed from the pensive consideration of death and rebirth, she finds herself astounded, not at the surprise gathering but at the "casual / accomplishment with which he has lied." That final observation opens a terrible vista, because it suggests that much of what she had considered to be true about their relationship is now in doubt.

Carolyn Kizer Bitch (p. 1119)

This poem depends upon the standard definitions of a bitch: first, as a female dog; second, as an unpleasant woman. The speaker manages a civil, even pleasant outward demeanor, while she struggles with the she-dog within when she meets her remarried ex-husband or lover. Lines 30–31 suggest that her bitchiness (sometimes groveling doglike devotion; sometimes, perhaps, howling rage) drove him away. His new friends have "well-groomed pets," and she has to restrain—drag by the scruff—her own bitchiness as she parts from her happily married ex. You might use this poem to illustrate extended metaphor and poetic conceit.

Etheridge Knight Hard Rock Returns to Prison from the Hospital for the Criminal Insane (p. 803)

The "bad nigger" is an archetype in African American life and literature. The term, no doubt coined by whites, describes one kind of black man (another is the Uncle Tom) American racism has produced: tough, mean, often violent, doomed (by his unwillingness "to take no shit from nobody") to prison or an early death or both. Whites use the adjective "bad" in its ordinary sense; but what is bad for whites can be good for blacks and thus, by a simple and ironic reversal, the adjective has taken on the opposite meaning among African Americans—the very best.

Hard Rock (in black slang the adjective "hard" is similar in meaning to "bad") is legendary even to his fellow-prisoners, who are themselves "bad niggers." The scars on his body are eloquent testimony to his indifference to physical intimidation and pain, to his refusal to submit to the standards of a (racist) society. Impervious to fear, Hard Rock has been defeated by the modern techniques of psychosurgery. The guards ("screws") and the "hillbilly" can now taunt him with impunity. The effect on the speaker and his fellow inmates is crushing, representing, as it does, the loss of hope and possibility. At the same time, conceivably, the speaker is warning himself and the other men against the dangers of hero-worship; they must resist and fight for themselves, rather than live vicariously in the legendary toughness of someone like Hard Rock.

Maxine Kumin Jack (p. 1121)

The elegiac tone and the pathos that drive this poem are so deeply personal that we cannot imagine that Kumin invented the roan gelding that got sold down the river. The poem begins with four stanzas quietly celebrating a comfortable old age lived in the company of "sturdy" friends and the two surviving horses. It is the end of summer. The last of the garden's corn, buttered, is consumed with red wine among friends in early September. How could this bucolic scene be made more pleasant? Traditionally, the end of summer, however lazy and golden, does invite grief and regret. In mythic terms, winter marks the death of the year, and spring marks its rebirth.

But the speaker's regret and grief reflect her response to a twenty-year-old decision that she cannot forget—that 1980 spring when she let Jack go to "a neighbor I thought was a friend." The neighbor sold the horse "down the river." Note the resonance of that expression reminiscent of slave families torn apart when close relatives were sold down the river. Bad enough. But worse, although she meant to recover Jack, "she never went looking for him, to buy him back / and now my old guilt is flooding this twilit table." The twilight clearly refers both to the time of day and the time of life (Kumin was seventy-eight when she published this poem).

We return to the present as the speaker muses on the inevitability of death. She is overwhelmed by the guilt she feels, the betrayal, not of just another roan gelding but of Jack—a family member. The "Oh Jack" of the penultimate line—the first time we hear his name within the poem—though profoundly understated, is absolutely devastating.

Maxine Kumin   Woodchucks   (p. 1411)

The central issue in this poem is the inescapable horror of killing, even when the killing is justified. In the final two lines, the poet muses about the differences between acquiescence in killing and active participation. Enlarging the world of the poem from the rural backyard garden to contain the Holocaust, she illuminates the incredible capacity for horror of a populace not required to participate in that horror personally. Had the gas bomb from the Feed and Grain Exchange worked properly, she would not have had to confront the woodchucks and would, presumably, have remained rather unmoved at their fate. But it did not work "underground the quiet Nazi way." She has to shoot them, the destroyers of her flowers and vegetables; she has to confront them personally—and that confrontation produces an insight into her own character that troubles her. First, she finds it thrilling to hunt and kill the woodchucks—but her first victim is the "littlest" one, and her self-justification immediately comes into conflict with her innate human compassion. That little woodchuck "died in the everbearing roses," almost as if it is lamented and mourned with flowers. Then, in quick succession, she kills the mother and another "baby." She has been ruthlessly shooting women and children—the old wily male, the proper antagonist, evades her. No wonder she wished for them the underground, out-of-sight deaths that would allow her, as it allowed the people of Nazi Germany, to distance herself from the guilt.

The "Darwinian pieties for killing," doubtless, alludes to her notion that she is more fit to survive than the woodchucks—since they are struggling over the same food.

Note the unobtrusive rhyme scheme, *abcacb,* reminiscent of the sestets of Italian sonnets.

Philip Larkin   Aubade   (p. 1409)

This "morning song" differs from those cheerful aubades that usually celebrate nature and all the possibilities of a new day. Morning here is that leaden hour before the dawn, four A.M., when one, lying sleepless in the soundless dark, can, perhaps must, contemplate his or her own mortality. No distractions interfere with the purity of that contemplation; no sensory intrusions divert one from the awful confrontation. And Larkin, in this remarkable poem, intricately structured yet translucent, describes the terror of death as few writers ever have.

The mind "blanks at the glare" of the inevitability of death, not because the speaker has failed some philosophical test—not for remorse at "good not done" nor even because he has not had time to get clear of "wrong beginnings." The terror cannot be softened by any such public notions about the life well lived. The terror comes from the idea of oblivion—"nothing more terrible, nothing more true."

Religion, here a "vast moth-eaten musical brocade," cannot dispel the terror. Specious philosophical analysis is even worse. The argument that "no rational being / can fear a thing it will not feel" misses the point. It is precisely the not feeling that we fear.

The fourth stanza describes the awareness that "slows each impulse down to indecision." How absurd, being mortal, to act at all. And the "furnace-fear" of that mortality, Larkin suggests, rages out at the early hour when neither the distraction of people nor the anesthesia of alcohol is available. Even "courage is no good." Courage is a way of "not scaring others." It does nothing to render the idea of death less terrifying for the speaker.

As the morning lengthens into light, and this aubade concludes with the intrusion of the mundane—a peculiarly absurd world, an "intricate rented world"—the speaker is released from the night terror. He will sally out into an absurd, charnel, white, sunless world where crouching telephones suggest the ominous weight of all the senseless work to be done; where postmen link us together in the business of life even as doctors minister to the dying.

Compare "Aubade" with Dylan Thomas's "Do Not Go Gentle into That Good Night" and Catherine Davis's response "After a Time." Our students might be too young to peer with Larkin's cold eye upon the inevitability of death. But the Larkin poem, with its unflinching desperation, makes the other two seem like literary exercises about death, a bit self-conscious, a bit self-dramatizing. "Aubade," with its restraint, its elegant understatement, doesn't so much illuminate the idea of mortality as remind its readers that though "most things never happen: this one will." And nothing, neither rage nor acquiescence, can ease the horror of extinction. You might discuss the relationship between poetry and belief. Can a religious reader, secure in the belief that death marks a transition to another form of existence, nonetheless appreciate this nihilistic poem?

Discuss the effect of the three-stress ninth line in each stanza juxtaposed against the essentially pentameter lines of the poem. The short lines have a hard force, a sort of finality that is then defeated by the pentameter (some have an extra syllable or two) of the final line. Might it be argued that the metrical variation contributes a sort of minor key quality that reinforces the consistent sadness of those last lines?

Philip Larkin   A Study of Reading Habits   (p. 173)

The speaker of this poem moves through three phases in his life and identifies with three quite different moral stances. As a prepubescent boy who hates school—a place where he was probably bullied and humiliated—he finds in books the pure poetic justice of childhood literature. He identifies with the heroes who defeat powerful evildoers, bringing down "dirty dogs" with the "old right hook." In the second stanza, the speaker—pubescent now and, no doubt, victimized by raging hormones—throws in with evil. His reading provides sexual fantasies much beyond any hope of fulfillment, what with those inch-thick specs. And finally, identifying not with the heroes but with the losers and villains in the books he has read, the speaker gives up reading in favor of alcohol—maybe drink-inspired fantasies are best. Though rendered in a set of belligerent colloquial expressions, the poem is intricately rhymed. These delicious rhymes—*specs–sex, fangs–meringues, dude–stewed, chap–crap*—contribute to its powerful effect.

Philip Larkin   This Be the Verse   (p. 173)

Using a form and vocabulary reminiscent of children's narrative ballads, Larkin makes a typically dark and bitter comment on the human condition. The psychological damage inflicted by parents on their children is understandable—the parents themselves were, in their turn, damaged children. And the inescapable conclusion opens the last stanza: "Man hands on misery to man. / It deepens like a coastal shelf." The net product of human history is an inexorable increase in misery; the only solution is a childless life and an early death. By contrast, Larkin's "Aubade" reflects on the terror of death with none of the whimsy of this poem. Written three years later, "Aubade" does not perceive death as a whimsical solution to the problem of the human condition, but rather as the utterly devastating problem itself.

Evelyn Lau Solipsism (p. 191)

One standard dictionary defines *solipsism* as "1. the theory that the self can be aware of nothing but its own experiences and states and 2. the theory that nothing exists or is real but the self." The poem describes the self-absorption of the speaker working out in a fitness gym and participating in the taping of a fitness routine (that requires the "makeup person" to tend her). She perceives herself engaged in the "process of making myself perfect." Though her neighbors at the exercise bar are perfect, her perfection will be unique (solipsistic)—not like theirs. Earlier, her exercise routine required that she pump her hips—and she muses on the lovers who will come "to smother us with their bodies." Lau's extraordinary life includes a period when she was actually on the street, surviving as a prostitute, and in some of her poems she considers the utter detachment that enables prostitutes to safeguard their emotional being. Here, in the gym, surrounded by "funhouse mirrors," she understands that audiences "would wave," "would stampede," in response to circumstances—but she will not "stray from the script or structure." And, in the telling final stanza, the speaker, though aware that "Journalists declare there are weather and wars / happening outside the fitness-club doors," remains impervious to such "outside" considerations. "Rarely," she concludes, "do I look outside, for something other or more." And that *outside* refers not only to the fitness club but also to her solipsistic self.

Philip Levine A Theory of Prosody (p. 1412)

The first thing students should note about this poem is the comic contrast between the grandiloquence of the title and the poem itself. Prosody, the study of poetic meters and versification, is a subject for scholarly research, for philosophical speculation on the nature of language. Levine exemplifies his theory in a story about his cat, Nellie, whose prosaic name contributes to the poem's comic, prosy tone. The comedy emerges from the poet's personification of his cat—when a line grew too long, Nellie would "paw at the moving hand" (l. 7); on sleepless nights, she would calm him (l. 17); and at the end, she played her part in an elaborate game or pretense (ll. 21–22).

The final three lines state the moral of this tale. The obvious referent for "it's" in line 23 is the poet's own writing of poetry, his theory of prosody. During her years of good health, Nellie functioned for the poet as the "alert cat / who leaves nothing to chance" (ll. 24–25). The year before her death, too decrepit to perform that necessary function, she faked it. Even though the poet faked obedience, the game (i.e., writing poetry) continued. But the "it's" suggests a more comprehensive referent—in a world devoid of meaning, we must create our own meanings. Nellie is a metonymy for those things humans do to create meaning, from games to God.

Audre Lorde Power (p. 1125)

Ten-year-old Clifford Clover was shot in April 1973; Officer Thomas J. Shea was acquitted more than a year later. The shooting occurred in South Jamaica (a section of the borough of Queens in New York City) when Shea and his partner stopped Clover and his stepfather for questioning and the two suspects fled. During the pursuit, the boy allegedly pointed a gun at the officers (though no gun was ever found at the scene). It was a high-profile, emotion-charged case from the outset. Clover was the youngest person ever killed by a New York City police officer, and he was shot in the back. The three days following the shooting were marked by what the *New York Times* characterized as "disturbances" in South Jamaica, culminating in looting and attacks on whites at the time of the young boy's funeral. Following the acquittal, again according to the *Times,* bands of African American youths injured two New York City patrolmen and several white civilians in random attacks and shattered car windows in South Jamaica. Shortly following the criminal trial, Shea was found guilty in a police department trial and dismissed from the force (as was his partner, for having lied to protect Shea).

Frantz Fanon, the black Algerian psychiatrist, points out in *The Wretched of the Earth* (1963) that his patients often fantasized that they had acquired superhuman physical strength. Thus they could take revenge with impunity on their white oppressors. In the lives and literature of oppressed peoples, power—political and physical—looms large.

Considerations of class and race rarely figure in reactions to police killings of a white; when a black is killed by a policeman, race and class are almost invariably at issue.

The very title of Lorde's poem evokes this central issue at both the personal and the societal levels. At the personal level, Lorde struggles to master and then channel the rage that Shea's acquittal released in her. The distinction made in the opening lines equates poetry with acting on the self and rhetoric with acting on one's children. Whatever this distinction means (she will return to it in the final section), it is clear that poetry is positive and rhetoric, negative. In contrast, the second section evokes a surreal, dream image, where the poet watches in rage the ten-year-old (her "dying son") bleed to death of gunshot wounds in a desert where she is lost "without imagery or magic"—that is, without power. In her declaration that she is "trying to make power out of hatred and destruction," the operative word is "trying," with its suggestion that the task may be impossible.

The second and third sections deal directly and literally with the event, focusing on two people, Officer Shea and the single African American member of the jury. Her comments on the officer are matter-of-fact and restrained, as if the racist motivation is obvious. The juror, however, is another matter, for in her Lorde is forced to confront the painful and horrifying truth that "four centuries of white male approval" have so deformed this black woman that she connives in the destruction of her own people (she could have created a hung jury).

In the final section, Lorde returns to "the difference between poetry and rhetoric." Rhetoric, she seems to say, is the abdication of power or the self-destructive kind of power (represented by the African American juror) that helps perpetuate a racist society where a policeman can, with impunity, shoot to death a ten-year-old African American boy. Poetry, on the other hand, is the willingness to exercise power, to put oneself (not one's children) at risk in order to achieve a society where murderous racism will not go unpunished. The final lines express just how deep and potentially uncontrollable—and mindlessly destructive—Lorde feels her rage to be. Without the power to command justice, one is left only with the corrupt and poisonous power to strike at the tormentor—in this case by raping and murdering an innocent white.

Lorde's epigraph, explaining how she came to write the poem, appears in *Black Women Writers (1950–1980)*, edited by Man Evans. This volume also includes essays by and about Toni Cade Bambara, Gwendolyn Brooks, Lucille Clifton, Nikki Giovanni, and Alice Walker.

Adrian C. Louis   End Prayer for Mogie   (p. 1418)

We asked the poet about the spider in the first stanza. Here is his response.

> "If you've ever been around hardcore boozers, the dregs of the bottle are referred to as 'spiders.' If you empty a bottle, there is still a small amount that will collect on the bottom, a spider."

The nitroglycerin pills are a common medication for treating angina pain. That "cheap hotel" in the third stanza doubtless represents the world of the living, with overtones of the degradation of life on Indian reservations. The speaker laments the passing of his alcoholic friend, particularly because Mogie still had love to give, Indian songs to sing, Indian dance to create (even if the dance was a cheap wine ballet). The juju summoned up by the speaker—the King's X, which is a part of a children's game in which one remains "safe" if he or she makes a certain hand sign—does not deter that anally fussy and frantic Sky God. Old Mogie's soul is vacuumed up presumably to keep the world tidy. The speaker leaves us with a tart taste of resentment, obviously annoyed with a frantic Sky God who sounds like one of those pathological neat housekeepers—only more deadly.

Adrian C. Louis   Tears of One Hundred Years: Wounded Knee, South Dakota, 1890–1990   (p. 183)

Presumably, this poem was written to recognize (*celebrate* would surely be the wrong word) the hundredth anniversary of the 1890 massacre of Indians at Wounded Knee,

South Dakota. Our students probably have some suitably vague notions of the conflicts between westward-moving settlers and the Indian populations they encountered. Perhaps the excerpt from Chief American Horse's testimony will put a human face on the horror that Indians suffered at the hands of their civilizers by revealing the indefensible and despicable aspects of a systematic genocide. But how does that horrid history relate to the poem it introduces?

The speaker, awakened from a (pleasant?) dream—not by the bucolic rooster call one would expect but by a "rooster raped" by the noisy car driven by drunken reservation Indians—begins with what sounds like a prayer to Lord Christ. The first line, starkly juxtaposed against the horrid epigraph, will immediately raise questions about the strange morality that allowed presumptive Christians to mercilessly slaughter unarmed women and children. His shattered dream a burst bubble, the speaker confronts the new day—but not with exuberance or joy. He is out of coffee; the dogs peed on the rug (again!). The best he can cobble up in memory of his ancestors' holocaust is a toast with warm beer—hardly a fitting commemoration for the event.

You might ask the students to debate the form of the poem. Does centering the lines add or detract from its effect? You might print it out flush left to consider whether the visual nuances provided by centering the lines justify the poet's decision. More important, what is the relationship between the poem and the epigraph? Can it be argued that such massacres were so demoralizing that they are, ultimately, responsible for the kind of degraded reservation life suggested by the poem?

Amy Lowell Patterns (p. 789)

Eighteenth-century England was famous for its elaborately landscaped and formally patterned gardens that reflected the period's belief in an orderly and rational universe. Thus, although "the Duke in Flanders" (l. 105) might refer to the Duke of Wellington's victory in 1815, the manorial garden, the gown, and, especially the sense of an orderly, patterned life in this poem indicate that Lord Hartwell died in 1708, the date of the Duke of Marlborough's celebrated victory in Flanders.

The speaker's meditation develops a powerful tension between the orderly, artificial patterning of the garden, symbolizing her outer life, and the dreams and images of her inner life. The garden paths, the "powdered hair and jeweled fan" (l. 6), and the lady's gown (which she repeatedly describes as "stiff") define that constricting life. In contrast is her inner life, evoked through her awareness of her soft flesh (l. 33), her dream of the gown lying crumpled on the ground (ll. 41–42), and of "melting" in the arms of her lover (l. 52). But as she returns to reality, she is overwhelmed with the realization that she will never escape the patterns; "the weight of this brocade" (l. 57) very nearly causes her to faint. The gown the young lady describes is literally heavy, but by this point in the poem, the gown is clearly symbolic, and its weight is emotional and spiritual. When she describes the delivery of the letter, her control and politeness contrast dramatically with the passionate dreams of the lines immediately preceding and help define further the social pattern of control and "stiffness" in which she is trapped.

The second-to-last stanza makes explicit what has been implicit in the earlier lines: the passion of lovemaking "would have broke the pattern" (l. 83). Underneath the lime tree, she would have cast off the weight of her brocaded gown and yielded to the passions of the naked body. But that is not to be. In the final stanza, the remainder of her life stretches before her like a patterned garden path, the "squills and daffodils" (representing spring and youth) will give way "to snow" (representing old age and death). Overcome by her loss, she identifies war, because it has taken her lover from her, with the other patterns that have imprisoned her. For like the garden paths and the stiff gown, war is the creation of a society that imprisons individuals, forcing them to suppress and control their innermost desires.

Katharyn Howd Machan Hazel Tells LaVerne (p. 187)

The poem depends on the reader's acquaintance with fairy tales. An important subset of that genre compels a beautiful, often haughty central figure to exhibit humanity and compassion by responding to an enchanted figure who appears to be ugly and repulsive. Hazel's problem results neither from her pride nor her beauty (we may reasonably assume). In her world, a frog is a frog, and the frog's request is perverse; in her world she will never be a princess. And she reports, with a touch of pride, the bedrock common sense that rejects the frog's slick talk and the illusions it attempts to generate. Hazel knows who she is, and Hazel has learned to cope with the various forms of perversity loose in the world. This frog has picked the wrong savior.

Get students thinking about the connotative energy of certain names. Are Hazel and LaVerne appropriate names for cleaning ladies who speak this dialect of English? (Is J. Alfred Prufrock an appropriate name for the ineffectual would-be lover of Eliot's poem?) As well, ask students to find the "poetry" in this rather prosaic piece that depends completely on allusion. Why do lines end as they do? Contrast line 13 ("me a princess") with the last two lines ('me / a princess") — what added effect does the second arrangement generate?

Aimee Mann Save Me (p. 1093)

See "Looking Deeper: From Poetry to Song" on p. 1085 of the anthology.

Christopher Marlowe The Passionate Shepherd to His Love
(p. 1086)

Sir Walter Raleigh The Nymph's Reply to the Shepherd
(p. 1087)

C. Day-Lewis Song (p. 1088)

The Marlowe poem provides the occasion for a discussion of poetic conventions in general and the pastoral tradition in particular. In the pastoral tradition the poet invites the girl to join with the poet in a carefree love. Students are not likely to find the invitation very convincing; it is doubtless too artificial, and the bribes offered in return for the girl's acquiescence are charming but modest.

Raleigh's reply is a better poem. It makes the pastoral tradition itself part of its target and opposes the realities that govern human relationships to Marlowe's vision of carefree love.

Note the allusion to Philomel in line 7. Philomel was raped by her brother-in-law, who then tore out her tongue so that she could not accuse him. The gods later turned her into a nightingale. Thus the allusion to a time of bitterness when the nightingale becomes mute is heavily charged with the tragic consequences of untrammeled lust. Raleigh systematically points out that the world offered by Marlowe's shepherd is illusory — shepherds lie, weather becomes bitter, flowers and nymphs fade and wither, as do gowns, skirts, and posies. Had joys no date, and age no need, the nymph might be moved to entertain Marlowe's invitation. But joys do pass, and the careless love of the shepherd is not likely to survive the loss of the nymph's beauty. Note the balance of lines 11 and 12. A "honey tongue" is "fancy's spring" (both season and source), but a "heart of gall" is "sorrow's fall" (both season and defeat).

Lewis's "Song" is another reply to Marlowe from a modern point of view. In a general way, it attacks Marlowe's poem on the same grounds as does Raleigh's. But whereas Raleigh focuses on the universal and inexorable process of aging, decay, and death, Lewis subverts Marlowe's timeless world of pastoral joy by focusing on the bleak prospects for a modern swain and his lady. The swain may be able to provide "bed and board" through "chance employment" (the phrase suggests the possibility of unemployment), which he ironically describes as handling "dainties on the docks" (i.e., the backbreaking work of a longshoreman). They will live beside "sour canals," weighed down by "Care" and "Hunger" and, as Raleigh also reminds us, the prospect of death.

Andrew Marvell To His Coy Mistress (p. 1102)

This poem incorporates a distinctly logical—almost syllogistic—structure that distinguishes it from other carpe diem poems. The three sections develop a tightly knit argument of *if-but-therefore*. *If* there was time, I'd woo you properly, *but* we will soon die, *therefore* we had better become lovers now.

The images of the first section—time, geography, and size—create a mood of languor. The rivers Ganges and Humber (on the southern boundary of Northumberland) are chosen for their locations, since they are approximately on opposite sides of the globe. The flood is, in effect, the beginning of time, and the conversion of the Jews is a hyperbole for never. The speaker's "vegetable" (as opposed to rational) love will grow "vaster than empires but more slow."

The second section introduces a note of urgency in the image of time's chariot, and we have—instead of an empire-sized vegetable love to look forward to—deserts of vast eternity. Then boldly and bawdily, Marvell sketches the consequences of too much coyness, driving his argument home with a series of powerful images of the utter decaying finality of death.

The logic then requires that the lovers behave differently, and the images change dramatically from those of the first section. In place of slowness, distance, and great size, the images radiate excitement—"fires," "sport," "devour," "roll," "tear," "rough strife," "run." Time is presented as a slow-jawed, devouring beast that will itself be devoured. The final couplet establishes the difference between chronometric time and subjective time—the difference between an hour of pain and an hour of pleasure.

Katherine McAlpine Plus C'est la Même Chose (p. 185)

This poem is a more complex achievement than may appear on first reading. The seventh-grade dance is the occasion for the speaker to express astonishment, as she does in the opening line, at how suddenly the little girls have turned into women. (If one of the little girls is the speaker's child, the poem does not say so.) Clustered in one part of the gym, the girls seem to know instinctively that their role is to be alluring not only in how they look but also in how they act. They affect an "elaborate indifference" (wonderful phrase!) to the boys who, fiddling with the audio equipment, perform *their* culturally assigned duties. The question of line 9 is a mock question, for the speaker clearly understands that while the boys and girls may not get around to dancing, in a deeper sense, everything that is happening is part of an elaborate mating dance.

In the final lines, the description of the boys gathering "in formation" and beginning a "migration" across the floor puts the entire event lightly but squarely in the context of those gender-defining activities and mating rituals that have from time immemorial characterized human (and animal) behavior. The bemused and comic tone is appropriately reinforced by the hilarious conclusion. Obeying the cultural (if not genetic) imperatives of their nature, the boys migrate to the girls, only to find that the girls, obeying their imperatives, have disappeared to make themselves even more alluring.

The formal skill of the poem is equally impressive. A fourteen-line sonnet, it alters and blends traditional sonnet forms. While it is not precisely a Shakespearean sonnet, the rhyme scheme (*abba cddc effe gg*) follows the formal three-quatrain structure of the Shakespearean form. Interestingly, though, the poem's meaning (or syntax) does not follow this formal structure. Line 4 runs into line 5, while the break in the poem occurs, in the manner of the Petrarchan sonnet, between the octave and the sestet. Finally, the prevailing iambic pentameter is varied throughout, notably in the first line, which has a (thematically appropriate) feminine ending.

J. D. McClatchy Jihad (p. 508)

If you search the Web, you will encounter many discussions of the concept of *jihad*. One source describes *jihad* as encompassing three aspects: struggling against a visible enemy, against the devil, and against the *nafs* (the lower or passionate soul or self).

McClatchy's poem perceives *jihad* as just such a struggle. When we asked the author to identify the Koranic verses quoted in this poem, he replied that they represent a pastiche of verses from the several *suras* that address martyrdom. But what the italicized "divinely revealed" verses signify is reasonably clear. The Koran provides Muslims with the promise of salvation if they lose their lives in conflict with infidels. And the poem concludes with a particularly inviting premise: you and your loved ones are saved by your martyrdom. Furthermore, who would value "the poverty of this world" above a place in paradise? But that salvation requires spiritual discipline as well as physical courage. In addition, McClatchy demands recognition of an ironic dimension, when he declares that the struggle addresses the "nothing both sides fight over / In God's name, a last idolatry / Of boundaries. . . ." And, with further irony, the speaker points out that the doomed Israelis travel "To buy or sell what goods they claim are theirs, / unlike our fates, which are not ours to say."

The poem describes a succession of actions, from practice stone-throwing at dummy tanks through a prayerful self-examination "to raze / The ziggurat of sin" to the self-immolation of the "skinny martyr" whose act kills not only himself but also thirty-four civilians on the bus he attacks. The ziggurat is an ancient Babylonian pyramidal temple tower. Jihadis must, first, through introspection and prayer, struggle to overcome the powerful sinful aspects of the human condition—the temptations sown by the devil and harvested by the *nafs*. Only then will they be equipped to struggle against their physical enemies and attain the promised salvation. And "only then, and at the Caliph's nod, / Are believers called to drown in blood the people / Of an earlier book." That earlier book is, of course, the Hebrew Bible. Though McClatchy reveals the context for the skinny martyr's act, he honors neither the victims, preoccupied with buying and selling, nor the martyr who kills, in the name of God, to worship the idolatry of boundaries.

Claude McKay   If We Must Die   (p. 487)

This call for militant resistance is direct and uncomplicated in language and rhythm. McKay handles the Shakespearean sonnet form with skill, though the occasional archaic phrases ("Making their mock," "accursed lot," and "let us show us") are jarring within the prevailing diction. When published in 1919, this poem was viewed with alarm by many whites (including Senator Henry Cabot Lodge, who read it into the *Congressional Record*), who saw it as evidence of a growing spirit of rebellion among African Americans. In later years, McKay asserted that the sonnet was a universal poem on behalf of all who were "abused, outraged and murdered, whether they are minorities or nations, black or brown or yellow or white, Catholic or Protestant or Pagan, fighting against terror."

Peter Meinke   Advice to My Son   (p. 174)

The poem deals with the tension between beauty and practicality, between the claims of intense emotion and mundane survival. The speaker urges squash, spinach, turnips, and tomatoes (the staples of a mundane life) along with the peony and rose (symbols for beauty and passion). The nectar is pleasure, but pleasure alone is insufficient sustenance for a human. The advice grows specific and literal. The pretty girl you marry is one day going to look like her mother, so temper your response to immediate attractiveness and consider the future. The friend to whom you bare your soul should not be in a position to use your confidences against you. Always recognize the humble reality symbolized by bread—but always at the same time reach for an intoxicating loveliness.

George Meredith   *from* Modern Love: Sonnet 17   (p. 1107)

In the cycle of fifty extended sonnets entitled *Modern Love* (1862), Meredith explored the discordant dying moments of his first marriage. This particular sonnet chronicles a moment at a dinner party for friends who are unaware of the couple's marital difficulties. The pair hide their situation and behave with such grace that they actually admire each other — exchanging "Warm-lighted looks." Their friends, reacting to appearance and ignorant of reality, envy them their apparent happiness. But all of those appearances are metaphorized as "Love's corpse-light!" — the marsh gas phosphorescence that, when seen in cemeteries, portends a funeral.

Robert Mezey My Mother (p. 175)

Some students will recognize this sketch of the soul-withering mother who equates wealth and business enterprise with happiness and success. Those who exhibit poverty (like Frank) are held up to scorn as horrible examples of a life-style to be avoided. For the poet's mother, to be a mensch — a human being — is to earn money and pay bills. At the outset she sounds encouraging: "you / are doing the best you can . . . you turned out very well." But she soon reveals her central concern. The writer Frank is a failure — save your money, I know better than you what is good for you, life is too short for art. In spite of the comic tone of the poem, the issue is a crucial one, and the mother's pressure on her son is fundamentally vicious.

This apparently colloquial poem actually embodies some rather sophisticated musical and rhythmic devices. Most of the seven-syllable lines contain three stressed syllables. Though there is little rhyme (and that mainly toward the end), there is considerable off-rhyme (*Trenton–bone; can't–went; said–did;* and so forth) and insistent consonance or assonance among the final words of the lines.

Edna St. Vincent Millay Love Is Not All (p. 1110)

As does Shakespeare's Sonnet 130, this sonnet plays off the traditional love sonnet that for four hundred years has celebrated extravagantly the nature of love and the qualities of the beloved. "Love," Millay tells us, "is not all." And then she goes on, using the irony of understatement finally, to suggest that love, *is* all — more significant than release from pain, from want, from hunger. Compare this poem to Elizabeth Bishop's villanelle "One Art," which uses a similar strategy to insist on the power of love. Both poems nicely contrast with such typical love sonnets as Shakespeare's 18 and 29.

Janice Mirikitani Suicide Note (p. 1416)

You might talk about this poem in tandem with Plath's "Daddy" and Lim's "Father from Asia." Those poems display the psychic scars left by the universal struggle between fathers and daughters. In this poem, however, the speaker's struggle is not to break free of excessive parental control but, without the necessary personal and intellectual resources, somehow to satisfy her parents' expectations. Unable to rise to that required standard, she perceives herself as a failure with no recourse but suicide.

Most chilling is the revelation that she kills herself because she is female. Being a male would have been enough to please the parents: "I would see the light in my mother's / eyes, or the golden pride reflected / in my father's dream." But as a female — an irreperable disappointment of her parents' expectations — she sees herself as not good enough, not pretty enough, not smart enough, not strong enough. She likens herself to a wounded, fragile sparrow, caught in winter, and crushed by her sense of her own mediocrity. Her broken body lies covered by the shredded notes that drift upon her like snow.

You might risk a classroom discussion on the relationship between culture and suicide. Could an American coed have done this, or would an American poet write this poem? A Chinese? A Korean? A German? Surely Americans, Chinese, Koreans, and Germans (along with all the other ethnicities that might be) have committed suicide. But for what reason? Why would a Japanese woman be more likely to kill herself under these circumstances? Or is that assumption simply not true? If acculturation were the rigid determinant of one's success or failure as a human being, would it not be wise to break free? But, if one breaks the constraining bonds of his or her own culture, what replaces them? What becomes the measure of a successful life? And how shall one deal with failure?

Felix Mnthali   The Stranglehold of English Lit.   (p. 980)

Like the other two pieces in this casebook, Mnthali's "The Stranglehold of English Lit." indicts the cultural influence of the West on Africa. Mnthali mounts his attack on Jane Austen as representative of English literature in its entirety—an attack that will lose some of its force for an audience of students unfamiliar with Austen's novels. A short description might help, but probably would not add much to those offered by Mnthali in the second, fourth, and fifth stanzas. Familiarity with Austen aside, the poet's feelings about the influence of English literature should still be clear from the title onward.

One good way to approach a discussion of the nature of that stranglehold would be the same way the poet uses—through the question a student in an English literature class seems to have had about why do the people in these novels "carouse all day / and do no work." This question highlights the irony of teaching novels written about the wealthy members of a foreign society—whose wealth came at the price of the labor and enslavement of another people—to the descendants of those enslaved. Mnthali most explicitly describes the effects of that teaching in stanzas four and seven. The initial question can also be connected both to the powerful images of the fifth stanza—it is the work done on plantations by branded slaves that made the leisure possible—and to the questions asked by the students mentioned in the final stanza who fought for independence—questions asked in the face of the influence of English literature.

Student resistance to the connection of novels of manners to the horrors of enslavement can be engaged by reference to the poem's form. The alternation between the calmer, more abstract moments in the poem with the few but powerful concretely violent moments can be read to illustrate that resistance—how can these quiet novels about country living be connected to that violence?—but it can also be read to demonstrate both the irony and insidiousness of the connection, in moments such as the abrupt transition from the fourth stanza to the fifth.

Lady Mary Wortley Montagu   Song   (p. 1103)

The history of literature is replete with lyric songs written by men attempting to seduce women—consider Marlowe's "The Passionate Shepherd to His Love" (p. 1086) and Herrick's all-purpose carpe diem lyric "To the Virgins to Make Much of Time" (p. 1091). Sometimes, the male lyricist creates an anti-love song (as did W. S. Gilbert in "To Phoebe" [p. 1092]). But here we have a woman (one of the very few eighteenth-century female English poets) singing a complaint common to all women. And her song embodies a venomous wit that a role-playing male is not likely to imagine. After all, Raleigh, imagining himself as the fetching country nymph, exhibits prudence, not scorn—as if "she" would welcome a roll in the meadow if only the shepherd could insure her future against the loss of her intoxicating beauty. But Lady Mary is a mature woman; she has endured the unwelcome attention of over-confident seducers; and her response is deadly, not prudent. The man pursuing her is a "powder'd fop," a "gaudy painted butterfly." Only some "giddy girl," some inexperienced childlike ditz, would take the trouble to "ensnare" such a worthless dandy (notice that the poor silly man is, finally, ensnared—the seduced, not the seducer). As for the speaker, well, she is "us'd to more substantial fare." Perhaps the opening lines provide the deadliest thrust in this poem. All the proud cocksureness of her would-be lover is impaled with one question: "Why should you think I live unpleas'd, / Because I am not pleas'd with you?" Surely the implication that a better man is already upon the scene is as devastating a blow to this fop's ego that a woman can deliver.

Lisel Mueller   Happy and Unhappy Families I   (p. 1118)

Leo Tolstoy's *Anna Karenina* opens with this rather famous line: "All happy families are alike; every unhappy family is unhappy in its own way." But Mueller argues that there is no difference. Unhappy families are as much alike as happy ones; furthermore, unhappy families are much more interesting. Early in the poem, Mueller asserts that the lives of unhappy families are "motion and heat," "they are what we think of as *life.*" These pronouncements are followed by a series of suggestive conditions that invite the reader to supply the circumstances that explain them. Why does someone lie? Why is that person being beaten? Why does this one weep, that one pray, the third one cower in the corner? It's a nice rhetorical trick—a bit like Johnny Carson's performances as The Answer Man. Recall that he would hold the envelope up to his turbaned head, provide an answer, and then open the envelope to discover the question.

Will our student readers just slide by, or will they respond to Mueller's desperate family members by recalling some moments of their own lives marked by weeping, by prayer, by cowering? Furthermore, has Mueller made her case? We might agree that unhappy families are more interesting, but her illustrations of unhappy behavior seem to validate Tolstoy's assertion rather than the poet's. As for those happy families, Mueller can barely contain her contempt for them because they "do nothing / to deserve their happiness." This might serve to agitate an argument in the class—ask the students what must people do to "deserve their happiness"?

Lisel Mueller Triage (p. 494)

Triage describes the process of sorting victims of, say, a battle or disaster to determine priority of medical treatment. Usually, priority is given to those having the greatest likelihood of survival. By extension, it can be applied to the determination of priorities in any circumstances.

Mueller confronts a fundamental conundrum: directing one's passionate concern to one aspect of her experience—in this case elm trees—by definition prevents a proper concern for other things that may be equally or even more important. What shall we do about the homeless and harassed who gather under them? The notion of applying triage principles to every aspect of our experience and concern leads, finally, to a reductio ad absurdum. "When I talk about myself, I cannot talk about you." On the other hand, we may reasonably ask, do triage principles apply to every human choice? May we not decide that some things are equally important? Or that assigning priorities is not the same as ignoring everything below the first priority? You might point out that political strategists are fond of defining "wedge issues" designed to create triage thinking in the electorate: this one issue is more important to me than any other, and therefore this candidate is my choice.

Prose poetry has always made us a bit nervous (Carolyn Forché's "The Colonel" [p. 511] is another example), and you might challenge the class to demonstrate that "Triage" is, in fact, a poem rather than a paragraph of prose. One exercise: arrange the piece in lines, flush left, jagged on the right. Where would you put the line breaks? Why? A second exercise: What elements in the piece are visual, substantial, image-like (for example, "elms," "homeless poor," "trash")? And what elements are less visual, more abstract and general (for example, "speak of one thing," "suppress another," "myself," and "you" in the last three lines). Perhaps this arrangement displays the speaker's movement from concrete particulars to a significant generalization—a common technique in poetry.

Susan Musgrave Right through the Heart (p. 1137)

This remarkable and unsentimental love poem provides a series of violent images quite different from what students might anticipate. Love, first characterized as a barbed arrow through the heart, produces a bloody wound that the speaker, nonetheless, wishes to welcome and embrace. Love then becomes a newborn infant that, paradoxically, you want to "crush to death" before it has a chance to die naturally. The poem provides a nice opportunity to generate a discussion of the agonies sometimes produced by the ecstasies of love. The "beast with two backs" (l. 3) alludes to Shakespeare's *Othello*, Act I, Scene 1, where Iago taunts Brabantio over the marriage of Othello and Desdemona.

Taslima Nasrin Things Cheaply Had (p. 813)

Because this poem emerges so directly out of the author's experiences in her native Bangladesh as a woman and a writer, students should be urged to read the entry on her in the "Biographical Notes on the Authors" at the end of the book. As noted there, her rationalism and feminism forced her into exile in 1994. She is being tried in absentia under the Bangladesh penal code on charges of "insulting religion and religious sentiment"; a conviction could lead to a prison sentence of two years.

The power of the poem derives from its quiet but graphic description of the status of women in a patriarchal society. Women, while not themselves literally sold, are nonetheless "bought off" by the objects cheaply available to men in the market: a bottle of decorative dye, bars of soap, a jewel, or a sari. In such a society, where women can be counted among the objects cheaply had, the more shocking fact, the speaker suggests, is that women become complicit in their own degradation and come to see themselves as their masters do. Why else, when "Even the mangy cur of the house barks now and then," do they not protest? Are the trinkets and baubles purchased in the market, the "golden lock," worth their dignity, their humanity?

Taslima Nasrin's case has been taken up by various international human rights groups. Writings about her difficulties with the authorities in Bangladesh, by her and others, can be found on the Web site of the Index on Censorship at <http://www.oneworld.org>.

Pablo Neruda The Dead Woman (p. 1398)

Although this poem begins as a traditional lament over the impending death of a beloved woman, it expands into a complex entwined lyric addressing political issues — justice and personal freedom — that require the speaker to "go on living." If the woman dies, the speaker asserts, "it will rain upon my soul night and day" and "my feet will want to march toward where you sleep." However, these traditional expressions of grief, including the suggestion that life is not worth living without the beloved, are tempered by the obligation to struggle for the rights of humankind. Thus, the speaker will "go on living" in order to give voice to the powerless, to racial minorities, to political prisoners. And the victory will be not his, but the "great victory" of social justice for all, and he will be "not just one man / but all men."

Neruda was a political man of the left, and a political writer who went into exile from his native Chile in order to avoid imprisonment himself. Unsurprisingly, he politicizes a traditional love lyric that, ordinarily, celebrates the most individual and private human relationships by insisting on his obligation to struggle with oppressors for the good of the public. Perhaps the private and the public aspects of the speaker are tied together by the woman who "wanted me to be, above all things, / untamable." The line suggests that her love for him was profoundly influenced by his passion for social justice — thus, his duty to continue his struggle after her death is altogether logical, despite his grief.

Sharon Olds Sex without Love (p. 1129)

Ask whether sex without love — the idea, not the poem — is good or bad. Many of us (at least publicly) would call it a bad idea. Then ask the students if that is the speaker's attitude. Here there may be differences of opinion or some confusion because parts of the poem seem to express admiration for "the ones who make love without love." One could argue (and if no one else does, the instructor might) that a good deal of the imagery of the poem seems to express admiration for these people.

The argument might run like this: If the speaker meant to condemn those who make love without love, why would she describe them as "Beautiful as dancers" (l. 2) and graceful as "ice skaters" (l. 3)? Is it consistent with moral disapproval to call them "the purists, the pros, the ones who will not / accept a false Messiah, love the / priest instead of the God" (ll. 14–16)? Why would she cap these positive comparisons with the final simile, likening them to "great runners" (l. 18) who compete not against others but, like the purists and pros they are, against their "own best time" (l. 24)?

Part of the answer is that these images have to be examined more closely and, above all, in context. For one thing, while they do express admiration, it is the admiration for a virtually nonhuman purity and obsession with self. The ice-skating image suggests coldness, as does that of the devotees who prefer the (cold?) abstraction of God over the real (warm?) priest. Alone with "the cold" (l. 19), these runners rise above what Yeats called "the fury and the mire of human events" and cease to be fully human.

This reading is supported by other images and language in the poem. These people have been cut off from a profound source of our humanity, like "children at birth whose mothers are going to / give them away" (ll. 7–8). The speaker's overwhelming astonishment at those who can make love to someone without loving the person is captured in the breathless repetitions of lines 8 and 9 and in the realization that for these people, "the partner / in the bed" (ll. 21–22) is simply a "factor," a thing, as road surface and shoes are to a runner, necessary but only instrumental in realizing "the truth" expressed in the last two lines. It is a cold truth indeed.

Mary Oliver   When Death Comes   (p. 1414)

Wallace Stevens's "Sunday Morning" turns on the speaker's paradoxical assertion that "Death is the mother of beauty." Essentially, this poem also celebrates mortality as the motivating force that challenges us to embrace experience, to live with awareness and passion, to not "end up simply having visited this world." But, unlike "Sunday Morning," which suggests that heavenly delights cannot measure up to those of earth, this poem suggests that death provides still another opportunity for experience, for satisfying curiosity.

Ask students to comment on the images associated with death—a hungry bear, a purchaser, a disease, an "iceberg between the shoulder blades." Are these images apt? Might students suggest others equally unclichéd? As well, ask students to consider the figures of speech used to suggest the possibilities of life, and the speaker's connection to it (i.e., as a bride and a bridegroom). Ask them to articulate (or perhaps write) how the speaker intends to avoid finding "myself sighing and frightened, / or full of argument" at the imminence of death.

Wilfred Owen   Dulce et Decorum Est   (p. 1394)

This poem is a reaction to the chauvinism and jingoistic patriotism of the civilian population during World War I. While the poem's dominant meter is iambic pentameter, variations in the meter insistently reflect the sense of the words. For example, line 6 has no weak syllables at all, with the possible exception of the first; hence, it reinforces the crippling infirmities described. Note also the sequence of participles that commences with line 2. As the cacophony echoes the very sounds of war, so the persistent participles create the nightmarish sense of present and ongoing action.

Dorothy Parker   One Perfect Rose   (p. 1110)

The fun of this poem is compounded by Parker's sensitive poetic ear. The first two stanzas, typical of a long and sentimental poetic tradition, capture the very rhythms of that older love poetry; "A single flow'r he sent me," "All tenderly his messenger he chose," surely generate the resonances associated with Spenser, Herrick, or Waller. Show students some of those older verses, and demonstrate that this poem embodies more than just the witty surprise ending. Note also that the language of the final stanza is quite different—distinctly modern—in its cynical response to single roses.

Molly Peacock   Our Room   (p. 184)

As in her poem "Say You Love Me," Peacock writes about her alcoholic father from the perspective of the mature adult looking back on the child she was. But the child of that poem seems older than the child of this poem. And whereas "Say You Love Me" deals with the fear of violence from a drunken, alcoholic father, in this poem she remembers an earlier time, when she "was in grade 5" (l. 9). The subject is not fear but shame. While fear is a primal, visceral reaction to some force or person (such as a drunken father) that threatens one's physical well-being, shame is a social emotion, a feeling that one is morally less than others. That is why shame often brings with it the overpowering need to confess, to bring to light the dark secret and thereby, perhaps, resolve the tension it creates. Why else did the fifth-grader submit to the inevitable taunts and ridicule of telling her classmates about her father? She apparently did so because she was an extraordinary, emotionally precocious child. She overcomes the ridicule and embarrassment by quietly sorting out the "junk / of my childhood for them" (ll. 11–12), subduing the children into serious questions. The poem ends with a quiet but remarkable triumph: Her actions not only quiet the other children but cause them to disclose "what / happened to them, too" (ll. 14–15). The aching, frightened child at the outset of the poem, who faced her classmates across an emotional abyss, has remarkably brought them all together. In the final line, "I" and "they" give way to "we" and "our," as they all recognize that the speaker's pain and shame is a version of their own, and "our room" becomes a metaphor.

Molly Peacock Say You Love Me (p. 1131)

In this poem, the mature speaker re-experiences a chilling experience of abuse at the hands of a drunken father when she "was probably fifteen" (l. 8). The very first line, seemingly casual, anticipatorily magnifies and focuses on the experience the speaker is about to recount by detaching it from the specific events that led up to it. The next line, with its matter-of-fact "Of course," makes it clear that the father's drunken abuse was a common occurrence. As he looms over her, his puffy, pink face reminds her of a ham on a hook, perhaps expressing an unconscious wish that he were dead. His menacing, insistent demand that she say she loves him causes her to wonder whether she is being attacked because her mother has "said or done something" (l. 10), a reaction that poignantly reveals the family's dynamics. In the midst of her terror and rage, she experiences a moment of extraordinary clarity as she sees her father turn into "a wet baby thing" (l. 18), sobbing in "baby chokes" (l. 20), an image whose pathos does not make him in any sense sympathetic.

Everything suggests a rape: the daughter locked, so to speak, in her father's arms as he towers above her, the description of the father's eyes as "taurean" (l. 30), the helplessness and the rage of the victim finally defeated. She collapses into "a cardboard image" (l. 34), suggesting the ultimate loss of humanity, dignity, and identity associated with rape. Her only direct reference to her father as "my monstrous fear" (l. 37) and, finally, her sense of utter abandonment, of being "completely alone" (l. 45) reveal the suffering inflicted by her abusive father. Note that in stanzas 10 through 13, the crescendo of terror approaches a hideous climax. The speaker's "fear ballooned" (l. 29), her sister "screamed" (l. 37), distracting her father and allowing the speaker to escape. What the impending horror is is not specified, though the implication seems to be that the father is about to physically assault his daughter.

The poem is comprised of fifteen three-line stanzas, many showing the characteristics of tercets, that is, groups of three lines with internal and adjacent rhyme. This rather complex stanzaic pattern contrasts with the colloquial diction, the lack of a regular meter, and the pervasive use of run-on lines both within stanzas and between them.

Marge Piercy The market economy (p. 499)

Prosaic as it may seem, Piercy's poem uses language in quite traditionally poetic ways. The first twenty lines have a rhetorical structure governed by the first word of the poem—the imperative "Suppose," repeated in line 9 and implied in line 17. The lines propose a hypothesis. A series of related questions invite the reader to respond, but the questions are rhetorical. The poet knows that our answer to these questions will be, "No, of course I would not agree to such an offer." The poem then turns at line 21 when the poet responds to our rejection, asking, what are your alternatives to this bargain in a world created—more accurately, corrupted—by the market economy? The final lines offer a bit of mordant humor. The watchword of the market economy has always been *caveat emptor* (let the buyer beware). The world of capitalism has always created sellers ready to take advantage of the unsuspecting buyer. We all know the world of duplicity and deceit evoked by the phrase "fine print." Piercy seems to be saying that in the present advanced stage of capitalism, where the market economy is becoming increasingly free of regulation and restraint, there is no longer any need for contracts with fine print. There is no opting out if your only alternative is to live in Smog City under a "yellow sky."

Marge Piercy   The truth according to Ludd   (p. 500)

The economic and environmental relationship of human beings to the machines they have created has been a common subject in our industrial/technological era among sociologists and historians. Karl Marx's *Das Capital* (1864) is one example. A more recent one is Edward Tenner's study, *Why Things Bite Back: Technology and the Revenge of Unintended Consequences* (1996). Our psychic relationship to machines is less commonly examined. Piercy's poem, alluding in its title to the early-nineteenth-century clash between men and machines that threatened workers' livelihoods, makes a serious point by exploiting the humor inherent in our often irrational relationship to machines. Who has not kicked or cursed a recalcitrant machine? Who has not felt that there was something sinister and conscious in the machine that was deliberately thwarting us? Murphy's famous law, "If anything can go wrong, it will," is an epigraph for the machine age, as is this, one of the hundreds inspired by Murphy's law: "It is a mistake to allow any mechanical object to realize that you are in a hurry."

"Who is to blame?" (l. 5), the poems asks. The Luddites, blaming machines for robbing them of their livelihoods, set out to destroy them. We engage in the same pathetic fallacy (pun intended) when we impute consciousness and purpose—moral awareness—to machines. We forget that morality applies only to humans. So vast is our egotism, the final stanza says, we fall in love with machines and then react like betrayed lovers when they fail us. In a nice irony, the poet—doing precisely what she has faulted us for—anthropomorphizes machines to make her point.

The Luddite movement is by no means dead. The Web site of the New Luddites, a group based at York University in Toronto, Canada, can be visited at <http://www.users.york.ac.uk/~socs203/luddites.htm>. The writer Kirkpatrick Sale is the author of *Rebels against the Future: The Luddites and Their War on the Industrial Revolution: Lessons for the Machine Age* (1995). His Web site, on which he has posted "Lessons from the Luddites," can be found at <http://www.io.com/~wazmo/luddite.html>

Robert Pinsky   An Old Man   (p. 503)

The celebrated opening stanza from Robert Browning's poem "Rabbi Ben Ezra" is the *locus classicus* for the optimistic view of growing old:

> Grow old along with me!
> The best is yet to be,
> The last of life, for which the first was made:
> Our times are in His hand
> Who saith "A whole I planned,
> Youth shows but half; trust God: see all nor be afraid!"

"Growing Old" (p. 1385), Matthew Arnold's response to Browning, takes an antithetical view of the aging process. While Pinsky's poem does not deal with the physical decay of old age, it is every bit as grim as Arnold's. As he sits alone, bent over his newspaper in a noisy café, an old man comes to the realization that he has no future to contemplate, only a past to regret. His life, he now sees, has been betrayed by caution, by timidity, by "brainless prudence" (l. 15)—in a word, by "Discretion" (l. 10). Looking back on a life devoid of impulsiveness and joy, he becomes dizzy with the realization of what he has lost. All that remains is sleep—and death.

Pinsky's use of triplets is effective. The first two lines of each stanza are rhymed couplets (many of them off-rhymes) and the third lines rhyme throughout, giving the poem something of the dirge quality of a requiem.

In addition to Arnold's poem, this poem can be effectively compared to Helen Sorrells's "From a Correct Address in a Suburb of a Major City" (p. 490) and Jenny Joseph's "Warning" (p. 495). It should also be compared to Ernest Hemingway's story "A Clean, Well-Lighted Place" (p. 107) for the striking resemblance between the portraits of an old man contemplating his life as he sits alone in a café. You might (perhaps in conjunction with the section "Looking Deeper: From Art to Literature," p. 1399) want to bring to class a reproduction of Edward Hopper's famous 1942 painting *Nighthawks*, which could at least in part have been the inspiration for Pinsky's poem.

Sylvia Plath   Daddy   (p. 1122)

In an unpublished typescript prepared for a radio broadcast that was never delivered, Sylvia Plath wrote of "Daddy": "Here is a poem spoken by a girl with an Electra complex. Her father died while she thought he was God. Her case is complicated by the fact that her father was also a Nazi and her mother very possibly part Jewish. In the daughter the two strains marry and paralyze each other—she has to act out the awful little allegory once over before she is free of it."

Although Plath is careful to speak of the voice in the poem as a third person, the poem certainly belongs to that contemporary confessional mode associated with such writers as Robert Lowell and Anne Sexton. The somewhat deranged voice in the poem seeks to exorcise the destructive power her dead father still holds over her life and seems to regress to a nursery-rhyme madness in her attempt to find the incantatory magic that will free her. In fact, Plath's father died when she was eight, and she, here, attributes a suicide attempt when she was twenty to her desire to be reunited with him.

In the second and third stanzas, she presents images of that overpowering father (always, however, speaking of him as "Daddy," assuming the little-girl posture) as a "bag full of God," and as a colossal statue with a toe in the Pacific ("Big as a Frisco seal") and its head in the freakish Atlantic. The German of the irritated summation—ah you!—signals the introduction of images of Nazism that grow increasingly ominous. She cannot recover his European sources—the Polish town (Grabow) from which he emigrated to the United States when he was fifteen. Indicatively, the speaker observes: "I never could talk to you. The tongue stuck in my jaw." That overpowering father-presence now becomes identified with the fear and consequences of Nazi totalitarianism, and her personal emotional disaster is described in images of the larger disaster—the Holocaust.

The lyrical images of Germany that begin stanza 8 call up memories of German romanticism and the concept of *der Volk*, concepts that were exploited in the propaganda of the Third Reich. But this Germany is rejected by the speaker, who prefers to identify with those despised minorities that attracted the venomous attention of the "Aryans." She perceives her father as one of those frightening Aryans—and if his ideas were "gobbledygoo," he was nonetheless dangerous and destructive. Identified now with the air force and the armored divisions of the Germans, he is no longer God but a sky-dimming swastika—a symbol of physically brutal fascism. The masochism reflected in lines 49 to 51 can no doubt be documented from the lives of at least some women.

In stanzas 11 and 12, the father becomes a devil—yet so attractive, even in death, that she attempts to join him through suicide and finally joins him through a surrogate—the husband—a torturer like the father. Now the two men, father and husband, are imaged as a vampire—one of the erotic undead. Her husband has drunk her blood for seven years, presumably as her father had before him. But she is released. And the Daddy-husband figure that imprisoned her emotional being in webs of fear, paradoxically both erotic and destructive, is ritually destroyed—lies truly dead at last, recognized by everyone (the villagers) as the force that, as father incarnate, can ravage the heart of a child and, as power incarnate, can ravage civilization itself.

Po Chu-i   Golden Bells *and* Remembering Golden Bells
(pp. 1081–82)

Po Chu-i was one of the most prolific ninth-century Chinese poets, and here we consider a pair of poems occasioned by the birth of a daughter when in his late thirties, and her death from illness three years later. Neither poem is likely to puzzle students. In the first, the speaker suggests that this daughter (not a boy, we are told in the second poem, but better than nothing) will be a great annoyance. Yet at the same time he reveals his more authentic feelings when he asserts that "My only reward,—the pleasure I am getting now" from watching her learn to walk and to speak. He frets that this unanticipated child will interfere with his life. He will (if she doesn't die young) have to get her married, and he will have to delay his plans for retirement. But the reader easily sees that, underneath, the speaker is wholly taken with his new baby—and his complaints are a sham. Alas, she does die young; the second poem clearly reveals both the understated love he feels for her and his grief at her death.

While the whimsical pseudo-complaints of the first poem cannot hide his affection, the bitter complaint of the second poem projects a more complex feeling. His beloved child's death teaches him that "the ties of flesh and blood / Only bind us to a load of grief and sorrow." And this complaint is not a sham. The fussing and trouble of the first poem, masking a deep affection for the baby, changes to a reflection on the inescapable and enduring grief at the beloved baby's death. The only way to deal with that grief is to push it away, to pretend she was never born, to immerse himself in other pursuits. And that therapy works, until an accidental meeting with the baby's former nurse jogs his memory. We can, perhaps, believe the speaker when he says, "for a little, the old grief came back." But we are likely to suspect that the old grief will never be laid to rest.

Deborah Pope   Getting Through   (p. 1130)

In a series of images, the speaker concretizes the futility of trying to communicate her feelings to an ex-lover. "Getting through" to such a person is like trying to drive a disabled car; to run, reflexively and aimlessly, like a beheaded chicken; to foolishly emulate a ringing phone in a deserted house. Her heart blunders on, but the words generated by her love are a derailed train—the words of a beautiful but dead language "no one else can hear." The images sustain this poem, and you might take the opportunity to discuss in general how images can intensify emotional response. Debate which images are most telling in the speaker's attempt to describe her desperation. Our own favorite is the endlessly ringing phone in the dust-skinned, deserted house. Except for *gone–on* (ll. 2–3), the poem doesn't use rhyme until the last four lines, in which the last word, *hear,* snaps the poem shut by almost rhyming with *years* (l. 21). Challenge students to confront the short free-verse lines. Do the lines display a self-contained integrity? Would it make a difference if the last word of each line became the first word of the next?

Wyatt Prunty   The Actuarial Wife   (p. 1134)

Make sure students know what an actuary is. The poem reflects on what seems to be a long and reasonably successful marriage, even if the wife is given to sardonic observations. The wife's first two witty and mildly acerbic comments suggest that the couple are at ease with each other, but the husband's smoking clearly irritates her. In the last stanza they discuss retirement options, and the ever-sensible, still sardonic wife makes it perfectly clear that her husband's smoking, as any competent actuary would predict, is likely to kill him. The poet provides a delicious image of the husband, living in the blue haze of tobacco smoke, settling into his favorite chair "like an accurate punt," lighting another cigarette, and crushing the butts "like punctuation marks / Down through an urgent argument." The wife makes her harsh actuarial comment, we may reasonably conclude, because she cares for her husband.

Wyatt Prunty   Learning the Bicycle   (p. 1133)

The speaker makes teaching his young daughter to ride her bicycle an emblem for a larger issue in the relationship between parents and children. At the end of this day, the daughter has not yet mastered her bicycle—but tomorrow she is likely to succeed and, with that mastery, create a significant distance (both literally and figuratively) between herself and her parent. The parent, sensitive to the obligation to keep his child safe, runs behind her with "arms out to catch her" but realizes that when her skills mature, he must "let her go."

Sir Walter Raleigh   The Nymph's Reply to the Shepherd
(p. 1087)

See the entry for Christopher Marlowe, "The Passionate Shepherd to His Love."

Dudley Randall   Ballad of Birmingham   (p. 491)

This poem commemorates the murder of four young African American girls when a bomb was thrown into the 16th Street Baptist Church in 1963, one of the early and most traumatic events in the modern civil rights struggle. The irony of the poem is the clear implication that if the mother had allowed her daughter to join the demonstration instead of going to church, she would not have died. (A historical irony is that six years later, when this poem was written, no one had yet been charged with the crime.) The poem is powerful, not least because Randall chose the ancient ballad form. Comparing this poem with the traditional, anonymous ballads "Bonny Barbara Allan" and "Edward" (pp. 1083 and 1376) will show students how closely Randall has followed this old form of folk origin. In alternating four- and three-stress lines, he narrates swiftly and without comment the tragic culmination of a complex event.

A further historical note: Within days of the bombing, four suspects, all Ku Klux Klan members, were identified by FBI agents. In November 1977, fourteen years after the bombing, one of the suspects, Robert E. Chambliss, was convicted of first-degree murder for the bombing and sentenced to life imprisonment. On February 18, 1980, a front-page story in the *New York Times,* datelined Birmingham, explained the long delay:

> J. Edgar Hoover [Director of the FBI] blocked prosecution of four Ku Klux Klansmen identified by agents of the Federal Bureau of Investigation as the bombers who killed four black children at the 16th Street Baptist Church here, in 1963, according to a Justice Department report.

Two of the suspects, Thomas E. Blanton and Frank Cherry, were finally indicted in 1997 (the fourth suspect, Herman Frank Cash, died in 1994). The case against Cherry was dismissed after a judge found him mentally incompetent. Blanton was convicted of four counts of first-degree murder and sentenced to life in prison.

Henry Reed   Naming of Parts   (p. 798)

In this poem an instructor is giving recruits a lesson on how to handle a rifle. It is the instructor we hear in the first lines of each of the stanzas (except the last)—his voice, appropriately, matter-of-fact and businesslike, the diction plain, the rhythm colloquial. The final lines of each stanza are the thoughts of one of the recruits, expressed in mellifluous lines of richly evocative imagery. As the instructor lists the various parts of the rifle and explains how they function, the recruit lets his mind wander over the beauties of life and nature. In dialogue fashion, the recruit's thoughts ironically counterpoint the instructor's lesson. The inert, cold, mechanical parts of the instrument of death are juxtaposed with the glistening flowers and the eloquent gestures of tree branches. The instructor's description of the sliding action of the rifle bolt that releases the tension of the spring evokes for the recruit the procreative urge of the spring season that causes bees to pollinate flowers. The double entendres throughout juxtapose a life-affirming sexuality with the lecture on an instrument of death.

Adrienne Rich   Living in Sin   (p. 1122)

This poem depends upon the ironic disparity between reality and the sentimental preconceptions governing love affairs. The studio apartment kept for assignations is, in imagination, characterized by "A plate of pears, / a piano with a Persian shawl, a cat / stalking the picturesque amusing mouse." In reality there is dust upon the furniture of love, grimy windows, depressing leftovers, a pair of beetle-eyes. The piano is out of tune; the woman's lover, stubble-faced, is out for cigarettes. The coffee boils over on the stove. But the day that so coldly jeers the romance of the night before passes. By evening she is in love again—but not so mindlessly that she doesn't already anticipate the dreadful following day that brings the relentless milkman who makes each stair writhe at 5 A.M.

One might, for fun, wonder whether the context makes the *p* alliteration of lines 4–6 amusing.

Edwin Arlington Robinson Miniver Cheevy (p. 481)

Satire derives not from subject matter or plot but from tone and style, as this poem illustrates. The second line, for example, alerts the reader to the tone, for who but a foolish person would assail the seasons? In Miniver's mind, the celebrated Medici represent nothing more than sensual pleasure, and he is so enamored of a romanticized antiquity that he sees the cumbersome armor of medieval knights as graceful. This pathetic infatuation with the past is, finally and devastatingly, exposed as the attempt of an ineffectual man to escape from a painful present through a bottle.

Edwin Arlington Robinson Richard Cory (p. 1390)

This poem provides the opportunity for a discussion of the uses of connotation. Note that the name itself and such words as "gentleman," "crown," "imperially," "arrayed," "glittered," "rich," "king," and "grace" all evoke the world of aristocracy. The envious speaker looks up to Cory as a commoner to an aristocrat. The shocking conclusion may be the occasion for a discussion of the suggested versus the particular. Would the poem be improved if we knew why Richard Cory killed himself? We can understand suicidal despair, but we are almost certain to quarrel over whether this or that is a reasonable cause of it.

Theodore Roethke Elegy for Jane (p. 1407)

This poem presents a series of images that contrast the intense life of Jane and her death. The poet, it would seem, speaks from beside her grave. He remembers her in terms of "tendril" neckcurls and "pickerel" (a narrow fish with a long mouth) smiles, as a "wren," "sparrow," and "skittery pigeon." A sense of her physical presence is brought out by "startled," "leaped," "balanced," "trembling," "kissing." The speaker, "neither father nor lover," has none of the ordinary rights to the exhibition of grief at her death, but as her teacher, he reveals an affection for her that was doubtless muted in life by their relationship.

Theodore Roethke I Knew a Woman (p. 1114)

This poem offers a good opportunity to discuss tone and figures of speech (as well as some difficult images). The speaker presents himself as the traditional lover overwhelmed by the beauty of his beloved. But there is a good deal of bawdy humor in his characterization of himself and his love for her. His subservience is embodied in images both traditional ("I nibbled meekly from her proffered hand") and unusual ("She was the sickle; I, poor I, the rake"). She, in the tradition of love lyrics, possesses beauty and virtues about which "only gods should speak," though the speaker goes on for three more stanzas speaking of them, often with a comic leer. As rake (roué?) and sickle, they make "prodigious mowing" (that is, make love). And following behind her, he is able to enjoy a "gander" and cop a "goose."

The description of the lady is dominated by images of nudity and motion ("undulant white skin," "flowing knees," "one hip quiver with a mobile nose," "She moved in circles, and those circles moved"), ardently admired by the speaker. His motion is dependent on hers, for she, as his master trainer, teaches him "Turn, and Counter-turn, and Stand; / She taught me Touch." Although the first part of this image is often glossed as an allusion to the parts of the traditional ode, as in Greek drama, where the chorus moves left, moves right, and then stands still (i.e., strope, antistro-phe, and epode), it seems to us to suggest dressage movements—certainly a more immediately appropriate image in the context of this poem, especially in light of the next line: "I nibbled meekly from her proffered hand." The image of the woman as the rider in perfect and absolute control of the speaker, as horse, works in ways that an allusion to the ode does not. He does, after all, declare himself a "martyr to a motion not my own."

In the final stanza, the speaker jauntily rejects the arguments of those who would decry his subservience and martyrdom to the lady on the grounds of some lofty notion that freedom should be used to know eternity. He boldly declaims that he will use his freedom not to "count eternity in days" (an impossible task) but to "measure time by how a body sways," that is, to continue to enjoy the physical delights of his lady.

Theodore Roethke My Papa's Waltz (p. 1113)

There is some disagreement about the tone of this poem. Most critics interpret it as an affectionate and comic tribute to the poet's father. It would be hard to argue that this scene of a drunken father boisterously dancing his young son around the kitchen does not have comic overtones. A waltz, after all, is a triple-time or three-beat dance, bouncy and happy (*waltz* also connotes ease and effortlessness, as in waltzing through a chore). The poem's three-beat iambic trimeter is, of course, the waltz beat. Other details support such a reading: the happy connotations of a word like "romped" (l. 5), the pans falling off the shelf (ll. 5–6), the disapproving mother (ll. 7–8), and the father's beating out time on his son's head (l. 13).

Others point out that there is little that is comic about a young boy, made dizzy by his father's breath and hanging on "like death" (l. 3), being violently waltzed around by a drunken father. Far from being comic, the boy is more than distressed; he is suffering pain as his ear scrapes against his father's buckle and his father beats time on his head (the father's hand is "caked hard by dirt").

These two readings need not be mutually exclusive. Roethke gives us a speaker who looks back upon a childhood event with the understanding of a mature adult while at the same time conveying the child's feelings. Roethke's speaker can see, from an adult perspective, the comic dimension of the event and still remember that to the child (as to most children), a drunken parent, even a loving one, is scary and disturbing.

It's worth noting that the only description of the father (besides his boozy breath) is the reference to his hands, once in the third stanza and again in the fourth. These descriptions skillfully convey what the child sees (his father's battered knuckle) and feels (the beating on his head), as he dizzily clings to his waltzing father. The descriptions of the hands also seem designed to characterize the father, for these battered, dirt-caked hands clearly belong to an earthy man who works as hard as he drinks.

Muriel Rukeyser Myth (p. 491)

Perhaps this poem alludes not only to the myth of Oedipus but also to the myth that sexist language is not unfair to women. Students may wonder what makes this a poem rather than a prose paragraph with a jagged right margin. Though the language is plain, the lines as verse units do contribute to the force of the piece. It might be interesting to discuss the difference in effect if the piece had been written as a solid paragraph with right margin justified.

In any case, the notion that Oedipus's troubles resulted not from a fate decreed by the gods but rather from his own insensitivity to the dignity of women is the sort of outrageous revisionism sure to delight even the men in the class.

Abbas Saffari Our Story (p. 1288)

To begin discussion of a literary work from the topic of genre can sometimes be to risk boredom, but in the case of Saffari's "Our Story" and parody in general, it is not so risky, and potentially quite useful. Students may have a hard time grasping just what kind of stance the poem is taking toward its subject—toward the biblical story to which it alludes and to the beliefs and values often found in or taken from that story. As instructors who have taught satirical works such as Swift's "Modest Proposal" have found, providing students with a generic way to think about parody and satire helps them figure out writers' use of irony as well as recognize that their confusion is not the result of ignorance so much as the intentional effect of the works.

Once students see that Saffari's parody is critiquing the ways the story of Adam and Eve has been told and interpreted, they can focus on the content of that critique and the variety of ways in which Saffari makes it. What might seem at first a maddening inconsistency of tone and frame and reference—a jumble of anachronism and geographical confusion—is seen instead as an intentional raising of the question of how we interpret ancient stories according to our time and place as well as a purposeful bringing down to earth of a story whose authority is often felt to be too great to brook any kind of critical reading. And once the poem is approached in this way, it is easier for students to see the way the poem questions the values that have been drawn from or imposed upon the story of Adam and Eve—concerning innocence and experience, the body, sexuality, the sacred and the profane, heaven and earth—and also to see the humor with which it does so.

Sappho   With His Venom   (p. 1081)

The unusual images associated with love provide the fun. Love is a poisonous snake. Its venom is "bittersweet" but irresistible (like good chocolate—even if that confection was unknown to Sappho). An interesting question is whether love here is a good thing or bad, this debilitating poison that loosens limbs. Take the occasion to ask students to suggest other unusual images to associate with love. The common red rose, you might point out, also has thorns.

Anne Sexton   Cinderella   (p. 800)

This poem, based on one of the more vigorous of the eight-hundred-plus versions of the Cinderella story, raises questions about the difference between the literary representations of reality (including newspaper accounts) and the experience of the people who read those versions with such avidity. We are raised on a body of children's literature consisting of cautionary tales that culminate in poetic justice. And we seem never to outgrow expectations that justice will triumph and folks will, indeed, live happily ever after. Perhaps one of the most ubiquitous tragedies of modern life is the painful perception that we do not participate in the heady triumphs of our literary or pop-cult heroes and heroines, nor does justice often triumph.

The catalog of human-interest stories from the press—punctuated with the sardonic tolling of the commentary "that story"—all represent mundane versions of the Cinderella story, the unlikely raises from poverty and dependence to wealth and independence. We read those stories with a kind of pleasurable envy. *If only I were that lucky, or skillful.* Sexton gives us the Cinderella story as the prototype of such tales. And we watch the development of the familiar plot with pleasure as the poet spices the retelling with modernisms. The kicker comes in the last stanza—a coda not only to the Cinderella story but to all the fairy-tale luck stories that supermarket newspapers love. She marries the prince. But what then?

These celebrated happy endings do not address what happens next in a complex world. They have no interest in the complexity of relationships, growing old, arguing. Consequently, such stories do leave us with grotesque Bobbsey Twins, "darling smiles pasted on for eternity." And Sexton's final judgment of Cinderella and her prince comments tellingly on those other stories that open the poem.

Students might notice the prosaic quality of this poem, a characteristic it shares with such poems as Mezey's "My Mother," Forché's "The Colonel," and Rukeyser's "Myth." You might ask them to try to change the line lengths—either in some arbitrary fashion or to try to match sentence length—and compare the revision with the original. With a little luck, this exercise will teach something about the line as a verse unit.

Have the students examine the poem for images, particularly those occasions when literary images are juxtaposed with slangy modernity: "all the warm wings of the fatherland came, / and picked up the lentils in a jiffy," or "The bird dropped down a golden dress / and delicate little gold slippers. / Rather a large package for a simple bird." Note that the deliberately antipoetic effects reinforce the poet's clear-eyed critique of sentimentality.

Finally, the sardonic refrain "that story" is made to carry an increasingly portentous weight. As the last words in the poem, the refrain creates an exasperation that a prose writer could not match with less than a paragraph.

Anne Sexton   The Starry Night   (p. 1403)

The Dutch painter Vincent van Gogh (1853–1890), usually grouped with Seurat, Cezanne, and Gauguin as a post-impressionist, began his career with starkly realistic paintings of life and landscape in his native Holland but was, by the end of his very short life, producing canvases pulsing with the vibrancy and violence of his own emotional state. One of the acknowledged masterpieces among these final paintings is *The Starry Night*, probably the artist's most widely known work. Sexton, who like van Gogh committed suicide responds first to the powerful contrast between the sleeping vilage in the lower right-hand corner and the extraordinary power of the night looming above, alive with color and movement, occupying roughly the upper two-thirds of the canvas. Compared to the starry night, the town indeed "does not exist" (l. 1). Or, as she continues, the only part of the town that exists at this moment is the cypress tree, which rises tall and tapering into the hot sky that boils with the energy of creation. The entire scene overwhelms Sexton as a powerful image of death. But the statement "This is how / I want to die" is puzzling, since the first four lines seem to describe the painting rather than a way of dying.

The second stanza, ending with the same line, is puzzling for the same reason. The speaker continues to describe the painting, its powerful illusion of movement: the serpent-like rushing energy that moves from left to right, circling back upon itself at the center of the painting and then rushing on; the pulsing moon in the upper left corner that seems to create a counter energy. Perhaps van Gogh's starry night symbolizes the primal forces of creation and destruction, life and death. "The old unseen serpent" may swallow up the stars, but it cannot extinguish all of them.

The final stanza clarifies the meaning of the refrain of the first two stanzas. Dominated by the verbs "sucked up" and "to split," the speaker passionately declares her wish to die by becoming part of the drama played out in van Gogh's starry night, departing life without fanfare, without pain, and without regret.

William Shakespeare   Fear No More the Heat o' the Sun
(p. 1379)

This dirge is sung over the supposedly dead Imogen by the sons of Cymbeline. Death releases one from a catalog of worldly cares—bad weather, labor, political oppression, need of food or shelter, lightning, slander, censure. Further, all, finally, will join in death: golden lads and girls, scholars, kings, physicians, lovers. The last stanza, in changed meter, prays for the protection of the dead body and its soul. This song may be compared with Nashe's "A Litany in Time of Plague" and contrasted with modern treatments of the theme in such works as Yevtushenko's "People."

William Shakespeare   *from* Hamlet, Macbeth, *and* Richard II
(pp. 1380–81)

The speech from *Richard II* is spoken by King Richard, whose crown is in danger from the revolt led by Bolingbroke (later Henry IV). His perilous situation suggests to Richard the leveling aspect of death, and he bitterly muses about the self-delusion of the powerful who are no stronger than the weakest subject before the power of death. Much concerned with his own kingship, he personifies Death as a king that keeps his court within the very crown that mortal kings wear. And Death is depicted as an amused and sardonic figure (an antic), scoffing and grinning at the self-important exercise of royal power by the mortal king as if he were immortal. In the last two lines of the excerpt, the mortal king is metaphorized as a castle—presumably imposing and stone-strong—and Death's weapon is a "little pin." But in the hands of Death, the little pin bores through the castle wall, in a remarkable verbal display embodying both overstatement and understatement simultaneously.

Hamlet finds himself in a situation quite different from Richard's. He is distressed at the death of his father, the incest of his mother, and the guilt of his uncle. It is he who must prove the guilt and avenge his father by punishing his uncle, the king. Here, in the middle of the play, he has yet to act, and he wonders in this famous soliloquy why people bear the anguish of life, the "whips and scorns of time," when they could escape that pain through suicide. But, for Hamlet, as for his Christian audience, death is not oblivion but a translation into another state. It carries one to "The undiscovered country, from whose bourn / No traveller returns," and the mystery, the fear of what one would find there, is sufficient to prevent suicide. The principal metaphors here are sleep for death and dreams for afterlife. Those "dreams" are the "rub" (literally a bump on a bowling green). The catalog of whips and scorns reveals that the sources of anguish have not changed in four hundred years, and the conclusion of the passage explains much modern behavior as well as it does Hamlet's. We do not know what color is "the native hue of resolution" (the color of commitment and action), but the color of "thought" (indecision, fear of consequences) is "pale" and makes sickly whatever it covers.

Macbeth is in much the same situation as Richard, except that he is old while Richard was young. Richard's cynicism projects forward; he sees a lifetime of delusion, made foolish by the inevitability of death. Macbeth measures his career and concludes that "all our yesterdays have lighted fools / The way to dusty death." Macbeth speaks these lines toward the end of the play upon hearing that his wife is dead, just as he is preparing to meet the challenge of a strong invading army. Ambition has driven him to betrayal and murder and won him the throne, and yet here he judges himself a fool, along with all men who act strongly to achieve status in life. The brief speech provides a curious mixture of images. It begins with time and history figures—tomorrow personified and the syllables of recorded time—but then moves to images based on light and darkness. Yesterdays, carrying torches or candles, lead fools to dusty death. Then the imperative, "Out, out, brief candle!" which refers both to the illumination provided by yesterday and to life itself. Life is nothing but shadows, and shadows are like play actors—those sham people who perform for an hour and then disappear. The train of thought ends with one of the bitterest judgments in literature. Not only is life foolish and transient; it is a tale told by an idiot—a disordered, senseless, and altogether insignificant sequence. Left balefully in the air are the human anguish and nausea generated by the absurdity of existence and the very meaninglessness of the word *significant*.

William Shakespeare   It Was a Lover and His Lass   (p. 1089)

See "Looking Deeper: From Poetry to Song" on p. 1085 of the anthology.

William Shakespeare   Sonnets 18, 29, 73, 129, and 130
(pp. 1095–96 and 1378)

These poems provide the opportunity to discuss the English sonnet form as well as some of the most recurrent Petrarchan themes among the Elizabethan sonneteers, notably immortalizing through verse and celebrating beauty. Shakespeare's syntax often forces words into unusual functions. The word "fair" is usually an adjective, but in sonnet 18, the first "fair" in line 7 is made to signify "fair summer's day," a substantive, while the second "fair" remains an adjective. In line 10 "fair" is again a substantive, standing for "beauty." While sonnet 18 exhibits a bit of pride—the sweetheart is to be immortalized by the poet's creation—sonnet 29 presents a poet whose emotional life depends on his beloved. Note that in both 18 and 29 the construction is essentially octave-quatrain-couplet—that is, the first eight lines represent a fairly continuous development which turns at line 9 to make the point and then concludes with a summarizing couplet.

Sonnet 73, dealing with the relationship between aging and love, moves, in its three quatrains, from a season of the year to a part of one day to a moment of recognition. The complex and bold figurative language pictures the aging speaker as a winter ravaged tree, the twilight moving into night, and a feeble fire choking on the ashes of its own expended fuel.

Sonnet 129 is quite different from the others. Here Shakespeare is dealing with the darker aspect of his own humanity. The poem has a 4-4-4-2 construction; each quatrain explores a different facet of lust, and the final couplet carries the truth derived from these explorations. Students often have trouble with the beginning of the poem. Lust in action spends (dissipates) the spirit (the better nature, the vitality) of man in a desert waste of shame. Possibly the word "waste" includes a pun on "waist." This sonnet makes notable use of variations in the meter to reinforce the sense. For example, line 4 exhibits three stressed syllables in succession—with only a very weak second syllable in "cruel" preventing it from being four—and the stresses fall almost like blows, echoing the violent temper of the lines.

The famous anti-Petrarchan sonnet 130 establishes, by implication, how widespread was the Petrarchan love sonnet, praising the matchless beauty and virtue of the poet's beloved. Shakespeare is confident that his readers have read numbers of those sonnets, and he turns their clichés to his own uses. The last line is a bit troublesome; the words "she" and "compare" are both nouns—I think my loved one is as rare as any woman ("she") misrepresented ("belied") through false comparisons ("false compare").

Percy Bysshe Shelley Ozymandias (p. 1382)

This sonnet makes an ironic comment on the pride of Ozymandias (the Greek name for Ramses II) but, as well, suggests the futility of all pride based on great works. Line 8 presents a problem: the passions of Ozymandias were well read by the sculptor who mocked them (imitated them on the face of the statue and derided them as well). Explicit in the ruined visage of the statue, the passions survive the sculptor who created the statue and the pharaoh's heart that produced them.

Charles Simic My Weariness of Epic Proportions (p. 501)

Aside from the footnoted identification of Homeric heroes, this quietly straightforward poem will be available to students. But those glory-mongering privileged Homeric heroes, together with the mischief wrought by those squabbling feuding gods, stand as a paradigm for the whole history of warfare from ancient Egypt to the present. The speaker confesses a preference for the death of military heroes and the silence of those (whether gods, tyrants, or congressmen) who sent them. And for his emblematic peace—birdsong, and a child walking to the well through the olive grove.

Before peace sets in, have some fun with the Trojan War, with Achilles sulking, with the story of his vulnerable heel. And ask the students to consider the word *winds* that describes the little path in the olive orchard. Would a different word— *runs* or *cuts* or *passes*—subtly change the feeling conveyed by the line?

Stevie Smith Not Waving but Drowning (p. 168)

Stevie Smith wrote this poem, she said, when she felt "too low for words," adding that many people "do not feel at home in the world" so they "joke a lot and laugh and people think they are quite alright [sic] and jolly nice too, but sometimes the brave pretense breaks down and then, like the poor man in this poem, they are lost" (quoted in Jack Barbera and William McBrien, *Stevie: A Biography of Stevie Smith,* 1985). The idea is familiar enough. Almost daily, the newspapers carry stories about someone who is dramatically discovered to be profoundly different from what he or she seemed: the hardworking, law-abiding neighbor who turns murderous; the loving parent and spouse who is living a second life with a second family; the well-adjusted, happy fellow worker who commits suicide. Often, in hindsight, friends and family remember things that now suggest something was amiss—signals, perhaps like "larking" around, that concealed the buried reality. We forget that the jester's buffoonery may conceal a sense of tragedy. We are astounded when a man of Richard Cory's advantages kills himself.

There are two voices in the poem. The speaker, who describes the scene in the first two lines, articulates the friends' feelings in the second stanza, and utters the parenthetical comment (a repetition of line 2) in the final stanza. The dead man speaks in lines 3, 4, 9, 11, and 12. It might be argued, however, that the words of the dead man are in fact the speaker's words, put into the mouth of the dead man for dramatic effect.

Finally, students might be asked to consider whether or not the poem loses or gains because it provides so little information about the dead man—who he was and why (and how) he died. Do "further out" (l. 3) and "too far out" (l. 11) constitute ineffective vagueness or satisfying suggestiveness?

Stevie Smith To Carry the Child (p. 167)

The first stanza asks and immediately answers a question. The answer, as the rest of the poem makes clear, is ironic. It is not good to carry the child into adult life—that is, preserve within ourselves the qualities of childhood—because those qualities are inimical to those the world demands of adults. The third and fourth stanzas define those contrasting qualities, best summarized perhaps in the contrast between mind and feeling in lines 15 and 16. If we allow the child in ourselves to survive, we become "defenseless" against the hard reality of adulthood and, therefore, come to despise the child within us. But, as the sixth stanza asserts, "if a child survive," it can "strangle the man alive." And so, as the heavily ironic seventh stanza declares, it is better for the child to die a child than to survive into adulthood and strangle the adult (with the additional suggestion that it is adults, not children, who spill one another's blood). In the powerful image of the final stanza, the child who lives in an adult "carapace," like an imprisoned anarchist, can only peer out with helpless rage.

Cathy Song Stamp Collecting (p. 812)

Some countries actually do depend on the export of unusual stamps to bolster their economies. And, at a critical moment in Wole Soyinka's The Lion and the Jewel, the village chief, in his attempt to seduce our heroine, promises to put her picture on a postage stamp! Here, the poet reflects on the relationship between the substance of countries and the stamps they issue. Sometimes, as in Tonga, the stamps show not the hanging bats that serve as a major tourist attraction, but fruits impressionistically pictured to resemble something else. Other countries, "without a thing to sell," design stamps showing their economic and social progress—doctors with stethoscopes, the new school building. And "the country that is bleak and stark" with no sense of beauty, with no sense of humor, place only "serious statements" on their stamps "commemorating / factories, tramways, and aeroplanes." Bring this poem to startling life by collecting a few stamps that illustrate the poet's assertions. And ask students to imagine the everyday life of a country (that is, its people) by looking at one of its postage stamps. There is no reason not to start with the United States. You might note that the most common U.S. stamp is the flag. But the U.S. Post Office systematically prints commemorative issues to sell to collectors. Have the class ruminate on the backroom political and cultural discussions that determine what will decorate those issues.

Helen Sorrells From a Correct Address in a Suburb of a Major City (p. 490)

This direct poem presents us with a portrait of the affluent, middle-aged matron who carries out her socially assigned role with grace and skill. But it is just a role, for inwardly she rages against a life that encases and constricts her like a hooded gown. The rage grows with the years that bring her closer to death and the clamoring realization that she may die without having tested her potentialities and talents. It is worth noting that her rage to escape is not fueled by some foolishly romantic dream of happiness but rather by the need to release "the soaring cry" within her. Outside the antiseptic suburb is a world of joy and pain and possibility that she will never experience from her correct address.

Gary Soto   Oranges   (p. 1138)

Surely students will recognize the event this poem celebrates, and recall from their own experience similar moments. We can look back smiling, but will, perhaps, remember the excruciating pains and pleasures of the first time we "walked out" with a potential girlfriend or boyfriend. The speaker here was fortunate—the lady store clerk knew "Very well what it was all / About"—but imagine the boy's feeling had the clerk not been so understanding. Doubtless the class could produce an album filled with moving reminiscences of those early and tortured first steps.

This poem resides among the prosy sort—the line lengths vary, there is no rhyme scheme, and no clear metrical pattern. Ask students what, then, distinguishes this piece from prose. Students will probably note the insistent images that render a banal December day in a nondescript neighborhood into a paean to child love, a defense of self-esteem, and that transform a humble orange into "a fire in my hands."

Wole Soyinka   Telephone Conversation   (p. 809)

The striking and frustrating thing about racism is its utter impersonality, its reduction of human beings to nothing more than their skin color. Soyinka's poem underscores the impersonality by describing a telephone conversation rather than a face-to-face encounter. The poem opens matter-of-factly, with the speaker in midconversation. The caller is satisfied that the room he is seeking to rent meets his criteria. He strikes the first note of irony when he makes the "self-confession" (l. 4). It is an interesting phrase in the context of the poem because what he has to confess is not something *about* himself but rather his very self—his African origin, his color. Before the lady breaks her shocked silence, the speaker resorts again to irony when he says, "Caught I was, foully" (l. 9), a line that befits a villain in a melodrama. But this is not melodrama; this is real life. The speaker, stunned by the lady's question about his degree of blackness, momentarily considers hanging up. As the polite interrogation continues, he turns the tables ever so gently by playing his assigned part in this surreal drama. Unable to convey to her in words the *exact* shade of his blackness, exasperated with the demeaning questions, he gives her a vivid physical description of his body colors, ending with his "raven black" bottom (l. 32). Clearly, this genteel, racist lady who finds it perfectly appropriate to interrogate the speaker about his color is shocked by the caller's crude reference to his "bottom" and abruptly hangs up.

The poem could very well be based on Soyinka's own experience. Soyinka published the poem in the year he returned from England to Nigeria, an accomplished and celebrated writer, eight years away from winning the Nobel Prize for literature.

For a poem that deals with a similar but much blunter version of the experience Soyinka describes, from the perspective of a child rather than a sophisticated adult, see Countee Cullen's poem "Incident" (p. 169).

David St. John   My Friend   (p. 1134)

There is a bit of the professorial in this poem that might pose problems for some students. Freshmen are not likely to connect emotionally with Mahler's music, Eliot's "Four Quartets," or the lyric poems of Rainer Maria Rilke. The allusions are designed to establish the nature of the speaker and his artist friend, who share a high culture and a profound intimacy that makes each transparent to the other. Meeting after seven years spent apart, the friend's first act is to play Mahler and comment, passionately, on the connection between the music and Eliot's poems. The detail illuminates the world these two live in and the insight they have into each other's emotional life.

Next they speak on the phone, catching up, and we learn more about the friend's romantic nature and his mourning over a broken engagement to a stunning but clearly unsuitable woman. The first thirty-seven lines of the poem introduce the friend and his easy relationship with the speaker. The remainder of the poem describes another kind of relationship — the astonishing liaison between the friend and the bisexual artist couple that "preferred him as a garnish." The scenes he describes on the phone — communal bathing, having his naked body painted by the women, being invited to share in a ménage a trois with the women on a trip to visit "the Holy Places of Art," "the constellations of coupling" — all seem like the fantasies of a hormone-addled postpubescent male. And, despite the obvious pleasure the friend takes in his situation, he wistfully confesses that he is "not quite so young / As he'd once been." As their conversation winds down, the friend, enthralled by his astonishing situation, blurts his final comment, bewildered by the sexual extravaganza he shares. What, in the world, has changed? How were things before? Was that a better world? Is the friend's comment a lament for a lost stabilizing moral vision, or a joyful shout of welcome for a newer, freer order?

Invite the students to comment on the formal structure of the poem. What (if anything) is gained by staggering the lines? Is there a dominant meter? If you don't look closely, the poem seems a kind of Shakespearean blank verse. But the poet has thwarted any easy regularity. The line lengths vary, and the tendency toward iambics is frequently broken mid-line. Have students look for some long logic that gives the lines shape, makes each a small independent construction.

Wallace Stevens Sunday Morning (p. 483)

The juxtaposition of the "Complacencies of the peignoir" in the opening line with the "Dominion of the blood and sepulchre" in the concluding line of stanza 1 states the theme of the poem. The richly sensuous surroundings of the lady on the Christian sabbath dissipate only momentarily her troubled vision of life on earth as merely a "procession of the dead." This vision naturally turns her thoughts to Palestine, to Christ and his crucifixion that assured eternal life after death for humankind.

Stanza 2 opens with the first of the many questions the speaker will ask and answer as he carries on a kind of dialogue with the lady. Why must the lady allow her pleasure in the concrete and sensuous beauty of this world to be destroyed by thoughts of a shadowy divinity? That beauty (evoked with images from stanza 1) is surely as worthy as "the thought of heaven." The speaker then provides his answer to the lady's dilemma: "Divinity must live within herself" (the line ends with a colon, indicating that the nouns that follow are in apposition to "Divinity"). Divinity is to be found in one's capacity to enjoy the sensuous splendor of the world, an enjoyment inseparable from the realization that everything, ourselves included, inexorably dies. "The bough of summer and the winter branch" evoke the endless cycle of life and death on earth.

Stanza 3 is wholly given over to the speaker's reflections on our human impulse to find divinity outside ourselves. The pagan Jove, inhuman in his birth and regally remote from humankind, gave way to the more human Jesus Christ. Now, asks the speaker, shall we fail to take the final step that will complete this process and accept the earth as all of paradise we shall ever know? If we do, the sky will represent not a "dividing and indifferent blue" separating earth from heaven but rather a part of paradise.

To the lady's declaration in stanza 4 that the beauty of the world is transitory, the speaker responds that no visionary heaven created by humans has endured "As April's green endures." Beauty and eternity exist in the never-ending cycle of birth, death, and rebirth. And while the lady (we may assume) agrees with the speaker, she nevertheless yearns for deathless, unchanging immortality, as she says in the opening lines of stanza 5. The speaker's answer states his attitude most succinctly and powerfully: "Death is the mother of beauty." Like Keats in his "Ode on a Grecian Urn," the speaker declares that it is mortality that creates joy and beauty and love.

This central idea is driven home in stanza 6 with a series of rhetorical questions about the kind of conventional paradise the lady yearns for. In such a deathless paradise there can be no beauty in ripe fruit or perfect skies, in rivers seeking for seas (they are "rivers like our own," suggesting the questing spirit of mortals), precisely because they are unchanging and untouched by the sadness that mortality gives to earthly existence.

And so, in stanza 7, the poet envisions a race of humans who, knowing that "Death is the mother of beauty," worship not some visionary deity who presides over a visionary paradise but the life-giving sun, exulting in a "heavenly fellowship / Of men that perish." The symbol of their paradise will be the perishable "dew upon their feet."

The concluding stanza appropriately returns to the lady, her musings abruptly interrupted by a voice crying that the grave of Jesus holds only the remains of a mortal man. His arguments accepted by the lady, the speaker now movingly summarizes his message. The earth and other planets are a fragment of the sun ("We live in an old chaos of the sun"), its fertility and beauty drawn from its rotations around the sun (the "old dependency of day and night") in the ocean of space (the "island solitude"), free of a supernatural deity ("unsponsored, free"), existing in inescapable time and space ("that wide water, inescapable"). This is the destiny of humans, who, like the pigeons of the final lines, exist in and are part of the world's beauty, a beauty "mothered" by the sinking "Downward to darkness."

Ruth Stone   Metaphors of the Tree   (p. 171)

There are many ways to look at a tree, to see it as a metaphor for one or another aspect of the relationship between nature and the human condition. The first tree provides an automobile tire swing—a positive artifact designed to encourage playfulness. But, ominously, the poet suggests that the tire hangs like a lynched person—the same tree that invites playful children can serve as an instrument of unjustified execution.

The second tree, like the first, is the "only tree in the yard." But that quality results from "a clump of trees . . . twisting up; a corporate tree." The image creates a threatening emotional context: trees cannot multiply freely, cannot become a forest. Rather, they twist together; they become the "tree with its thousand subsidiaries." They become the metaphor for a giant tyrannical corporation—not merely General Electric or General Motors, but General Everything. That conglomerate tree dominates the air above and the ground beneath. Some key words reveal the poet's attitude toward this metaphor of the tree: "growing chemicals," "pulling the guts," "involved with fungus." Chemicals, guts, fungus—hardly inviting or joy-inducing nouns.

Next the tree becomes an unabashedly positive source of life-giving air. This tree can "capture bullets of light," and use those dangerous projectiles as a tool for converting pollutant gases into indispensable oxygen.

But, finally, with what surely is a pessimistic comment on the power of the corporate tree—inexorable degradation fueled by insatiable greed—the tree disappears altogether. The "play yard is paved with asphalt," another distressing impingement on the natural world. Here, the absent tree becomes a "space," a void, unnoticed by birds, unmoved by the wind.

Sir John Suckling   Song   (p. 1092)

See "Looking Deeper: From Poetry to Song" on p. 1085 of the anthology.

Wislawa Szymborska   First Love   (p. 1117)

Somewhat like Victoria Chang's "Morning Ritual," this poem plays off the clichéd sentimentality that governs certain popular conceptions. In Chang's case, response to a dying grandmother; in Szymborska's case, the notion of the importance of first love. The speaker here rejects the views that "first love's most important," and that it remains a sentimental memory. Her hands do not tremble over "silly" keepsakes. At the only subsequent meeting with her first lover, two chairs conversed at a chilly table—the formerly warm and, presumably, passionate lovers are not emotionally present; the conversation is wooden, like the conversation between pieces of furniture. The tone is chilly.

Nonetheless, there is one thing special about that "unremembered" first love. By marking the magical transition from innocence to experience, it signifies the end of a childhood characterized, perhaps, by a sense of immortality, and the beginning of responsible adulthood chastened by its awareness of mortality. Thus, paradoxically, one's first sexual experience is not so much the source of giddy memories as the impetus that requires one to confront the inevitability of death.

It would be interesting to discover the feelings of our eighteen-year-old students in the matter; it would be particularly interesting to discover whether males and females respond differently to their own experiences and to the poem.

Alfred, Lord Tennyson   Ulysses   (p. 475)

Students' reactions are likely to divide rather sharply on this poem. Some will see Ulysses as a grand and noble man who recalls the heroic events of his past life in order to justify his refusal to submit quietly to old age and death. Ulysses finds the very meaning of life in action, and the action of the past provides, he says in lines 19 to 21, not a fund of dead memories to relive imaginatively in old age but rather a prologue and guide to the future. Ulysses is determined to struggle not against physical death—he is acutely aware of his own mortality—but against the spiritual death of exchanging life for mere breathing, action for memories, satisfaction for yearning. Other students will react to Ulysses as a bombastic and arrogant old man, contemptuous of family and subjects. The latter he describes as a "savage race / That hoard, and sleep, and feed, and know not me" (ll. 4–5). It might be suggested that his subjects do not know him because he has spent most of his life pursuing adventure rather than governing and that, consequently, he cannot know them either. He patronizingly dismisses his wife, though there is no reason why an old man should not be "Matched with an aged wife" (l. 3). And while he professes to love his son Telemachus, his comment on Telemachus's aptitude for governance ("the sphere / Of common duties," ll. 39–40) is hardly flattering. This disdain and haughtiness reach the most concentrated expression in the bombast of the final three lines.

But whatever view readers take, most agree that Tennyson is superb in his handling of sound, rhythm, and image. For example, it can be argued that line 22 is repetitious, yet the image is extremely effective. The heavy-stressed, monosyllabic, irregular opening lines, heavy with plosives and sibilants, help to create the description of the dull world Ulysses wishes to leave. In contrast, when Ulysses describes his past and the future he is determined to have (ll. 19–23, for example), the verse is mellifluous and flowing.

The poem divides into three sections. In the first, Ulysses recalls the past and sets forth his philosophy of life in general terms. In the third section, beginning with line 44, he addresses his sailors. In contrast to the first section, the scene is now much more specific and concrete as he describes the sights and sounds of the port from which he will sail. The details in this final section (the dying day, the moans), as well as Ulysses' direct statements, will make it clear that this will be his final voyage.

Dylan Thomas   Do Not Go Gentle into That Good Night
(p. 1408)

The poem is a villanelle, an intricate French form customarily used for light verse, consisting of five tercets and a final quatrain all employing the same rhyme. The first tercet of the poem opens with an arresting line. The adjective "gentle" appears where we would expect the adverb "gently." The strange diction suggests that "gentle" may describe both the going (i.e., gently dying) and the person (i.e., gentleman) who confronts death. The speaker addresses his dying father, and in contradiction to the usual poetic injunctions to die with confidence and serenity, he urges his father to "burn," "rave," "rage," and shed "fierce tears" at imminent death. Yet the poem is not an exhortation to die fearfully so much as a rhapsodic celebration of life and living. On behalf of life, the poet alludes to four types—wise men, good men, wild (i.e., poetically inspired) men, and grave men. Wise men, though they understand death, do not go gently because their wisdom had not made sufficient impact ("forked no lightning"). Men devoted to good works rage against death because death prevents them from enjoying even their rather "frail" accomplishments ("deeds" that "might have danced in a green bay). The inspired men, whose poetry arrests time ("caught and sang the sun in flight"), discover that their own time is not arrested. Grave men (punning on their mortality, since they are "near death") perceive the stunning insight that gaiety might transcend even the infirmities of age and relieve them of gravity. Despite their recognition of failure, all these men value life too much to acquiesce in death. The speaker urges his father to refuse that acquiescence as well. The "sad height" implies that maximum of experience and insight that ends with death. And in the second line of the final quatrain, the speaker prays to his father to either curse him or bless him (suggestive of Old Testament events, such as Jacob's deathbed blessing and cursing of his children) that is, to act and deny acquiescence with "fierce tears."

Dylan Thomas   Fern Hill   (p. 169)

"Fern Hill" is Dylan Thomas's superb evocation of the innocence of youth, that period in our lives before we grow into the adult world of evil, corruption, and mortality. The poignance of the poem derives from the fact that the poet looks back from the vantage of maturity and adulthood. The juxtaposition of "Now" and "was" in the very first line shadows the lovely period of childhood with a foredoomed change. Only now, with innocence lost, can the poet re-create it and understand it. He now sees that in his youth the entire world revolved about and seemed to focus on him, as if he were some Adam before the fall from "grace" (l. 45). And for him, as for Adam and Eve ("maiden," l. 30) before the fall, everything was bathed in green (evoking youth, spring, life) and gold (evoking purity, radiance, royalty); everything was holy and full of wonder. Each day he looked upon the sun with unjaded and wondrous eyes, as if he were seeing it for the first time. But all of this happened "once below a time" (l. 7), and now he has grown up, into time and mortality, heralded in the final stanza by the vaguely ominous "swallow thronged loft" (l. 47), the imagery of darkness, the shift from the constantly reborn sun to the rising moon. The final lines powerfully fuse the complex point of view by juxtaposing "green" with "dying" and singing with the chains of time.

Edmund Waller   Go, Lovely Rose!   (p. 1101)

This song, like so many love lyrics, employs the rose centrally. Here, the rose is personified and sent to carry the lover's message. The poem is structured in a sequence of imperative directions to the rose: go, tell, bid, die. The most prominent words are "waste" (l. 2), in its control of two objects (it is one thing, relatively minor, to waste time; it is rather ominous to waste the poet—with all the overtones of pining and lovesickness), and "die" (l. 16), for its startling impact. Carpe diem poems characteristically raise the specter of age and death in their arguments for pleasure, but that imperative "Then die!" is unique in the tradition.

Phillis Wheatley   On Being Brought from Africa to America
(p. 473)

Our editor asked us to include some women poets to fill a huge gap that ran from Sappho to Emily Dickinson. She suggested this poem, and when we pointed out that the poem is likely to offend black students, her response was "They should be offended. Let it fire up a lively discussion." You might acquaint students with Cain, the first murderer and, presumably, a patriarchic forebear to the black African races, though clearly, the principal biblical patriarch is Noah's son Ham, the father of Canaan who managed to get himself roundly cursed by his grandfather: "Cursed be Canaan; a slave of slaves shall he be to his brothers" (Genesis 9:25). The biblical admonition justified slavery to generations of Americans. Students need to understand that Wheatley was an incredible phenomenon in her time. She was taken to England and introduced into the highest social and political circles because she rose from the position of a kidnapped eight-year-old slave to the position of a black woman who not only could read and write but actually compose poetry. Taken from Africa as a child, perhaps she can be forgiven for feeling that a nurturing household and the promise of Christian salvation were more attractive than the pagan alternative. And if the poem yearns for refinement, a kind of spiritual "whiteness," what other symbols of success and salvation could the poet look to in 1773?

Walt Whitman *from* Song of Myself (p. 1105)

This self-contained section from Whitman's celebratory "Song of Myself" doubtless contributed somewhat to the rage that impelled John Greenleaf Whittier to hurl the wicked *Leaves of Grass* into the fire. Though our modern sensibilities find this frankly sexual lyric rather tame, many in the mid-nineteenth century thought it bordered on the pornographic. Not only is it unabashed, but it celebrates a woman's sexual desire and need—an idea quite foreign to the conventional notions of the period. Certainly, one of Whitman's great contributions to literature was his insistence that the body's claims upon our interest and respect were as valid as the soul's.

The poem provides the opportunity to discuss some of the characteristics of Whitman's long-line free verse. It uses parallel grammatical structures to provide formal design in the absence of repetitive meter and rhyme.

Walt Whitman When I Heard the Learn'd Astronomer (p. 11)

See "Reading Poetry" on p. 11 of the anthology.

Richard Wilbur Museum Piece (p. 493)

Wilbur's poem is a marvelous illustration of Alexander Pope's celebrated definition of poetry as "what oft was thought but ne'er so well expressed." The sentiment expressed in this poem is an old one: many of the great works of art, created by young, intense, disreputable artists who in their lifetimes were deplored by respectable circles, come to expensively rest in museums patrolled, paradoxically, by "good grey guardians," the elderly, featureless counterparts of those who ignored or condemned the artists in their lifetimes. Then and now, these bourgeoisie with philistine tendencies would be "suspicious of Toulouse" because he made great art out of the morally suspect nightlife of Paris.

The freshness in this old idea derives from Wilbur's skill with imagery, rhythm, and rhyme. In four stanzas, within the constraints of an iambic tetrameter meter, each with exact rhymes in the second and fourth lines, Wilbur pays clever tribute to great modern painters while at the same time noting the paradox inherent in the enterprise of a museum. These great, passionate paintings, pulsing with life, are hung on walls and thereby reduced to "museum pieces." The uneasy relationship between the painting and the museum is powerfully caught in the image of the guardian dozing in a funeral chair beneath the painting of a Degas dancer, who seems to be dancing on the guard's head. It is of course another paradox that real life (the guard) is associated with somnolence and death while art (the dancer) represents "Beauty joined to energy." The anecdote related in the final stanza brings the poem brilliantly to a close. Degas, unlike the museum and the guard, did not look upon his El Greco as a sacrosanct and priceless object to be protected and separated from real life. Hanging his pants on the painting, far from being a desecration, merely demonstrated that this beautiful painting had its practical uses as well.

Oscar Williams A Total Revolution (p. 488)

This poem is discussed on p. 111 of this manual.

William Wordsworth The World Is Too Much with Us (p. 474)

In this sonnet Wordsworth protests a world most students will understand, a world so devoted to materialism that it is in danger of losing its soul. The contrast between "world" and "Nature" is established in the first three lines. The images that dominate the poem—sea, flowers, Proteus, and Triton—define what the poet means by Nature. Not only is modern man insensitive to the natural beauties of the world (sea and flowers), he has, more significantly, cut himself off from that sense of wonder and mystery that, in the ancient world, gave rise to myth (Proteus and Triton). Yet if Wordsworth indicts the soulless "world" man has created, he makes clear that "Nature" abides always and is there to "see" if only we will. The sea and the winds, he tells us, "are upgathered now like sleeping flowers" (l. 7) ready to awaken in their perennial splendor and beauty when man awakens.

William Butler Yeats   Easter 1916   (p. 478)

Few great poems have been written about specific political events, but "Easter 1916" is certainly one of them. Its success results from the fact that while the political event is never lost sight of, Yeats focuses upon the human participants and upon his own feelings and reactions to those participants before and after the event.

Yeats opens the poem by describing his attitude of casual aloofness and near contempt for these political activists, who worked at dull jobs while they hatched foolish conspiracies. But the distance Yeats establishes between himself and the conspirators is not absolute, for lines 13 and 14 suggest that all Irishmen, in their futile struggle to gain independence from England, are foolish and comic, like the court jesters who wear "motley." In the second stanza, Yeats sketches portraits of four of the conspirators he knew. The first is Constance Gore-Booth, born into the Irish aristocracy (ll. 17–23); the second is Patrick Pearse, a promising poet (ll. 24–25); the third is Thomas MacDonagh, a poet and dramatist (ll. 26–30); the fourth is Major John MacBride, who married the woman Yeats had hopelessly loved for years (ll. 31–38). They are bound together in the poet's imagination because their background and temperament seem to Yeats utterly inconsistent with a desperate, doomed rebellion. In the third section, Yeats attempts to penetrate the mystery of their involvement through a series of images that contrast the beauty and flux of the world with the single-mindedness of revolutionaries, whose dedication turns them into stones. The images of changing life pick up and further develop the attitude of the opening section, while the "stone," which opens and closes the stanza, remains the unmoved and durable symbol of their single-minded purpose.

In the opening lines of the final section, Yeats turns, as if the pressure of feeling is too intense to bear, to a direct statement that interprets the imagery of the preceding section. With the question "O when may it suffice?" Yeats again evokes the long and bloody struggle of the Irish. But the question is beyond the power of man to answer; man can only lament the tragic deaths with the love of a mother who broods over a sleeping child. The poet then rejects this analogy, for those he celebrates do not sleep. They lie in graves, dead. He, therefore, returns to the question of line 59, only this time its formulation is specific and personal: "Was it needless death after all?" Politics will not yield an answer—England may or may not grant Ireland independence. What remains, finally, is the power of the rebels' dream and excessive love that paradoxically transcend the political goal that inspired them. Before that inexplicable mystery, Yeats can only name those rebels and affirm that the terrible beauty of their act is enshrined beyond the reach of time and history.

William Butler Yeats   The Great Day   (p. 481)

Robert Frost   A Semi-Revolution   (p. 482)

Oscar Williams   A Total Revolution   (p. 488)

These three poems ride on varying degrees of wit and cleverness: the mock enthusiasm of Yeats, Frost's personal gibe (Yeats was a Rosicrucian) and his humorous rhymes (*revolution–Rosicrucian, salves–halves*), and Williams's multiple rhymes as he picks up Frost's and adds another: "calves." Since their target remains abstract, their casual if not flippant tone is appropriate. In this context, "revolution" functions much like the term politician," a byword for negative actions or qualities. Obviously, we're not dealing with a particular revolution but rather the political concept of revolution, which the dictionary defines as "a complete and forcible overthrow and replacement of an established government or political system by the people governed."

Yeats sees the consequences of revolution as simply the exchange of one set of beggars for another, while the objective conditions ("the lash") remain the same. Frost, interpreting Yeats to mean that a revolution "brings the same class up on top," calls for a "semi-revolution," a kind of public relations revolution that leaves the same class, the "Executives of skilful execution," in power. If we assume that Yeats was deliberately playing on the word "beggar," which means both a penniless person and a rogue, his meaning is slightly different: when the powerful rogues on horseback are overthrown by the powerless and penniless beggars on foot, power corrupts them as readily as it corrupted the rulers they have replaced. Like Yeats and Frost, Williams relies on abstractions ("Compromise, Complacence and Confusion"), but his poem is more specific. He suggests in line 7 that "The old saw [that] says there's loads of room on top" is a bromide meant to keep the poor in their place. While Yeats's and Frost's poems take conservative positions—beware the unintended consequences of revolution—Williams argues in favor of revolution as a means of improving the lot of the downtrodden.

William Butler Yeats Leda and the Swan (p. 163)

"Leda and the Swan," generally regarded as one of Yeats's most brilliant poems, is written on a theme that fascinated him all his life: the great historical or mythical event that heralded profound changes in man's history. Here Yeats meditates upon the meaning of the rape of Leda by Zeus, disguised as a swan, and manages to re-create the event with a powerful immediacy from the point of view of Leda without in any way diminishing its legendary force or allowing his own reflections to be submerged. The octave is remarkable for its description of the rape (note, for example, the harsh, emphatic stresses of the first words). It is a violent event, inspiring terror in Leda. And at precisely the point where the sestet begins (l. 9), the momentous orgasm that is both an ending and a beginning, the sonnet turns as if it were at its own climax. Out of Zeus's shudder comes the future, a future that he knows will result from his act. Caught up in Zeus's passion, the mortal Leda, chosen by the god for union, has "put on" his power. But did she at the moment of annunciation, the poet asks, share his knowledge? Did she know, as Zeus did, what the profound consequences of the act would be?

William Butler Yeats Politics (p. 1109)

This delightful commentary mocks the self-importance of nations and international politics by insisting on the emotional primacy of certain well-known masculine tendencies. In what is almost a ballad stanza (alternating tetrameter and trimeter lines rhymed abcb), Yeats addresses Thomas Mann's portentous observations about politics and the destiny of man. The poem reminds its readers that, ancient and modern political history notwithstanding, the speaker pursues a destiny that embodies his ardent desire to recover his lost youth so that he can embrace "that girl standing there." Certainly students will smile, but there are some desperately serious issues here. What is it that men and women most desire? How does international politics—trade, treaties, war (when all else fails)—satisfy those desires? The destiny the speaker—as well as all individual men and women—wishes to achieve differs markedly from some abstract "destiny of man."

William Butler Yeats Sailing to Byzantium (p. 1388)

In stanza 1, music is life, but in stanzas 2 and 4, it is art—more particularly, poetry. That "country" is the natural world of cyclic change that the poet wishes to escape—the "sensual music," the "dying generations" (with its overtones of sexual procreation and mortality). The speaker wishes to escape from life and the mortality that finally overtakes the generations; he wishes to become an "artifice" free of the inevitable debilitation of time. The natural world is no country for old men who cannot enjoy the sensual music; it would be better to be such a form as Grecian goldsmiths make—a golden bird that survives the dying generations. Yeats conceives of Byzantium as a symbol of immortal art where the sages can teach the soul to sing, consume away the poet's heart "fastened to a dying animal" (i.e., the body), and make him eternal. There he will sing, not of whatever is "begotten, born, and dies" but of "what is past, or passing, or to come." The speaker leaves the world for Byzantium in order to transform himself from a "paltry" old age into an immortal singer-artist.

William Butler Yeats   The Second Coming   (p. 480)

Although this poem nicely fits Yeats's theory of historical cycles, it remains quite intelligible independent of that theory. In the first stanza, the speaker images a breakdown of society and order. The falcon, spiraling out, escapes from the control of the falconer. Perhaps as a response to the Russian Revolution of 1917, Yeats describes the dissolution of social order as "Mere anarchy." Later, Yeats himself asserted that the poem (published in 1920) was a prophecy of the rise of fascism in Europe. But it is more than that—it is the vision of the end of an era, the Christian era that culminated in a scientific rationalism. A new era is at hand (they come, in Yeats's view, every two thousand years). Appropriately he speaks of the new era as the Second Coming, a term from Revelation that refers to the return of Christ after a time of great upheaval and disorder. But this advent is not of Christ but of an anti-Christ—a Sphinx that presumably held sway during the twenty centuries before the birth of Jesus. Christianity is finished, the poem says, and it will be replaced by some "pitiless" force that slouches toward Bethlehem to be born.

Line 20 is troublesome. The Sphinx has been sleeping for the twenty centuries of the Christian era, the era that began with a "rocking cradle" at Bethlehem. Now that rocking cradle is the Sphinx's and has vexed him to nightmare. The Sphinx awakens and will replace Christ as the dominant force for the next historical period; its pitiless and blank gaze, its roughness, its slouch connote the quality of the next two thousand years.

Yevgeny Yevtushenko   I Would Like   (p. 805)

Allen Ginsberg and, ironically, Yevgeny Yevtushenko are the two most Whitmanesque of contemporary poets. And here, Yevtushenko gives us his own condensed "Song of Myself' that, like Whitman's, ranges over time and geography, and includes animals, vegetables, and minerals in its inclusive hug. However, underlying Yevtushenko's chirpy assertions about all the animals and people (including the sick and disfigured) he would like to be, there are some people he judges through exclusion—he would not like to be a tyrant, for example. He would rather be one of the miserable of the earth than Rambo; he would suffer any indignity to avoid infection by the "microbe of superiority" (l. 54). And he rejects both the "elite" and the "cowardly herd." His sympathy with rebel causes and underground movements suggests a suspicion of government and authority in any form. It would be instructive to ask students to identify the things he dislikes, among them drinking Coca-Cola (ll. 106–8) and ask them what those things symbolize and suggest about the poet's values. Why not drink Coca-Cola? Note also the conclusion—is it crude jingoism or warm patriotism for the poet to wish, finally, to be buried in "our Russian, Siberian earth" (ll. 161–64)?

Have the students analyze the prosody of the piece. Why are the lines divided as they are? Note that repetitious passages ("I would like to be") and repeated syntactical patterns ("a victim of . . . / a homeless child in . . . / a living skeleton . . . / a holy beggar . . .") establish certain formal expectations similar to those created by metrical patterns and rhyme schemes.

Yevgeny Yevtushenko   People   (p. 1413)

The poem addresses human mortality not as a biological fact but as a psychological fact; what is significant about death is not the end of an animal but the end of all the experience that animal has acquired. In this sense, no person is uninteresting, not even the most obscure, for death marks the end of "his first snow and kiss and fight"—

standing, of course, for the unique world of memory that constitutes a human life. Each person's life is the creation of a world, and thus "Not people die but worlds die in them." Those who survive are left some of the furniture of that unique world — books, bridges, painted canvases, machinery — by which the dead will be remembered. But the world that death has ended is "also not nothing." The works remain as only vague, obscure hints of the "secret worlds" we never knew in life and now, because of death, can never know.

Yevtushenko's attitude toward death is among the most humane in the poetry of the anthology's "The Presence of Death" section. Compare it with the attitudes revealed in such poems as Owen's "Dulce et Decorum Est," in which an untimely and horrible death is dominant, or Yeats's "Sailing to Byzantium," in which mortality itself and the human experiences associated with it are rejected for an ideal immortality.

Tawfiq Zayyad   Here We Shall Stay   (p. 495)

Zayyad, for several years the elected mayor of Nazareth, is an important writer in the Palestinian struggle against Israel. This poem, written almost forty years ago, is a passionate declaration of Palestinian determination to both endure and triumph over what they perceive as an illegitimate occupation of their land by Israel. The poem marshals a series of violent images depicting the retribution to be visited on the oppressors — "in your throat / like a splinter of glass, like spiky cactus / And in your eyes / A chaos of fire." But adjacent to the fiery threats, the poet describes the abysmal lives of Palestinians struggling to survive — "If we get thirsty / We'll squeeze the rocks. / If we get hungry / We'll eat dirt." The speaker's aim is to encourage his disadvantaged countrymen by emphasizing their determination to stay. And, at the same time, discourage Israelis (characterized as blue-fanged, exploitive employers) at the prospect of a never-ending struggle with those same determined Palestinians. The final stanza refers to a holy book — it could be either the Koran or the Hebrew Bible — which requires a reckoning for sinful behavior. You might compare Zayyad's poems with 'Ashrawi's. Her poems engage at a personal and psychological level, while these seek to engage nationalistic fervor.

Tawfiq Zayyad   A Million Suns in My Blood   (p. 497)

Like "Here We Shall Stay," this lyric is a passionate lamentation at the injustice of an oppressive occupation. Somewhat overwrought (how has the speaker been stripped of the shining sun and the warm sea?), the song, nonetheless, embodies the powerful emotion of one who has been materially impoverished, but remains emotionally dedicated to his perception of justice. They (the Israelis) cannot strip the speaker of his heart, his conscience, and his tongue. And those qualities that embody his national pride are at the service of his oppressed people. The lyric displays some of the qualities of lamentation psalms in the Hebrew Bible. Compare it, for example, with Psalm 137, "By the waters of Babylon, there we sat down and wept," a lament decrying the oppressive exile of Israel in a foreign land (Iraq, as it happens).

Drama

Edward Albee   The Sandbox   (p. 1423)

Perhaps more than most modern absurdist playwrights, Albee works through certain aspects of his own life in his work. The exceedingly wealthy Frances and Reed Albee adopted Edward as a two-week-old baby; the beloved grandmother this short play is dedicated to was Frances's mother. Albee's adolescence was troubled — he was expelled from two prominent prep schools — and he left home at twenty-one. His adoptive short-statured, soft-spoken father co-owned a chain of theaters. His brassy adoptive mother, a foot taller and twenty-three years younger than her husband, was a domineering and snobbish social climber. Moreover, she bitterly disapproved of young Edward's choice of friends, his homosexuality, and his choice of profession. And while some of his best works, notably *Who's Afraid of Virginia Woolf?* importantly refer to a lost child (surely some reflection on being abandoned by his birth mother), this play depends for its force on a mother discarded by her middle-aged daughter.

The short play (it performs in less than fifteen minutes) presents a dysfunctional married couple presiding over the demise of the wife's eighty-six-year-old mother. The relationship between husband and wife is distressing — he is weak and whiny, she is arrogant, controlling, and opinionated. Despite her obscene cruelty, she determinedly embraces the social clichés — she weeps for her dying mother, but, when the sun comes up, she brightly announces, "We must put away our tears, take off our mourning . . . and face the future. It's our duty." One wonders how often Frances Albee lectured young Edward on his "duty." And we can, perhaps, understand why the thirty-year-old Albee, somewhat maliciously, strikes back at his wealthy and socially prominent adoptive parents for their failure to understand and nurture him. In effect, the play, with ironical propriety, celebrates the death and funeral of Grandma — Mommy and Daddy perform the requisite vigil; music is provided; a buff Angel of Death, fluttering his wings, waits for the proper moment; Mommy exhibits socially required tearful grief. But the event is an empty form. And Grandma makes her wealthy daughter's deficiencies as a human being pretty clear: "[T]hey moved me into the big town house with *them* . . . fixed a nice place for me under the stove . . . gave me an army blanket . . . and my own dish . . . my very own dish!" In short, they turned her into a housedog.

The play endures because it embodies more than Albee's attack on his own hypocritical adoptive parents. It endures because it exposes the counterfeit feelings that social pressure demands. As well, it exhibits dramatic techniques that tear down the fourth wall between stage and audience as characters direct certain details of the action. And tearing down that wall may well have consequences, may well destroy the "distance" that protects the audience from the insistent revelations that emerge from the hypocritical characters and their behavior.

Woody Allen   Death Knocks   (p. 1430)

"The prospect of death," said the great Dr. Samuel Johnson, "wonderfully concentrates the mind." Those familiar with Woody Allen's films will know that death is one of his continuing preoccupations and will probably agree that his is the kind of mind that could turn the solemn subject into an uproarious farce. From the medieval play *Everyman* to Ingmar Bergman's *The Seventh Seal*, the appearance of Death to announce to the protagonist that his time has come has been the subject of the most solemn examinations of the meaning of life. We might say of Allen's farce that it is typically modern in its implication that death (like much of life) can best be seen as a farce.

Allen's play depends on a long literary tradition in the dramatization of Death's calling. Death is in black, of course, as he must be, but Allen hilariously has him in a black hood and skintight black clothes. Death appears, as he always does, unannounced, but Allen's figure is a fumbler and bumbler who barely makes it into Ackerman's house in one piece. Ackerman, who has probably seen *The Seventh Seal*, naturally wants to play chess to gain time, but Allen's unintellectual Death doesn't play chess—he plays gin rummy and, of course, loses. And, having lost, he is turned out of doors penniless, with no money to pay for a motel. What a humiliation for the most awesome figure of the human imagination!

Margaret Edson W;t (p. 1438)

At the time these notes were written (September 2004) this Web site, http://faculty .smu.edu/tmayo/witguide.htm, provided a comprehensive eleven page guide to Margaret Edson and her play headed with an amiable invitation to "[f]eel free to print out all or some of this guide." We commend it (if it is still posted) to you and your students. As well, the play has been made into an HBO feature film starring Emma Thompson and directed by Mike Nichols. We warn you that the movie, as serious and compelling as it is, fails to project much of the dark humor that will surely tickle readers.

W;t examines the relationship between research and scholarship, on the one hand, and the experiences that constitute a life on the other. And that semicolon in the title, placed where an "i" should appear, is the witty first detail in the examination of that relationship. John Dryden and Samuel Johnson characterized John Donne (1572–1631) as one among several "metaphysical poets" whose work exhibited and depended on "wit." Those critics meant that Donne's work exhibited distinctive word play, strange, even perverse imagery. Johnson spoke of this metaphysical wit as a "kind of *discordia concors*; a combination of dissimilar images, or discovery of occult resemblances in things apparently unlike." As well, he found that metaphysical poetry displayed "the most heterogeneous ideas yoked by violence together."

Those characteristics, together with the innate difficulty of Donne's work, appealed to Vivian Bearing, and made her the preeminent Donne scholar of her time. Ironically, though immersed in the "humanities," neither she, nor her mentor E.M. Ashford, had much interest in humanity. They approached their subject with the detachment of science researchers, exhibited contempt for softer artists (like Shakespeare and modern novelists), and, consequently, dehumanized their students. Paradigmatically, Professor Ashford sternly criticized her young student Vivian for erroneously substituting a semicolon for a comma in the text of a Donne poem—an unforgivable gaffe given the scholarly edition of Donne's work she should have consulted. Thus tutored, Professor Bearing enshrined the brainy research that became the foundation of her reputation and her career. But at what cost?

That metaphysical wit described by Dr. Johnson celebrated the ingenious manipulation of image and language in poetry. It appealed to the intellect, not the heart, to a recognition of the poet's skillful technique, not to his ability to touch (or alter) the lives of his readers. And the schism (perhaps *abyss* is a better word) that separates knowledge from love, technique from caring, is revealed to pain-wracked Vivian Bearing contemplating herself as a laboratory animal in the research design of Doctors Kelekian and Posner. They treat her precisely as she was treated by Professor Ashford, and precisely as she treated her students. They perform research in the healing arts, but perceive attending physicians as troglodytes. They wish to discover techniques that cure, but have no interest at all in the humanity of those that may (or, as in this case, may not) benefit from their work. Only the relatively witless Susie Monahan rises above all the learning, all the science, all the intellect to the simple loving humanity that both poetry and pharmaceutical research presumably enhance.

Yet, Edson introduces wit enough into her exposé of doctors who patronizingly ask their nauseated distressed patients "How are you feeling today?" The names of some key players merit attention: Vivian (ironically echoing *viva*) Bearing (enduring, weighed down [as in bearing a cross], imposing weighty difficulties [as in overbearing]). Then we have Professor E(velyn). M. Ashford. The *Ash* part is easy—perhaps have some fun with the *ford* part—crossing a river(?). And why the initials?—sometimes a device used by women to hide their feminine names. This ultimate pedant cannot even read a children's book without turning it into a scholarly article. Then there's Jason Posner. Jason and his argonauts were the prototypical voyagers (in some sense, early researchers). Posner is uncomfortably close to *poser*, and he takes Professor Bearing's class not out of any desire to engage with the humanities but because it will look good on his medical school application. Nonetheless, we may assume that he, too, has been transformed by Vivian's fate and Susie's humanity.

The formal structure of the play exhibits a deft command of dramaturgy and allows Edson to solve what would be extraordinarily difficult problems in a more realistic (say Ibsenesque) presentation. Using novelistic techniques, similar to Elizabethan soliloquies, she moves Vivian from her bed to provide omniscient voice-over viewpoints on the progress both of her illness and the lessons she learns from her suffering; she slips Vivian into flashbacks that illuminate the choices she made in life. But, at the same time, Edson displays, with a dogged realism, the progress of Vivian's terminal illness. In these respects, the form of the play reflects the flashback techniques used by Miller in *Death of a Salesman* that were simply not thinkable for Sophocles, Shakespeare, and Ibsen.

Susan Glaspell Trifles (p. 1236)

Although *Trifles* was written three-quarters of a century ago, when the disabilities imposed on women were far more numerous than they are today (in 1916, for example, women were still denied the vote), the advances women have made since then have not lessened the power and the relevance of the play. America has, in the intervening years, changed from a predominantly rural to an overwhelmingly urban society. But the man/woman, husband/wife relationship depicted in the play is not difficult to transpose imaginatively to a modern tenement or suburb. It could be argued that the play is all the more powerful precisely because the appalling events unfold in a rural America that has always been associated with ruddy good health and loving family life (not to mention the Jeffersonian ideal of a nation of sturdy yeoman farmers, the version memorably set down in John Greenleaf Whittier's poem "Snow-Bound").

The incongruity is apparent before a word is spoken, in the contrast between the expectations evoked by the rural farmhouse and the disarray of the kitchen. Something is clearly wrong. That feeling is strengthened by the opening dialogue. The kitchen is not only in disarray but it is also bitterly cold. The atmosphere established, the following exchange between the county attorney and Hale provides the necessary exposition. The theme of the drama is introduced when the sheriff and the attorney, filled with the self-importance of male authority, treat the two women with contempt and condescension.

When the men disparage Mrs. Peters's observation on Mrs. Wright's preserves as a feminine preoccupation with "trifles," "The two women move a little closer together." When the attorney patronizes them with his remark about "the ladies," "The women do not unbend." The attorney's criticism of Mrs. Wright's housekeeping and his reference to the lack of "the homemaking instinct" provoke Mrs. Hale to defend Mrs. Wright. From that moment on, the men become indistinguishable as pompous and insensitive male egos, while the two women are delineated as different individuals ultimately drawn together by their sense of womanly solidarity. In fact, except for the end, the men appear only once again, just long enough to ridicule Mrs. Hale's question about the quilt, "I wonder if she was going to quilt it or just knot it?"

As the women examine the house, the drama of Minnie Foster's life unfolds, as does the motive for the murder, through the "trifles" the men could never see. (It is noteworthy that Mrs. Wright is the only one identified by her maiden name, perhaps to underscore the tragedy of a woman whose identity and being were destroyed by marriage.) The overall "nice and even" work of the quilt refutes the attorney's callous criticism of her housekeeping; the final, carelessly done block is mute testimony to her state of mind just before the murder.

The discovery of the bird cage, immediately following the examination of the quilt, not only deepens the women's understanding of Minnie Foster's state of mind but gives them insight into her motive. Mrs. Hale, we have already seen, knows that Mrs. Wright has had to endure years of a cold and joyless marriage. The discovery of the bird cage and then the rotting bird suggest violence as well. In killing the bird, Mr. Wright killed his wife's last link with something that meant joy and hope. Mrs.

Hale's observations that Mrs. Wright "was kind of like a bird herself" and that "she used to sing" suggest that the killing of the bird ended Mrs. Wright's life and drove her to murder. The effect is especially strong on Mrs. Peters, who has up to this point remained somewhat more intimidated by law (i.e., male authority) than Mrs. Hale. She recalls a childhood experience when a boy killed her kitten with a hatchet and vividly remembers that if she had not been restrained, she would have "hurt him." Although she protests once more that "the law has got to punish crime," the memory of the dead kitten and her dead first child bring her round completely to Mrs. Wright's defense. Her final words before the men reappear are heavy with bitterness against male pride and cruelty:

> My, it's a good thing the men couldn't hear us. Wouldn't they just laugh! Getting stirred up over a little thing like a—dead canary. As if that could have anything to do with—with—wouldn't they *laugh*!

Mrs. Hale's response to the attorney's derisive question, the last line of the play, is perhaps the final irony of this ironic play. The "knot" evokes not just the quilt (and the sad life of Mrs. Wright) but the rope by which Mrs. Wright avenged herself.

A final and more general observation on the relationship of literature and the literary canon might be appropriate here. One of the many consequences of the great civil rights upheavals of the 1960s was the permanent alteration of our conception of literature. For example, no introductory literature text or anthology of American literature could conceivably, like those of the 1950s and earlier, exclude African American writers. The feminist movement of recent times has likewise altered the literary landscape. *Trifles,* to take the example at hand, now often described as a classic, was (along with most writing by women) rarely if ever to be found included in the literary canon and anthologies of a few decades ago.

Lorraine Hansberry A Raisin in the Sun (p. 815)

The originality and historic importance of *A Raisin in the Sun* received immediate recognition when the New York Drama Critics gave it their 1959 award for Best Play of the Year. Written four years after *Brown v. Board of Education,* the Supreme Court ruling holding that the doctrine of "separate but equal" schools was unconstitutional, and in the same year that Rosa Parks triggered the Birmingham, Alabama, bus boycott by refusing to move to the back of the bus, *Raisin* was the first Broadway play ever about a black family. Inevitably, reactions to Hansberry's drama about a working-class family's struggle to overcome the debilitating disadvantages of economic and racial oppresson reflected the complex nature of racial relations in America at the dawn of the historic civil rights movement of the 1960s. (One of the best accounts of this period can be found in Taylor Branch's two volumes, *Parting the Waters: America in the King Years, 1954–1963* [1988] and *Pillar of Fire: America in the King Years, 1963–1965* [1998].)

While the popular success of the play has steadily grown (it was made into a highly successful film in 1961), it has not received universal critical praise. Some critics, both white and black, have attacked the play as yet another variation on the "accomodationist" or "assimilationist" theme of much literature written by African Americans, especially in the late nineteenth and early twentieth centuries. These works appealed to the conscience of white America to right the injustices of racism, often by citing the precepts of Christianity or the principles of the Declaration of Independence and the Constitution. Paul Laurence Dunbar's "We Wear the Mask" (p. 787) is one example of this kind of writing.

Faced with the ineffectiveness of these appeals, black writing became more assertive and direct. Appeals gave way to demands and protest, a literature warning America that it could not indefinitely deny some of its citizens their rights without risking serious consequences. Toni Cade Bambara's "The Lesson" (p. 136) is an example of this tradition of writing, as is Richard Wright's explosive 1940s novel *Native Son.*

But as time has passed, the growing consensus among audiences and critics alike is that in *Raisin,* Hansberry created a powerful drama that for the first time in American theater history focused on a struggling black family. Amiri Baraka, who in the 1960s (writing as LeRoi Jones) created some of the most militant, antiwhite dramas ever written in America, made a remarkable acknowledgment of this fact in 1987. In an essay titled "A Critical Reevaluation: *A Raisin in the Sun*'s Enduring Passion," he conceded that he and his militant colleagues had been mistaken in their dismissal of Hansberry's play, declaring that "Hansberry has created a family on the cutting edge of the same class and ideological struggles as existed in the movement itself and among the people." (This essay appeared in *A Raisin in the Sun* and *The Sign in Sidney Brustein's Window*, ed. Robert Nemiroff.)

Act I opens on a cramped, Chicago south side apartment, home to three generations of the Younger family: Lena (Mama), her thirty-four-year-old son Walter Lee, his wife Ruth, and their young son Travis, and Lena's daughter Beneatha, a student who is hoping to enter medical school. The stage direction and the action make clear that the family's struggle to keep financially afloat has exacted a toll of weariness. But hope has been revived by the imminent arrival of a $10,000 check, the payoff from "Big Walter's" life insurance policy. The money becomes a focal point of the action, opening up fissures among the family members but at the same time providing a challenge that ultimately affirms the values of love and caring over individual, self-seeking desires.

Walter Lee, enthralled at the prospect of becoming a big-shot businessman but impervious to the moral ambiguities of this aspiration, wants to use the money to open a liquor store. Beneatha wants the money for her medical education, though she seems more drawn to the prestige of being a doctor than aware of the rigors of medical school. Lena, determined to escape the stifling atmosphere of the ghetto, has quietly made a $3,500 down payment on a house in a white neighborhood.

The play takes up a range of issues related to African American life. Beneatha's two suitors, George Murchison and Asagai, offer her diametrically opposed futures, one a bourgeois life of self-indulgent affluence, the other a life of selfless activism and the rediscovery of her African heritage. By the time the check arrives, the tensions within the Younger family are extreme. The first act ends with Walter's bitter comments about his bleak future and Lena's angry demand that Walter not allow Ruth to abort their child.

Act II opens with Beneatha, dressed in African robes, dancing wildly to the drunken accompaniment of Walter's shouting. This caricature of what Asagai represents is interrupted by the arrival of George Murchison to pick up Beneatha for their date. George expresses nothing but contempt for Beneatha's new fascination with her African heritage. Walter seizes the opportunity to tell George about his plans for some big business projects that George's rich father might want to bankroll. George brushes him off and leaves with Beneatha. Walter, confronting a crisis in his inability to take charge of his life, lashes out at Ruth in a scene that turns painfully tender as they wonder, in Walter words, "How we gets to the place where we scared to talk softness to each other" (p. 853). But before they can say much, they are interrupted by the arrival of Mama, who discloses that she has used part of the insurance money for a down payment on a house. Walter's bitter reaction is, "So you butchered up a dream of mine—you—who was always talking 'bout your children's dreams . . ." (p. 857).

A few weeks later, on the eve of the Youngers' move to their new home, the quiet courage of the family is underscored by the visit of a neighbor, Mrs. Johnson, who, under the guise of congratulating the family on "moving up" in the world, in fact attacks and attempts to frighten them for their arrogance in attempting to escape the ghetto. Her quotation from Booker T. Washington, "Education has spoiled many a good plow hand—" is the quintessential Uncle Tom reaction, timid and acquiescent in the face of the historic oppression of black people. Beneatha's reaction, in contrast, defines the new spirit of militancy that by 1959 was propelling America into a decade of civil rights strife: "Mama, there are two things we, as a people, have got to overcome, one is the Ku Klux Klan and the other is Mrs. Johnson" (p. 862).

In the moving dialogue that follows between Mama and Walter, and then the tenderness elicited by Walter and Ruth's gift of gardening tools to Mama, we see a growing understanding between mother and son that foreshadows the play's climax and denouement. In the meantime, however, the intense centrifugal pressures become even heavier when Karl Lindner attempts to dissuade the Youngers from moving into his all-white neighborhood. As the act ends, Walter learns that his business partner Willy has absconded with the money Walter has entrusted to him.

Act III opens with the family at its lowest point. Beneatha's cynicism is impervious to the hope and idealism insisted on by Asagai, Mama is so shaken she has lost her bearings and her strength, and Walter bitterly declares that he has finally figured out that life is about looking out for number one, whatever the cost. But the countertide of hope and resistance to servile acquiescence is stronger than these setbacks and, when the climax arrives and a choice must be made, Walter rises to the occasion with his powerful response to Lindner's offer to buy the family out: ". . . we have decided to move into our house because my father—my father—he earned it for us brick by brick. We don't want to make no trouble for nobody or fight no causes, and we will try to be good neighbors" (p. 888). The play ends on a note of triumphant affirmation of the family's love and strength. But any possibility of feel-good sentimentalism is kept in check by the realities that the Youngers will face in their new lives.

Finally, it should be noted that *Raisin* is a tightly constructed play, observing the traditional unities of time, place, and action. Its three acts provide a beginning, a middle, and an end, with no digressions. It could be argued that the appearance of Mrs. Johnson in Act II momentarily deflects the play from its trajectory, that she does not serve to advance the plot in any way. That is no doubt why she was dropped from early versions of the play. Yet her presence reminds the Youngers and the audience that the family is embarking on a new life that will entail many dangers and difficulties.

Václav Havel Protest (p. 605)

Protest is one of a trilogy of short Vaněk plays (written in the late 1970s; the others are *Audience* and *Unveiling*) in which the brewery worker/political dissident Ferdinand Vaněk appears. Vaněk shares some of the experiences endured by his creator—Havel, too, was sent to prison for political dissidence, and forced into hard physical labor in attempts by authorities to discourage him from voicing his opposition to the Soviet-installed rulers of Czechoslovakia. Perhaps the most effective aspect of *Protest* is its quiet understatement. Although Havel had reason enough to pen a drama featuring agitated rants by innocent victims against their unprincipled tormentors, he chooses not to vent angry rage. Rather, he places two characters (with interestingly similar names—almost as if they were shadows of each other) who seem to share all the desirable aspects of human decency in a setting where each is attempting to beg a favor of the other. If only one of them appears to be principled, the other at least confesses to his human failings. And while that confession does not rise to expiation, it does attempt an explanation—one that exhibits a certain (merited) self-loathing. That awareness, that self-loathing is for Vaněk (and Havel as well) sufficient punishment for those whose fecklessness caused so much grief.

The issue (if not the moral stature of both characters) is abundantly clear: How must one act in response to political repression? Staněk, who does most of the talking precisely because his behavior requires the most justification, envies Vaněk and his dissident friends for their moral courage in the face of dangerous retribution. But, at the same time, he complains bitterly of the outrages he endures from the authorities who distort his work and compromise his integrity; but he fails to oppose those depredations, because any display of moral conviction would endanger his comfortable position. And all the while, he treats Vaněk as if he were a heroic intervener—even a savior. His recognition of Vaněk's courage (a courage he envies but does not possess) leads him to remark, "who knows—perhaps the hope of a moral rebirth of the nation hangs on it."

The great irony, of course, is that Staněk has called the well-known dissident Vaněk to ask him to write a protest demanding that the authorities free an imprisoned musician (his pregnant daughter's lover). Vaněk has not only already written that protest but also gathered fifty signatures. He has come to ask his important and well-known friend Staněk to add his name to the protest. That request leads to two consequences. The first is the long aria during which Staněk examines every conceivable ramification of his signature on the document. That speech is a virtual seminar on pragmatic, self-interested politics and its relation to moral behavior.

Pragmatism, once again, triumphs. Staněk, despite agreeing with the protest in principle, refuses to sign the very document he wished Vaněk to prepare. The second consequence is more rapid and more subtle. Deeply embarrassed at his own moral cowardice, Staněk turns on Vaněk. He accuses him (despite Vaněk's demurrals) of feeling morally superior and charges him with his own moral failure. "As far as I know," Staněk complains, "in prison you talked more than you should have!"

A revealing stage direction follows this speech: "Vaněk jumps up, wildly staring at Staněk, who smiles triumphantly. Short tense pause. The phone rings. Vaněk, broken, sinks into his chair." His behavior suggests that Vaněk was not able to endure the extraordinary pressure of interrogation and jail—that he may, indeed, have betrayed some of his co-dissidents. Ask students to determine who, finally, holds the moral high ground? Is this play about Staněk's moral cowardice, or is it about human fallibility in general? Is Staněk's analysis of the consequences of signing the protest relevant only in an oppressive tyranny, or does it apply in truly democratic power structures as well? What, for example, characteristically happens to whistle-blowers, particularly those in government, here in the United States? Does that one stage direction restore the balance between the two men, or is Vaněk, finally, the moral savior that Staněk claims he is early in the play? Does the release of Javurek moot the issue? Or does moral intention count even when it is not put to the test?

Henrik Ibsen   A Doll's House   (p. 546)

For students who have grown up in an era of strong liberationist movements among women and insistent demands by minorities for equal rights, not to mention the alternative lifestyles associated with drugs and rock music, the theme of A Doll's House may seem rather ordinary. Such students need to be reminded that when Ibsen wrote the play, over a century ago, it generated an explosive response. In writing a play that ends with the wife walking out on her husband and children, Ibsen challenged one of the pillars of middle-class society. For the way in which a society defines its institutions subtly and pervasively permeates the way in which its members define themselves. The sound of the door Nora slams shut at the end of the play reverberates far beyond her house; it becomes an aggressive assertion that the successful bourgeois marriage turns a human being into a doll, an ornamental possession for the social and sexual pleasure of the husband, who does the serious work and thinking the world requires.

The portrait of the wife in this sort of ideal marriage is rapidly and skillfully sketched in the opening of the first act. Bubbling with happiness, her first thoughts are of children and husband. She is a mother but also a child indulged by an amused and tolerant father, as her first dialogue with Helmer reveals. When Helmer reproaches Nora for spending too much money, we not only see a predictable quality of a middle-class housewife but also learn that the Helmers are at a typically middle-class stage in their lives: Helmer is about to get the big new job that will put them on easy street (it is amazing how many middle-class marriages still fall apart precisely at that moment when the years of scrambling for affluence finally pay off). With the arrival of Nora's old friend Christine, we learn something of her past (as a rich and spoiled child) and, with Krogstad's first appearance, of the forgery that will destroy her marriage (though not in the way she fears).

By the end of Act I, the portrait of Nora is full and ominous. She is a thorough prisoner of that wifely identity that comes with middle-class marriage (though, as the references to her father indicate, it is an identity that her entire life has trained her for). The coy and kittenish child/wife, she cannot forbear exulting in her good fortune even though her old friend has had a life of hard work and unhappiness. A forger herself, Nora is nonetheless haughty and unsympathetic to the desperate Krogstad. What is most vivid in her mind at the end of this act is not the plight of either Christine or Krogstad, or even her own plight contained in the latter's threat, but rather the impending party.

The direction of the action is effectively foreshadowed by the opening stage direction of Act II. The bright and centrally placed Christmas tree of Act I is now in a corner, "stripped of its ornaments and with burnt-down candle-ends on its dishevelled branches." As in Act I, there is an early dialogue between Nora and Helmer in Act II.

But in contrast to the opening act, Nora is preoccupied and increasingly somber. Nora, the hapless victim, watches as her best efforts to avert disaster—at this point keeping the knowledge of her forgery from Helmer—fail in the face of Krogstad's desperation and her husband's insufferable moralism. The role of the giddy child/wife is now counterpointed by her growing premonitions of disaster and death (underscored by the more prominent role of the dying and morbid Dr. Rank).

Under increasing pressure, a critical change begins to take place in Nora in Act II. She confesses the truth to Christine and declares that she, herself, is responsible for the consequences. With that statement, Nora begins her transition from helpless victim to strong human being. And nothing could more powerfully capture the stage Nora has reached than her violent, hysterical dancing at the end of this act. It is a dance of terror as Nora faces the implications of independence and liberation. Helmer's remark after he stops her dancing, "You have forgotten everything I taught you," is heavy with unconscious irony.

Significantly, the final act, which will end with the breakup of the Helmers' marriage, opens with a dialogue between Krogstad and Christine in which they decide to marry. It is a dialogue of great thematic importance to the major action. In contrast to the relationship between Nora and Helmer, Krogstad and Christine are frank with one another about their past and, chastened by their difficult lives, recognize that they can fulfill important and real needs for one another. Further, they are agreed that "concealment and falsehood" have poisoned the Helmers' marriage. The resolution of the subplot thus makes clear that Ibsen's attack is not on marriage *per se* but rather on the kind of marriage the Helmers' represents.

This opening dialogue of Act III occurs while the Helmers are attending the party, the anticipation of which has functioned as an effective structural device in the preceding acts. As much as anything, the preparations for and discussions of the party throughout have served to reveal the kind of marriage the Helmers have. But the mindless wind-up doll of the first act, who so eagerly participated in preparations for her starring role at the party as Helmer's prized possession, becomes the frantic dancer of Act II. Now, the party over, Nora signals her new consciousness by rejecting the sexual advances of her husband (whose final argument in the attempt to seduce her is typically, "Am I not your husband?"). It is a moment of brilliant dramaturgy, focusing this climactic moment on an aspect of middle-class marriage that has been only implicit up to now: the sexual exploitation of women.

The Nora who has spent such frantic energy keeping her husband away from the mailbox now calmly suggests that Helmer ought to read his mail. He does, discovers the truth, shamelessly attacks Nora, and retreats when Krogstad's saving letter arrives, remaining all the while utterly unaware that he is talking to a human being rather than a doll. When, after all this, Nora momentarily leaves the room and Helmer asks what she is doing, Nora replies, with an irony that escapes her husband, "Taking off my fancy dress."

When she reappears (with the words, "I have changed my things") she announces her decision to leave. Helmer's arguments starkly summarize the dehumanizing duties expected of women. When his arguments for home, husband, children, and reputation ("And you don't consider what people will say!" Helmer declares) leave Nora untouched, he reminds her of her religious duties. But no arguments from duty or social convention or religious traditionalism can move Nora now. The only meaningful truths are those arrived at by the critical intelligence of an independent "human being." Thus, as shocking as it may appear, it is surely right that Nora walk out on everything (children included). We have seen enough of the Helmer household to say confidently that it could not possibly provide her the freedom and breathing space in which to wage successfully the battle for her humanity.

Under strong pressure from the German producers of his play, Ibsen provided the alternative "happy" ending in which Helmer dissuades Nora from leaving by forcing her to look at her sleeping children and reminding her that if she leaves, they will awaken motherless. Nora's final words are, "Oh, it is a sin against myself, but I cannot leave them." The curtain falls as Helmer joyously utters his wife's name.

A notice of this production appeared in a Danish newspaper in February 1880 with the comment that the new ending had Ibsen's approval. In a letter to the same newspaper, Ibsen characterized the alteration as a "barbaric outrage" and declared that its use was completely against his wishes. But in the absence of a copyright agreement between Denmark and Germany, the Germans were free to alter his work in any way they wished. "I prefer," he explained, ". . . to commit the outrage myself, instead of handing over my work for treatment and 'adaptation' to less careful and less competent hands." (*The Oxford Ibsen, Volume V*, trans. and ed. James Walter McFarlane, Oxford University Press, 1961.)

A final comment: It has become fashionable in Ibsen criticism to assert that *A Doll's House* is not about women's rights but about the more universal question of human rights. In this view, based on Ibsen's statement in 1898 that "I . . . must disclaim the honor of having consciously worked for women's rights. I am not even quite sure what women's rights really are. To me it has been a question of human rights" (quoted in Martin Meyer, *Ibsen*, II, 297), the play's "real theme has nothing to do with the sexes. It is the irrepressible conflict of two different personalities which have founded themselves on two radically different estimates of reality" (Robert Martin Adams in *Modern Drama*, ed. A. Caputi). In our view, such a reading proceeds from the uneasiness many critics feel when faced with works of art that deal with specific sociopolitical problems. One does not have to deny that the struggle for human rights takes many forms for both sexes to assert that *A Doll's House* is about the deadening effects of a marriage in a society that has a vested (male) interest in binding women to home, husband, and children. Whatever Nora's fate beyond the end of the play, one may insist that *A Doll's House* is about a "social problem" — that is, a problem created by, and therefore remediable by, society. In our view, Ibsen's comment, quoted above, in no way contradicts such an interpretation. Nora's "human rights," we can assume, include the right to face whatever reality she is able to discover, including the pervasiveness of evil and injustice in the world, perhaps, and the ultimate mystery of human existence. Before she can do that, however, she must free herself.

Arthur Miller Death of a Salesman (p. 251)

As the play opens, we hear the sounds of a flute "telling of grass and trees and the horizon." We see the Lomans' house, dominated by the "angular shapes" of a "solid vault of apartment houses." The grass and the horizon evoke the pioneers and yeomen of an early America moving ever westward to create new settlements in the open spaces, where they could rear families by working the land. The Lomans' "small, fragile-seeming home" suggests a later stage of American history, linked to and growing out of the pioneer era, of modest homes in a human-scale community. Their home is fragile indeed, a "dream rising out of reality" represented by the faceless apartment buildings of modern, urban America. In the very opening words of the first stage direction, Miller provides a notation on American history and thereby introduces one of the play's major themes.

For surely Willy's tragedy arises in part from the fact that he is a victim. He has uncritically accepted the softest and easiest parts of the American Dream and guided his life by them. Success is to be measured by outward, visible signs, primarily material wealth. And material wealth is to be achived through an outgoing personality, physical beauty, and luck. It is in every way appropriate that Willy is a salesman, for that calling, as Charley poignantly declares in the Requiem, requires only "a smile and a shoeshine." Willy has spent a lifetime committed to those propositions ceaselessly drummed into American consumers: "personality always wins the day"; big advertising means high quality; and physical beauty, athletic prowess, and being well-liked assure success.

But if Willy is a victim of forces outside himself that he neither creates nor controls (as Oedipus is a victim of the gods), he is also a victim of his own deeply flawed character. He has lived a long life of confused values, double standards, and hypocrisies that ultimately tear him apart. He knows that his responsibility as a parent is to see that his sons do their homework, and yet he encourages Biff to slight his studies (and ridicules Bernard for being studious); he condones when he should condemn his boys' theft of lumber and Biff's theft of the football. And, most devastatingly, he is exposed to Biff as a tawdry philanderer. It is not an exaggeration to say that his relationship to Biff captures all the contradictions of Willy's pathetic life, those false values that have destroyed him. But, until the very end, Willy is unable to recognize and accept Biff's offering.

Many critics of *Death of a Salesman* have argued that Willy cannot be a tragic figure because he lacks, among other things, that ultimate self-awareness of the tragic heroes of classic dramas. In the introduction to his *Collected Plays,* Miller responded to this criticism by saying, "Had Willy been unaware of his separation from values that endure he would have died contentedly while polishing his car, probably on a Sunday afternoon with a ball game coming over the radio." The point is an important one, for while Willy does not achieve the depth of insight of an Oedipus or an Othello, he does come to recognize the falseness of the life he has lived, his "separation from the values that endure, as Miller puts it. In fact, his entire play could be described as Willy's unsuccessful struggle to fend off that awareness.

While the action in the present is realistic and objective, the flashbacks occur inside Willy's mind (Miller's original title for the play was *The Inside of His Head*). These flashbacks serve a number of functions. For one thing, they powerfully dramatize Willy's precarious emotional state and reveal a protagonist increasingly unable to live in the present. Sometimes, Willy returns to a happier period, when the boys were young and everything still seemed possible. But, as noted earlier, these events represent more than a simple flight from an unbearable present to a happy past, for Willy seems to select episodes that he half-consciously realizes provide clues to why he has failed so miserably. The sequences involving Ben are more complex, primarily because it is difficult to know how much those reminiscences represent objective reality and how much Willy's fantasy. In any case, as the play progresses, Willy's conversations with Ben cease to be flashbacks from a possibly "real" past and become creations in Willy's mind that mark the depths of his despair. His final conversation with Ben is clearly a dialogue with himself on the advantages of suicide.

Many critics of the play have found Linda one of its weakest characters on the grounds that she is sentimental and obviously a mouthpiece that Miller uses to make generalizations about Willy. She seems to understand the falseness of her husband's life and yet to encourage him in that falseness. The problem, perhaps, is that Miller suggests more complexity in Linda than he dramatizes. In the first stage direction, he tells us that "she has developed an iron repression of her exceptions to Willy's behavior," but those exceptions we never see. In the same stage direction, he goes on to remark that Linda shares Willy's "turbulent longings," but again there is little evidence of that side of her character in the action.

In one of her most important comments, Linda tells her sons that, whatever Willy's faults, "he's a human being . . . So attention must be paid." But if we are to pity Willy only as a helpless human being destroyed by an impersonal society and his own confusions, what we have is merely pathos that leaves us sad but unenlightened. Yet Miller himself has declared that a work that relies on pathos presents a false view of life. Tragedy, on the other hand, brings "not only sadness . . . but knowledge" because it "makes us aware of what the character might have been" and thus of "man's possibilities" (Arthur Miller, "The Nature of Tragedy," *The New York Herald Tribune,* March 27, 1949; reprinted in *The Theatre Essays of Arthur Miller,* ed. Robert A. Martin, New York: Viking Press, 1978, pp. 9–10). In any case, it is clear that the numerous references in the play to the outdoors and the West, to Willy's skill and joy in working with his hands, are meant to represent those possibilities that Willy might have realized. More specifically and concretely, Biff, albeit imperfectly, seems to represent the possibility of escape from the forces and delusions that destroy his father. Standing at his father's grave, it is Biff who recognizes that "there's more of him in that front stoop than in all the sales he ever made" and that "he had the wrong dreams." While Happy remains pathetically bound to the values that destroyed his father, Biff is able to say, "I know who I am."

Whether this recognition is enough to support Miller's contention that his play is a tragedy remains debatable. His own vigorous defense—"Tragedy and the Common Man"—appears in the anthology on p. 247.

Milcha Sanchez-Scott   The Cuban Swimmer   (p. 1486)

The narrative pull of drama, even when read, can be a double-edged sword, as it can keep students interested but at the same time pull them through the text too quickly. Without ignoring the special experience of reading a play, it can be useful to slow students down by reading passages closely in class so that they don't miss the ideas Sanchez-Scott is exploring in *The Cuban Swimmer*. While the suspense of the race and the question whether to pull Margarita out of the water will be clear to students, many things, including moments of satire and the motivations and tensions resulting from the Suárez family's immigrant status, may need to be pulled out of the text.

One way to approach the latter would be to start from an obvious surface characteristic of the play, its mix of English and Spanish. This discussion could even start from the frustration that some students will feel (even with footnotes) at the presence of the Spanish. Rather than skipping past it, stopping and asking those students how their frustration actually illustrates the experience of Abuela and other immigrants can get them thinking about the ways in which different members of the family are motivated by their sense of identity as Cuban Americans. Asking students why the playwright included the helicopter-riding reporters can get them thinking about how public that sense of identity is, how much it is affected by the way Cuban Americans are seen by the majority of Americans and the media.

One other aspect of the play that warrants discussion is the ending, which should be reread carefully in class so that students can work through just what it is that happens and how the playwright presents it (making sure they notice the walking on water and then connect it to the ways in which Margarita is a sacrificial, Christ-like figure should help here).

William Shakespeare Othello (p. 1144)

There are a number of issues to attend to when dealing with *Othello* in an introductory course: (1) What motivates Iago? (2) How is it that so noble a figure as Othello crumbles so badly? (3) What are the implications of Othello's blackness? (4) Why does Desdemona resign herself to Othello's judgment? (5) What is the time scheme of the action? (6) How much of one's response to the play depends on Shakespeare's poetry?

Much critical ink has been spilled in controversy over Iago's character. Is he reasonably motivated to seek his revenge by (1) his anger at being passed over for promotion in favor of an unsoldierly dandy accountant and (2) his suspicion that Othello may have cuckolded him? Or is he a devil incarnate—a man who is evil by disposition, requiring no serious motivation for his destructive actions? Those who urge that Iago is reasonably motivated accept his statements as the basis for his hatred of Othello and Cassio (though he has no grudge against the innocent Desdemona, of course). Those who urge that Iago personifies motiveless human depravity argue that the weak suspicion that Othello has cuckolded him (which Iago himself scarcely believes, saying that it needn't be true—the suspicion itself is enough) is hardly sufficient cause for an experienced, apparently capable, and still well-trusted soldier (he is after all Othello's aide-de-camp) to shatter the lives of all around him. His anger at Othello for advancing Cassio instead of himself also seems a weak motive for bringing about the death of Cassio, Othello, and the innocent Desdemona. Further, his use and treatment of the foolish Roderigo bespeaks a character that cannot be understood as a noble and decent fellow who has been so wronged as to justify his revenge. It may be argued that Iago doesn't from the outset plot to destroy Othello and Desdemona. He asserts that he hates the Moor, but his initial plan results in the disgrace of Cassio. That Cassio loses his commission, however, doesn't at all satisfy Iago, who begins to enmesh Othello in a tragic web of jealousy.

Traditionally, Othello has been played as a large-minded, dignified figure. Such a portrayal raises questions about the rapidity of his emotional collapse. In the third scene of Act III, the very scene in which Iago plants the seed of doubt, Othello already resolves on the murder of both Cassio and Desdemona. And his encounters in Act IV reveal him as a shattered and hysterical shambles of the man he was. Laurence Olivier, in his movie version of *Othello*, cleverly avoids the difficulty by playing Othello as a trifle vain, a successful soldier and an able man, but not a lofty and dignified romantic hero. In Othello's vanity, from the beginning, there is fertile ground for the seeds of jealousy and insecurity that grow so rapidly rank.

Critics have generated some controversy, as well, on the importance of Othello's blackness. Some say it would be wrong to apply modern attitudes about a marriage between a white woman and a black man to Shakespeare's audience. But there is some evidence that Othello's blackness has much to do with his vulnerability to Iago's machinations. The marriage horrifies Desdemona's father—he dies of grief shortly after. It is seen as "unnatural." Othello's blackness is the object of contempt in speeches of Iago. In Act I, he obscenely calls out to Brabantio that a black ram is tupping Brabantio's white ewe and refers to Othello as a Barbary horse. Iago assures Roderigo that Desdemona will soon tire of such exotic and unnatural fare. A good part of Iago's conversation with Roderigo about Desdemona suggests that Desdemona is possessed of a passionate and insatiable sexuality. That is why she mates with the Moor (who, by implication, is a mythically supersexed black man). And it is certainly Othello's blackness at stake when in Act III, Scene 3, Iago succeeds in prompting Othello himself to say, "And yet, how nature erring from itself. . . ." Iago himself supplies the obvious conclusion to that thought, pointing out that Desdemona rejected "many proposed matches / of her own clime, complexion, and degree, / whereto, we see, in all things nature tends; / Foh! one may smell in such, a will most rank, / foul disproportion, thoughts unnatural." The daring Iago, in effect, asks Othello how he can trust a woman so unnatural as to marry a black man like himself. And Othello's self-esteem has been so weakened that the argument is effective. In *White Over Black: American Attitudes Toward the Negro* (1968) the historian Winthrop D. Jordan writes:

> . . . the presumption of heightened sexuality in black men was far from being an incidental or casual association in the minds of Englishmen. How very deeply this association operated is obvious in *Othello,* a drama which loses most of its power and several of its central points if it is read with the assumption that because the black man was the hero English audiences were friendly or perhaps indifferent to his blackness. Shakespeare was writing both about and to his countrymen's feelings concerning physical distinctions between kinds of people; the play is shot through with the language of blackness and sex. Iago goes out of his way to soliloquize upon his own motives: "I hate the Moor, / And it is thought abroad that 'twixt my sheets / He has done my office." Later, he becomes more direct, "For that I do suspect the lusty Moor hath leaped into my seat." It was upon this so obviously absurd suspicion that Iago based his resolve to "turn her virtue into pitch." Such was his success, of course, that Othello finally rushes off "to furnish me with some means of death for the fair devil." With this contorted denomination of Desdemona, Othello unwittingly revealed how deeply Iago's promptings about Desdemona's "own clime, complexion, and degree" had eaten into his consciousness. Othello was driven into accepting the premise that the physical distinction *matters*: "For she had eyes," he has to reassure himself, "and chose me." Then, as his suspicions give way to certainty, he equates her character with his own complexion:

> Her name, that was as fresh,
> As Dian's visage, is now begrim'd and black
> As mine own face.

This important aspect of Iago's triumph over the noble Moor was a subtly inverted reflection of the propositions which Iago, hidden in darkness, worked upon the fair lady's father. No one knew better than Iago how to play upon hidden strings of emotion. Not content with the straightforward crudity that "your daughter and the Moor are now making the beast with two backs," Iago told the agitated Brabantio that "an old black ram / Is tupping your white ewe" and alluded politely to "your daughter cover'd with a Barbary horse." This was not merely the language of (as we say) a "dirty" mind: it was the integrated imagery of blackness and whiteness, of Africa, of the sexuality of beasts and the bestiality of sex. And of course Iago was entirely successful in persuading Brabantio, who had initially welcomed Othello into his house, that the marriage was "against all rules of nature." Brabantio's first reaction betrayed a lurking fear: "This accident is not unlike my dream." Then, as he pondered the prospect, he could only conclude that witchcraft — the unnatural — was responsible; he demanded of Othello what other cause could have brought a girl "so tender, fair, and happy"

> To incur a general mock
> Run from her guardage to the sooty bosom
> Of such a thing as thou.

Altogether a curious way for a senator to address a successful general.

These and similar remarks in the play *Othello* suggest that Shakespeare and presumably his audiences were not totally indifferent to the sexual union of "black" men and "white" women. Shakespeare did not condemn such union; rather, he played upon an inner theme of black and white sexuality, showing how the poisonous mind of a white man perverted and destroyed the noblest of loves by means of bringing to the surface (from the darkness, whence Iago spoke) the lurking shadows of animal sex to assault the whiteness of chastity. Never did "dirty" words more dramatically "blacken" a "fair" name. At the play's climax, standing stunned by the realization that the wife he has murdered was innocent, Othello groans to Emilia, "'Twas I that killed her"; and Emilia responds with a torrent of condemnation or, rather, of expulsive repudiation: "O! the more angel she, / And you the blacker devil." Of Desdemona: "She was too fond of her filthy bargain." To Othello: "O gull! O dolt! / As ignorant as dirt!" Shakespeare's genius lay precisely in juxtaposing these two pairs: inner blackness and inner whiteness. The drama would have seemed odd indeed if his audiences had felt no response to this cross-inversion and to the deeply turbulent double meaning of black *over* white.

It required a very great dramatist to expose some of the more inward biocultural values that led — or drove — Englishmen to accept readily the notion that Negroes were peculiarly sexual men. Probably these values and the ancient reputation of Africa upon which they built were of primary importance in determining the response of Englishmen to Negroes. Whatever the importance of biologic elements in these values — whatever the effects of long northern nights, of living in a cool climate, of possessing light-colored bodies which excreted contrasting lumps of darkness — these values by Shakespeare's time were interlocked with the accretions of English history and, more immediately, with the circumstances of contact with Africans and the social upheaval of Tudor England.

Modern women will doubtless find it difficult to understand why Desdemona acquiesces in her own tragic demise. When Othello strikes her before Lodovico and mocks her, why does she remain submissive? But what else can she do? She is Othello's wife at a time when wives had few rights. She is on an island separated from her family and friends. She has, in short, no alternative but to hope that her virtue and innocence will triumph over whatever strange disorder afflicts Othello. Instructors who wish to pursue the character of Desdemona further might deal with her and her relationship with Othello (and her father) in Freudian terms.

Stephen Reid, in an essay on "Desdemona's Guilt" (*American Imago*, Fall 1970), finds Desdemona a woman bearing so large a burden of guilt for her treatment of her father and for essentially incestuous motives in desiring Othello (a father figure to her) that she not only acquiesces in her punishment at Othello's hands but actually seeks it. It is of course inconceivable that any Elizabethan audience perceived her this way, and only a very few psychoanalytically oriented among a modern audience might. But this play is after all clearly a psychological drama. Iago acts in ways not explained by his rationale. So does Desdemona in marrying (unnaturally) the older Moor. So does Othello, consumed so quickly and thoroughly by jealousy. Hence a psychoanalytic discussion might prove quite stimulating and provide provocative insights, however foreign it appears to the conventional response the play generates. Perhaps, using the method of Norman B. Holland in *The Dynamics of Literary Response*, the viewer or reader of *Othello* might ask, How do I feel as the play ends—

terrified, upset, purged (of "bad" emotions), calm . . .? The attempt to illuminate the source of that feeling may provide substantial psychoanalytical insight into the work of art itself.

Critics have often noted that the elapsed time in the play is extremely short. Othello elopes with Desdemona and on the same night takes ship for Cyprus. Cassio is disgraced the first night after their arrival in Cyprus, and Desdemona is killed on the second night. Despite the rapidity of the action, audiences do not seem to feel that events transpire too quickly. Yet close examination of the text reveals many references to a more remote past. Iago tells Othello that "I lay with Cassio lately" (Act III, Scene 3); Bianca complains of Cassio's long neglect (Act III, Scene 4) despite the fact that he has been on Cyprus only one day; Othello questions Emilia about his wife's behavior, though they married only the night before taking ship; Emilia finds the handkerchief Iago had "a hundred times" asked her to steal—but when and why? There are other illusions to past time, but these suffice to illustrate the way the dramatist provides a backdrop for the impetuous action of the play. Close examination reveals that many of these allusions are quite senseless, yet they seem to work well.

The language of *Othello* is doubtless a serious obstacle for many students. Not only the archaic language but the verse speeches themselves may interfere with students' response to the play. Yet, finally, it is the poetry upon which much depends. Note that characters speak differently. Iago, in his prose discussions with Roderigo, is direct and colloquial, in contrast to his verse speeches to Othello. Cassio, in Act II, Scene 1, speaks a particularly mannered and artificial language. He is here the dandy courtier, straining the language for wit and fulsome praise of Desdemona. On the other hand, Othello speaks quite differently of his beloved (Act III, Scene 3). Consider the images Iago uses in his speech on the supposed lechery of Cassio and Desdemona (Act III, Scene 3). And in Act IV, Scene 1, when Othello believes he has seen Cassio boast to Iago of his conquest of Desdemona and determines that both shall die, he thinks of Desdemona's virtues and reveals his condition in a finely cadenced line: " —but yet the pity of it, Iago! O! Iago, the pity of it, Iago!" And discuss the poetic qualities of Othello's last long speech, beginning "Soft you, a word or two before you go." No one speaks like this; the dialogue is not realistic. But its poetic qualities, to those who listen carefully with an ear for appropriate imagery, are a most pleasing part of the drama.

Sophocles Antigonê (p. 514)

Most students will have little difficulty in understanding the great theme that the play explores: the head-on clash between the duty imposed by divine authority and the duty imposed by the state. In contrast to much modern drama, however, *Antigonê* explores questions of great religious and political moment in the lives of characters whose destinies are inseparable from the destiny of the city-state. It is important to understand that the public nature of *Antigonê* was characteristic of all ancient Greek drama. Drama apparently developed out of the religious dances of primitive tribes, and the few early Greek plays that have survived, including *Antigonê,* were written for public festivals.

By Sophocles' time, the dramatic tragedy seems to have been fully formalized. It opened with a prologue that provided the necessary exposition for the story about to unfold. The parodos, which followed immediately, marked the entrance of the chanting chorus (in *Antigonê,* the parodos reminds the audience of the events immediately preceding the action of the play, the chorus expressing a joyful optimism that the action will belie). The major part of the play consisted of episodes—that is, the dramatic narrative itself, interspersed with the commentary and lyric odes of the chorus. The play ended with the exodos, which concludes with the commentary of the chorus.

The Greek playwright invariably based his play on a famous legend or half-legend whose outlines were no doubt familiar to his audience. The story of the divine curse pronounced on the Theban royal family—to which Oedipus and his children, Antigonê, Ismenê, Eteocles, and Polyneices, belonged—was known to Sophocles' audience in many versions. Sophocles' originality lay not in inventing a story but in creating out of a well-known legend a particular plot that embodied his own interpretation of the legend's meaning.

This historical knowledge will help students cope with the unfamiliar form of the play and help them to understand why the play seems to lack the careful motivation and exploration of character that we associate with modern literature. We expect character development in dramatic narratives, and yet Antigonê remains unchanged from beginning to end. It is Creon, of course, who changes profoundly during the course of the action, but many students will find his change so abrupt that it is unbelievable: at one moment, he is accusing everyone of being anarchists and sell-outs; the next he admits he has been wrong and desperately tries to undo what he has done.

Protagoras, the famous Sophist and a contemporary of Sophocles, formulated the most celebrated statement of the fifth-century secular attack on religious truths: "Man is the measure of all things." It is not a large step for a king to move from this position to the assertion that "The State is the King," as Creon declares to Haimon. But Sophocles' play itself is evidence that this kind of secularism was by no means triumphant — on the contrary, it constituted for many a dangerous and arrogant blasphemy that the gods would punish. With Antigonê, Teiresias, and (to a degree) the chorus ranged against him, Creon is not so confident of his rectitude as he pretends. Indeed, the intemperateness of his reactions — to Antigone, to Haimon, to Teiresias, to the sentry — suggests that Creon is in fact beset by doubts and fears. If such a reading is correct, then his sudden reversal makes a good deal of sense.

Creon's character is more complex than students may at first perceive and is certainly more complex than the character of Antigonê. This, coupled with the fact that Antigonê disappears two-thirds of the way through the play, has led many critics of the play to view Creon, rather than Antigonê, as the protagonist. These critics note that it is Creon who suffers doubts and fears and is finally shown to be wrong, whereas Antigonê remains, from beginning to end, unwaveringly convinced that she is right. If we expect the protagonist to exhibit doubts and uncertainties, some weakness of character or judgment, then Creon rather than Antigone is certainly the protagonist.

Others see Antigonê as the protagonist, the tragic heroine. The play bears her name, she dominates the prologue, and, despite her absence from the stage during the final part, it is her heroic defiance that sets everything in motion and permeates the action, even when she is not present. In the name of honor, family, and divine injunction, and in the face of the overwhelming physical and temporal power of the king and state, she risks everything, including her life, to do what she never doubts is right.

A third view is based upon Hegel's conception of tragedy as the dramatic representation of the clash between two opposing and antithetical forces, both of them right but (tragically) irreconcilable. In this view, then, it is not that Creon is wrong and Antigonê right, but rather that both represent forces that have clashed throughout human history: the family versus the state, the laws of God versus the laws of man. The tragedy, according to Hegel, results precisely because the opposing claims are both valid.

The role of Haimon is interesting, especially in light of the fact that he and Antigonê never appear together. It is probable that Sophocles does not bring them together because he wishes to keep the attention of the audience focused on the single and central issue: the confrontation between Antigonê and Creon. It would be difficult to imagine a love scene between Antigonê and Haimon that would not significantly alter the characterization of Antigonê, either by showing her momentarily weakening out of love for her betrothed or by showing Haimon agreeing with Antigone and thus exhibiting disrespect toward his father. In addition, the absence of such a scene effectively underscores the tremendously disruptive forces set in motion by Creon's obstinate refusal to let Antigonê bury her brother. These forces doom their love and, as Haimon points out to his father, are creating dangerous unrest among the citizens of Thebes.

The critical consensus is that the play vindicates Antigonê's position. Yet her character deserves some comment. From the confrontation with her sister in the prologue to her final appearance, she appears to be virtually untouched by doubt and human compassion. She explains to Ismenê in the prologue what she has decided to do and then invites her not to join with her or discuss the matter but flatly to "prove what you are: / A true sister, or a traitor to your family." While she later asserts that "I'll join anyone in loving, but not in hating," she coldly rejects the contrite Ismenê's decision to share the punishment: "don't / Lay claim to what you haven't done." Antigonê seems, in fact, to be dominated not by the living reality of sister, lover, and king but rather by the abstract sense of family duty. She appears in part to desire her death as the conclusive means of triumphing over Creon and as the foreordained result of her birth.

Frequently, the chorus in Greek tragedy served as a commentator on the action from the point of view of traditional or normative values. In *Antigonê*, the chorus is an integral part of the whole, functioning not so much as a "norm" but as a concerned and at times bewildered participant in the unfolding events.

Sophocles Oedipus Rex (p. 194)

Oedipus, like *Antigonê*, deals with the question of secular versus divine authority. But students will probably find *Oedipus* more difficult because, unlike *Antigonê*, it does not dramatize a conflict of institutions—the laws of God versus the laws of man—that has numerous and familiar modern analogues. In both plays (as in all classic tragedy) the destiny of the state is inseparably linked to the fate of the protagonists, but in *Oedipus*, Sophocles focuses upon the eternal mystery of human existence—of fate, or destiny, versus free will—without the explicit theme of political power that gives *Antigonê* its sharp clarity. Unlike Creon in *Antigonê*, Oedipus confronts no human and intransigent antagonist. As he comes to learn, to his horror, he faces only himself and the gods.

Accustomed to the facile and flattering dramatizations of human existence in slick fiction and television, where justice usually triumphs, students may be distressed and baffled by the fate of Oedipus. What has Oedipus done to deserve such a horrible fate? Incest and patricide certainly deserve severe punishment, but Oedipus is guilty of neither, since he did not know that the man he murdered was his father or that the woman he married was his mother. Add to this the fact that these critical events in Oedipus's life were divinely preordained before his birth and it would seem that Oedipus is the passive victim of some mordant cosmic joke, certainly not responsible for what happens to him.

In one sense, there can be no satisfactory answer to this question, since such an answer would penetrate that irreducible mystery of human existence that is the very subject of Sophocles' drama. No matter how strong one is, no matter how wealthy and powerful, one may abruptly be reduced to dishonor and despair. Indeed, this plunge from the heights to the depths is the peculiar province of tragedy, which tells us that happiness and power are never fully within our control and that when we are actively working for our own happiness, power, loved ones, and civic good, the results may be disastrously different from what we had hoped for.

Yet the great classic tragedies, notably *Oedipus*, do not present us with a vision of a mechanical universe, one in which moral choices have no meaning. Central to Sophocles' vision is a paradox or mystery similar to that of Christian theology: God is omniscient and has foreknowledge, and yet human will is free and humans therefore create (and must take responsibility for) their destiny. If, then, Oedipus seems on the one hand the hapless victim of divine vengeance, he is on the other hand a man whose success and power have induced an arrogant pride that leads him to contemptuously deny divine authority.

In the prologue, we see Oedipus at the height of his power. While there is a suggestion of both the irony that saturates the action as it unfolds ("Sick as you are, not one is as sick as I," l. 63) and the pride that will contribute to his downfall ("Then once more I must bring what is dark to light," l. 134), Oedipus is dignified and self-possessed, admirable in his genuine concern for the plight of Thebes. Perhaps most significant in terms of Oedipus's character, however, is his speculation, upon learning that the old murder of Laios must be avenged before the plague will be lifted, that the motive for the murder was political and that, therefore, he himself may be in danger (ll. 140–43). While Oedipus seeks the help of Apollo, his first reaction to the news suggests a narrowly secular and political view.

That view is given full expression in Scene I. When Teiresias ("the holy prophet / In whom, alone of all men, truth was born," ll. 82–83), under Oedipus's peremptory prodding, directly tells the king that he is the source of the city's pollution, Oedipus becomes abusive and accuses him of complicity with Creon in a political plot. His attack on Teiresias in this scene reveals the two related traits of his character that make him responsible for his own ultimate fate: a fiery, explosive temper and blasphemous contempt for Apollo's holy prophet.

These traits are exhibited further in Scene II. None of Creon's reasonable arguments can touch the irrational fury of Oedipus (it is interesting to note that in *Antigonê* Creon the king falls into precisely the same trap as Oedipus). The first part of this scene provides further and deepening evidence of Oedipus's inability to entertain even the mere possibility that he might be anything but the savior of Thebes or that he, rather than Creon, is "evil incarnate" (l. 111). In the long dialogue that concludes the scene, Iocaste recounts the story of her child left to die in the mountains in order to convince Oedipus that Teiresias could not be right. It is a consummately skillful scene, for while it provides important expository material (for both Oedipus and the audience), the information is charged now with dramatic tension and irony. Iocaste's information seems to prove that he could not be Laios's murderer and yet evokes ominous recollections that point directly at him. And Oedipus's description of the murders at the crossroads ("I killed him. / I killed them all," ll. 287–88) offers further evidence of his rash and violent temper.

Irony deepens in Scene III as Oedipus and Iocaste seize upon and exult in the messenger's news that Polybos is dead. The joy is short-lived, for almost immediately the messenger informs Oedipus that Polybos was not his father. With the ringing declaration that "the truth must be made known" (l. 146), and in the face of Iocaste's desperate attempts to dissuade him, Oedipus insists upon pursuing the question of his parentage. From the point of view of Oedipus, what began as a search for the murderer of Laios has become a search for his identity—a supreme irony, since, as Oedipus will soon learn, both quests are one. Despite the mounting evidence that Apollo has spoken through Teiresias, Oedipus turns away from the truth with the facile assumption that the queen is fearful that he was born of lowly parents. Thus, poised on the edge of the horrible truth, Scene III ends with Oedipus at his most optimistic, declaring with outrageous pride that "I / Am a child of Luck: I can not be dishonored" (ll. 160–61).

Scene IV is, appropriately, the shortest of the four scenes. Oedipus's character is fully developed and all the relevant facts but one are known to the king. With the revelation by the shepherd in this scene that Oedipus is the son of Laios, the door of Oedipus's fate clicks closed. That fact fixes all the others into a single and unambiguous pattern from which there can be no escape. The haughty king, "child of Luck," can now describe himself accurately: "damned in his birth, in his marriage damned, / Damned in the blood he shed with his own hand!" (ll. 72–73).

The exodos serves a number of functions. Most importantly, it reminds us that the intensely personal quest of Oedipus was undertaken to rescue the *community*. Now restored to health and with Creon in firm control, Thebes will flourish with a renewed faith (we can assume) in Apollo's divine power and justice. The exodos underscores that justice by showing us the chastened Oedipus accepting responsibility for the fate that has befallen him. The acceptance involves a total recognition of the mysterious interaction of fate and free will, for when the choragos asks Oedipus what god drove him to blind himself, he replies that Apollo "brought my sick, sick fate upon me. / But the blinding hand was my own!" (ll. 112–13).

The chorus and the choragos often represent the feelings and attitudes of the community. The chorus responds to the unfolding events with temperateness and compassion and a constant concern that the major characters not lose sight of their civic responsibilities, though as Ode III, for example, makes clear, it is not privy to any special insight or knowledge. The choragos, in contrast, often plays an important role in the dramatic action, introducing characters, providing exposition, mediating arguments, and, above all, reminding the characters (especially Oedipus) in their passions that obedience to Apollo requires reasonableness.

Since Sophocles' audience knew the story of Oedipus, its interest for them (as for us) lay in the artistic skills the dramatist brought to the task. Nowhere is that skill more powerfully demonstrated than in the irony that saturates the play, particularly in the images of light and dark, blindness and vision. When, in the prologue, Apollo's will is made known, Oedipus nobly declares that "once more I must bring what is dark to light" (l. 134), unaware that — unlike the darkness he brought to light years earlier by answering the riddle of the Sphinx — in so doing he will bring a terrible darkness into his own life. When, later in the prologue, he mocks Teiresias's blindness, Apollo's prophet declares that it is he, Oedipus, who, despite his eyes, is blind.

The equation of physical blindness with the capacity to know spiritual truth (the blind prophet appears throughout history and literature) underscores the religious conviction that human physical senses and human ability to reason can never lead to truth. It might be fair to say that they are a trap, leading one into disastrous pride. In this connection, it might be said that the trap for Oedipus was sprung when, through the use of his rational powers, he answered the riddle of the Sphinx. The memory of that great event, which he reminds his antagonists of in the prologue contributes significantly to his overweening confidence that he "sees." Unlike the earlier riddle, however, the one he must now solve — the identity of Laios's murderer — will not lead to fortune and power but to disgrace and exile, and also to humility and insight.

Wole Soyinka   The Lion and the Jewel   (p. 891)

The fundamental issue in this lighthearted, romantic comedy is the struggle between traditional Yoruba village life and the relentless incursion of western attitudes and technology that threaten to undermine those traditions. And, though the play dates from 1963, that struggle continues throughout an Africa enduring the commotion and pain of a difficult postcolonial rebirth. Furthermore, the very form of the play exhibits certain aspects of the cultural collisions that it seeks to illuminate. The European formal structure of the drama (Soyinka, after all, studied drama in England) is wonderfully modified by the mime, drum, and dance sequences that reflect Yoruba performance traditions. Those sequences might well be the most impressive part of a performance of this play; alas, few readers will be able to fully imagine the visual and emotional excitement of such a performance.

Commentaries on this play generally ignore its verse form — a loose arrangement of free verse lines that vary in the number of stressed syllables per line — that bestows a distinctive rhythm to the dialogue. Though one can't be sure what Soyinka was up to (formally speaking), he might have been attempting to weave a weft of lilting Nigerian speech rhythms into a warp of Shakespearean blank verse. The durable test to determine whether the lines are poetry is to add or subtract a word at the end of each line and evaluate the result. As poetic entities, most of the lines of dialogue here would be damaged by that experiment.

The village beauty Sidi creates the tension that drives a simple plot. Two men, representing wholly different attitudes, are infatuated with her. Lakunle, the village schoolmaster, presumably represents progress and enlightenment — but Soyinka lampoons him. Dressed in ill-fitting English clothes, given to pompous pronouncements, his foolish attempts to project progressive views become a mockery of modernity. And the hypocrisy of his westernized courtship gallantry is revealed by his peculiar medieval pronouncements about the proper place of women. The wily and somewhat corrupt village chief Baroka, despite his age, wishes to add Sidi to his contingent of wives. And as the play unfolds, we discover that the buffoonish Lakunle has no chance against the crafty old chief. Despite her tearful complaint at being seduced by the presumably impotent Baroka, ultimately, Sidi chooses power and status in the village over the ersatz Europeanization offered by the schoolmaster.

The Morning section of the play establishes the principal relationships and issues that impede Lakunle's courtship. He refuses to submit to the Yoruba tradition that requires him to pay a "bride-price" to Sidi's family. Either he is, as Sidi suspects, too miserly to make that payment or, as he repeatedly asserts, too principled to submit to the commercialization of his grand romantic commitment. By insisting on European conceptions of romantic love that prevent him from "purchasing" Sidi as a chattel, he blinds himself to a tradition that perceives the bride-price not as the retail price of a bride but as a concrete and public display of the value the suitor places on his beloved (a western parallel might be a lavish diamond engagement ring). Lakunle simply refuses to understand Sidi's position. She frets that marrying him without the payment of a bride-price would be the ultimate humiliation—marrying a man who perceives her as having no value at all would destroy her status in the village. Add to this substantive impediment Sidi's mocking responses to Lakunle's overblown and poetic courtship rhetoric. What could be more devastating to a lover than having his figurative speech reduced to inane foolishness? When Lakunle croons: "Sidi, my love will open your mind / Like the chaste leaf in the morning, when / The sun first touches it." She savagely responds: "If you start that I will run away. / I had enough of that nonsense yesterday."

The return of the "stranger with the one-eyed box" introduces the second part of this first act. That photographer has returned with a "book" (more likely a magazine) featuring a sexy photo-spread of Sidi. Worse, the diminutive picture of the village chief places him next to the village latrine—both the size and context represent a serious breach of protocol that adds a perilous dimension to Sidi's untrammeled pride in her celebrity. The photographer's return is also the occasion for a remarkable mimed and musical retelling of his earlier visit to the village. The scene ends with the humiliated Lakunle chased offstage by a band of women, and the stirring of a new idea in Baroka's head: "Yes, yes . . . it is five full months since last / I took a wife . . . five full months. . . ."

The brief Noon section provides three elements. First, it displays Sidi's enormous vanity, the result of the photo-spread that, in her own mind, has made her a world-famous celebrity. Second, it provides Lakunle the opportunity to direct the mimed scene illustrating Baroka's wiliness. The chief bribes the engineer to reroute the train tracks that would have threatened the village's isolation and thus threatened not only its traditional values but also his own authority within the village. Third, it reveals Baroka's desire for Sidi, whose haughty rejection he plots to circumvent by "confessing" to his gossipy head wife, Sadiku, that he has become impotent. Thus Sidi would have nothing to fear from dining with him.

The Evening section displays the carefully calibrated seduction of Sidi against a background of what must be, for her, exciting wrestling games. These are power struggles, and though they occur between men, they foreshadow the struggle between Sidi and the chief. Baroka (knowing that she thinks him impotent) plays her like a fish, and capitalizing on her vanity, easily nets her by offering to put her face on the village postage stamps. The seduction occurs against a series of wild drumming and musical miming that, ironically, portrays, first, a man in flight from aggressive women, then the dance of Baroka's early virility and the satisfied response of Sadiku to the (false) notion that she, and his other wives, have finally drained him of potency. When the deflowered Sidi runs on to the scene, sobbing, we know what's happened. Poor Lakunle, in his final and most foolish gesture, magnanimously offers to marry the damaged Sidi anyway. He is clueless. She will opt for the real, the powerful man—Baroka—and become his jewel, an appropriate tribute to the Lion of Ilujinle.

Some summing up (which might create more questions than answers) needs to be done. Did Sidi do the right thing? Is Baroka the "hero" of the play? Are their any heroes or heroines? When, some years later, Ilujinle is finally swamped by the sophisticated culture of Lagos, will it be a better or a worse place? Will the Lakunles of Nigeria ever find clothes that fit and a nourishing African culture? Will they learn to stop mouthing alien western platitudes, and look to Africa for durable guides for the future?

This play would be a particularly good subject for postcolonial critical analysis (see Glossary of Critical Approaches, p. 1519).

Wendy Wasserstein   Tender Offer   (p. 1250)

This wonderfully rendered moment will not trouble students. Its charm lies in the understated but authentic emotional energy lying beneath the dialogue. The situation is quickly made clear. The father has missed the dance recital in which his nine-year-old daughter performed, and she, disappointed and determined to hide her feelings, retreats to the age-old technique of routine monosyllabic answers. The extraordinary quality of the scene emerges as the antagonists move from the shallow, tense discourse that masks the underlying feelings of father and daughter to the father's recognition of his child's hidden feelings. She, of course, masterfully manipulates him into that recognition by irritating him into a display of anger that allows her to reveal the intensity of her own anger at his nonchalance. "I hate you, Daddy! I hate you!" she shouts as she throws her second-place trophy into the trash. Now she has his full attention. Now he is no longer anxious to just get home. Now, finally, he begins to understand the feelings seething below her terse answers to his clichéd question, "How'd it go?" And now, it is he who procrastinates, he who is no longer so anxious to get home. Perceiving himself guilty of disrespecting his daughter at several levels, he marshals his wits to serve his deep parental love. He makes her a White Knight "tender offer" — the perfect pun to illuminate his deep feelings for her. By the end of the brief scene, he is no longer a harried father, but a loving parent attuned to his daughter's world—a world that is, perhaps, as demandingly complex as his own.

Essays

Maya Angelou Graduation in Stamps (p. 967)

This essay opens with a long and vivid description of and paean to graduation day, one of the most important events in the life of a community, a wonderful time, when "the student body . . . acted like an extended family." The joy and sense of community are, if anything, enhanced by the fact that Lafayette County Training School, as we learn from the next paragraph, is a black school whose physical environs are meager and shabby compared with its white counterpart. Among the graduating seniors, "Only a small percentage would be continuing on to college at one of the South's A&M [agricultural and mechanical] schools, which trained Negro youths to be carpenters, farmers, handymen, masons, maids, cooks and baby nurses" (para. 3).

Angelou then returns to the festive atmosphere of the day, focusing on herself, the "birthday girl" (para. 6), her appearance, her proud academic achievements, and her high hopes for the future: "I was headed for the freedom of open fields," she confidently asserts (para. 9). Henry Reed, the class valedictorian and her academic competitor, has spent weeks preparing his speech, entitled "To Be or Not to Be." Students should note how skillfully Angelou weaves scenes and various time periods into a coherent narrative that moves toward the climactic event, graduation day (beginning with para. 19), and then the ceremony itself (beginning with para. 29).

With the principal's comments (para. 32), the tone of the essay begins to shift. Whereas the first half of the essay has been predominantly descriptive, with a few matter-of-fact references to racism and its effects, the tone now becomes angrier as Angelou reflects on the messages conveyed by both the black principal and the white commencement speaker. The principal's approving references to Booker T. Washington as well as his remarks introducing the speaker evoke an older generation of African Americans, often called Uncle Toms, who accepted the teachings of Booker T. Washington and the racist assumptions underlying Mr. Edward Donleavy's address (paras. 34–39).

Beginning with paragraph 40, the essay becomes a meditation, often angry, on the destructive effects of racism, buttressed by the Washington philosophy that Donleavy's speech represents. The graduating students, so memorably described in the first half of the essay in all their individuality, diversity, ambitions, and disappointments, children of a warm and supportive community, are all reduced to the uniformity of stereotypes. It is indeed, as Angelou recognizes, "the ancient tragedy" of racism being played out in a black school in Arkansas (para. 43). Overwhelmed for a moment by the realization of what it means to be black, she yields to self-doubt, that most destructive effect of racism, and declares, "Donleavy had exposed us" (para. 44). This in turn leads to her rage (para. 46) and violent fantasies (para. 47). She then returns to the ceremony and describes the conclusion to Donleavy's speech (paras. 48–49).

The concluding moments of the program—the reciting of "Invictus" and the valedictory address, "To Be or Not to Be"—ring hollow and impertinent to her ears (paras. 50–54) until suddenly, unexpectedly, Henry Reed, "the conservative, the proper, the A student" (para. 55), turns his back on the audience and begins singing James Weldon Johnson's "Lift Ev'ry Voice and Sing," the Negro national anthem. Slowly, everyone, children and adults, teachers and parents, joins in the singing, which swells into a mighty anthem of healing and hope. "The depths had been icy and dark, but now a bright sun spoke to our souls" (para. 61).

The words of Booker T. Washington quoted in paragraph 32 are drawn from his so-called "Atlanta Compromise" speech, delivered before a predominantly white audience at the Atlanta International Exposition in 1895. Students may find interesting this relevant passage:

> To those of the white race who look to the incoming of those of foreign birth and strange tongue and habits for the prosperity of the South, were I permitted I would repeat what I say to my own race, "Cast down your bucket where

you are." Cast it down among the eight millions of Negroes whose habits you know, whose fidelity and love you have tested in days when to have proved treacherous meant the ruin of your firesides. Cast down your bucket among these people who have, without strikes and labour wars, tilled your fields, cleared your forests, builded your railroads and cities, and brought forth treasures from the bowels of the earth, and helped make possible this magnificent representation of the progress of the South. Casting down your bucket among my people, helping and encouraging them as you are doing on these grounds, and to education of head, hand, and heart, you will find that they will buy your surplus land, make blossom the waste places in your fields, and run your factories. While doing this, you can be sure in the future, as in the past, that you and your families will be surrounded by the most patient, faithful, law-abiding, and unresentful people that the world has seen. As we have proved our loyalty to you in the past, in nursing your children, watching by the sick-bed of your mothers and fathers, and often following them with tear-dimmed eyes to their graves, so in the future, in our humble way we shall stand by you with a devotion that no foreigner can approach, ready to lay down our lives, if need be, in defense of yours, interlacing our industrial, commercial, civil, and religious life with yours in a way that shall make the interests of both races one. In all things that are purely social we can be as separate as the fingers, yet one as the hand in all things essential to mutual progress.

Finally, reprinted below are the texts of "Invictus," the poem that Elouise recites and whose message so infuriates Angelou (para. 50), and of "Lift Ev'ry Voice and Sing" (para. 55):

Invictus

Out of the night that covers me,
    Black as the Pit from pole to pole,
I thank whatever gods may be
    For my unconquerable soul.

In the fell clutch of circumstance
    I have not winced nor cried aloud.
Under the bludgeonings of chance
    My head is bloody, but unbowed.

Beyond this place of wrath and tears
    looms but the Horror of the shade,
And yet the menace of the years
    Finds, and shall find, me unafraid.

It matters not how strait the gate,
    How charged with punishments the scroll,
I am the master of my fate:
    I am the captain of my soul.

Lift Ev'ry Voice and Sing

Lift every voice and sing
Till earth and heaven ring,
Ring with the harmonies of Liberty;
Let our rejoicing rise
High as the listening skies,
Let it resound loud as the rolling sea.
Sing a song full of the faith that the dark past has taught us,
Sing a song full of the hope that the present has brought us,
Facing the rising sun of our new day begun
Let us march on till victory is won.

Stony the road we trod,
Bitter the chastening rod,

Felt in the days when hope unborn had died;
Yet with a steady beat,
Have not our weary feet
Come to the place for which our fathers sighed?
We have come over a way that with tears has been watered,
We have come, treading our path through the blood of the slaughtered,
Out from the gloomy past,
Till now we stand at last
Where the white gleam of our bright star is cast.

God of our weary years,
God of our silent tears,
Thou who has brought us thus far on the way;
Thou who has by Thy might
Led us into the light,
Keep us forever in the path, we pray.
Lest our feet stray from the places, our God, where we met Thee,
Lest, our hearts drunk with the wine of the world, we forget Thee;
Shadowed beneath Thy hand,
May we forever stand.
True to our God,
True to our native land.

Meredith Besser   Perry Mason, Parakeets, and Gorgonzola
(p. 1273)

Students will understand this essay without difficulty. Hence, it might be interesting to direct attention to the artfulness of the piece. The dreamt escape of the caged parakeet, for example, suggests a sort of Freudian symbolic foreshadowing of the real flight of the speaker's lover that follows. Neither the bird in her dream nor (presumably) the ungrateful lover will submit to caging. As a matter of style, the speaker's short, rhetorically parallel sentences create and then satisfy expectations in the reader. For example: "Perry Mason appears to be. . . . Perry Mason hasn't met. . . . Perry Mason is someone I would probably date. Why can't men be more like Perry Mason?" Then later, "Why can't men be more like parakeets?"—particularly that successfully rescued, tamed, and grateful parakeet in her apartment. And finally, "Why can't men be more like gorgonzola?" Perry Mason, parakeets, and gorgonzola, unlike the men she dates, all function properly in her life. They champion justice, reveal gratitude for attention, and provide pleasurable tastes. Alas, unlike those three stable features of her life, the men she systematically improves—who become more confident, find better jobs, cars, and homes under her tutelage—invariably flee. And with cooler weather coming, she will keep the front door shut—not only to keep the parakeet in, but also to keep those miserable men, who infect her life, out.

Judith Ortiz Cofer   American History   (p. 347)

The unusual title of this gentle essay raises questions. In what sense does the essay investigate American history? It begins by describing the effect of Kennedy's assassination on the Puerto Rican residents of "El Building"—the Paterson, New Jersey, dilapidated apartment house where the author lived. But Kennedy's assassination is part of America's political history, and Cofer seems to be more concerned with America's social history. She describes the migrations through her neighborhood "the Italians, the Irish, the Jews, . . . the Puerto Ricans, and the blacks." The narrator is deeply conscious of roots and race, and this essay, simultaneously, speaks of the cultural divide that separates and the human condition that brings together.

The evidence of a pervasive racism in Cofer's school and city permeates the essay. The African American girls taunt Elena for eating pork chops, rice, and beans for breakfast. Though she is a straight-A student, she is denied entrance to the honor classes open to Eugene (because English is not her first language). Mr. DePalma, stung by the insensitivity of the African American and Puerto Rican children, calls them idiots. "I should have known [the president's death] wouldn't mean anything to a bunch of losers like you kids." And the narrator herself reveals a systemic awareness of race and religion. She watches the Jewish couple who live in the building. She notices a Jewish man in Mario's drugstore. She is aware of the energy and the heat of the African American girls in a climate that always chills her. She is aware of Eugene's white southern origins.

At the same time, we learn that Elena's and Eugene's mothers are both unhappy, both feeling bitterly displaced. Both mothers exhibit profound sorrow and regret at the death of Kennedy. Both yearn for a better life. Elena's family dreams of owning a house in the suburbs and, one day, retiring back to their native Puerto Rico. Eugene's mother clearly yearns to return to some idyllic southern grace nonexistent in dingy, industrial Paterson. One excuse for her brutal rejection of Elena is that "We won't be in this place much longer."

Elena's confrontation with American history is devastating. A charismatic president much admired by the underclass is murdered. And, certainly much worse for Elena, her attempt to make a friend who shares her passion for reading is destroyed by the deeply ingrained racism that her mother understands. "You are forgetting who you are. . . . You are heading for humiliation and pain," her mother warns. But what could prepare Elena for Eugene's mother, whose first observation about Puerto Ricans is "I don't know how you people do it." And because she has been relegated to "you people," Elena is denied even the simple pleasure of enjoying a friendship with a fellow student who is her emotional and intellectual peer. Her tears that night are not for the dead president but for herself. The common human aspirations of both mothers are insufficient to bridge the deep abyss of racism.

At the end of the essay, Elena watches the beautiful lacelike white snow fall. She does not look down to see it turning gray in the dingy streets of an American city where, apparently, most things are sullied by an American history incorporating both the death of Kennedy and the murder of a young girl's spirit.

Bernard Cooper   A Clack of Tiny Sparks: Remembrances of a Gay Boyhood   (p. 339)

Coming of age, along with love and death, is surely one of the main themes of literature, and this remarkable autobiographical examination of a middle-school boy's struggle to understand his emerging homosexuality invites students to consider their own green dreams and adolescent insecurities. You might want to pair it with James Joyce's "Araby"—a fictional, though even more anguished, account of heterosexual yearning.

The essay begins and ends with the enigmatic Theresa Sanchez—a hopelessly cosmopolitan sophisticate in the eyes of the speaker, but a fourteen-year-old schoolgirl nonetheless. Only as an adult does the speaker realize that Theresa and the reviled Bobby Keagan would have been his natural mates. As a child, he feels socially inferior to Theresa, and dares not risk the taunts that a friendship with Bobby might cause. And when Theresa cooly asks, "Are you a fag?" his conditioned response is predictable—he denies the characterization that would devastatingly stigmatize him. Like all adolescents, he wants to be accepted—not shunned like the "gentle, intelligent, introverted" Bobby Keagan. Out of ignorance and fear, he "became the scientist of my own desire, plotting ways to change my yearning for boys into a yearning for girls." Boyish enough to be invited to a make-out party, he discovers the implacable truth. His dutiful kisses serve no purpose—he yearns for the popular and athletic Grady.

Concrete and detailed images characterize Cooper's writing. In an interview, he revealed a distaste for abstractions. He avoids "Large Issues and Big Ideas. The world seems real and vivid and meaningful to me in the smaller details, what's heard and felt and smelled and tasted." From the outset, this essay illustrates Cooper's skill with details, down to the "gauzy photograph of a woman biting a strand of pearls, head thrown back in an attitude of ecstasy" that decorates the cover of Theresa's illicit book.

The speaker's seminal mistake is asking his mother (though he knew quite well) what a "fag" is. Her hysterical response (does she, after all, have the same prescience that Theresa exhibited?) makes his precarious position clear to him and, of course, adds to his misery. The discussion around the lox reveals his parents' essential hypocrisy. They urge him to taste the smoked fish, to live a little: "Expand your horizons. Try new things." One new thing was the high school make-out party, but that experience only served to reaffirm his dilemma — he is drawn to Grady, not to the girls he awkwardly embraces. That whole scene, under the direction of the determined hostess, sounds more like a military exercise than a sexually charged event.

Our favorite line in this essay is Mr. Hubbley's evaluation of Theresa Sanchez: "No wonder she flunked out of school. . . . Her head was always in a book." The observation is more than an easy joke. Theresa, we discover (despite the wild rumors surrounding her disappearance), has transferred to a "progressive" school, where they "don't have grades or bells and you get to study whatever you want." This voracious and omnivorous reader will surely flourish there. And it is not difficult to agree with her evaluation of Joseph Le Conte Junior High — "this place is so . . . barbaric."

Had this been fiction, Cooper might have ended his essay without the last two paragraphs. Contrast Cooper's ending with the ending of Joyce's "Araby." What might Joyce have added, were he writing an essay? Certainly, Cooper has an agenda. Now an adult and at ease with his sexual life, he regrets the terror that bedeviled his childhood, and wants others just now coming of age to profit from his experience. He regrets that he didn't level with Theresa, but true to the power of concrete detail, his final words imagine that other path, enriched by both Theresa's cooking and a delicious nimbus of alliteration: "hamburger Stroganoff, Swedish meatballs in a sweet translucent sauce, steaming slabs of Salisbury Steak."

Joan Didion   On Morality   (p. 334)

We find, among the earliest written records, law codes and stories that depict the vengeance of angry gods. Doubtless, questions of morality — including definitions of "right" and "wrong" — tormented humans even before writing was invented. Joan Didion, asked to "think . . . in some abstract way" about "morality," finds the task both difficult and troubling. She asserts at the outset that she distrusts the word *morality*; it is a powerful, hence dangerous, abstraction, and she prefers particulars to abstractions. Yet there is a kind of wagon-train morality she respects, manifested in particular acts — protecting dead bodies from coyotes or keepng a vigil during the search for a drowned husband. For Didion, such acts represent deeply felt humanity. Similarly, she perceives the tragedy of the Donner-Reed party as a moral failure — these people had "somehow breached their primary loyalties, or they would not have found themselves helpless in the mountain winter" (para. 4). Didion is not uncomfortable with a definition of "morality" that celebrates simple humanity — the "promises we make to one another."

As she sits in her motel room, Didion is content that the jukebox song "Baby the Rain Must Fall" (a nice allusion to the essentially amoral quality of nature) drowns out the old folks' prayer sing. The old folks' belief that the *rock of ages* is, in fact, *cleft for me* threatens her sanity — she distrusts the fierce moral codes that are based on abstract religious conviction.

She goes on to demonstrate her profound distrust of abstract morality — of adherence to a set of principles that justifies betrayal and murder in the name of "conscience." The standard litany of traitors and murderers is, "I did what I thought was right." Among them Didion lists Klaus Fuchs, who, while working for the United States and Great Britain, sent atomic bomb secrets to the Soviet Union; the Mormons who planned and incited the massacre of over one hundred "gentiles" at Mountain Meadows; and Alfred Rosenberg, the "Grand Inquisitor" of Nazi Germany. Students should have little trouble compiling an up-to-date list of others who justify and commit terrorism against innocents in the name of "morality." The horror generated by those who argue that "I followed my own conscience" puts Didion in mind of a passage from Norman Mailer's *The Deer Park* in which a character invokes a nuclear cataclysm to "clear the rot and the stench and the stink" once and for all.

Didion quotes Lionel Trilling's pithy observation that the "enlightened interest" of the powerful ultimately ends in coercion. This tendency toward coercion is precisely what Didion fears from those who act upon abstract "moral imperative[s]."

"Then is when we join the fashionable madmen, and then is when the thin whine of hysteria is heard in the land, and then is when we are in bad trouble" (para. 9).

E. L. Doctorow Why We Are Infidels (p. 667)

"Why We Are Infidels" is one of the William E. Massey, Sr., lectures in the history of American civilization, published, together with the others, as *Reporting the Universe* (Harvard University Press, 2003). Doctorow examines a curious paradox: Americans, on the one hand, inhabiting a "God-soaked country" must, by law, relegate their religious behavior to the private sector, while at the same time allowing a plethora of contending and contentious religious groups to enjoy the freedom to pursue whatever theological grail they desire. We are "infidels" because our government is forbidden to promote any religion, and we are infidels because the diversity of religions that flourish here prevents us, presumably, from embracing the one true faith, and we are infidels because many of us are atheists. Technically, of course, infidel means unfaithful—but, alas, the term *infidel* applies not only to atheists but also to those that someone in the know perceives to be devoted to the wrong conception of god.

And the mind-boggling variety of religions we Americans "tolerate" owes their existence, Doctorow suggests, to our desire to find "spiritual release from the society we have made out of secular humanism." The sentence, concluding paragraph 3, provides a nice focus for a number of debates. Do we, here in America, really have a secular, humanistic society? How does such a social and political order differ from a theocracy? Would a majority of Americans choose a theocratic state if they could? What would be its nature? Would the extraordinary diversity of religious organizations in America preclude the possibility of a theocratic state in the absence of our constitution? Might religious diversity create warfare in America as it has done in the Asian subcontinent, in Africa, and in the Middle East? And most significantly, why do citizens need "spiritual release"? Just what is spiritual release, and what relationship does it bear to secular humanism?

The word *infidel* is associated with Islamic theocrats. But when Christian fundamentalists, whose political aims became increasingly insistent and successful at the time this essay was written (October 2004), interpret disastrous events as God's well-deserved judgment on our apostate nation for tolerating abortion, homosexuality, feminism—anything they disapprove of—they join as equal partners with those orthodox Islamists who dedicate themselves to finding a final solution to the existence of infidels anywhere. The two prominent Christian fundamentalists Doctorow alludes to are Jerry Falwell and Pat Robertson—both media-savvy televangelists. And as Doctorow concludes, they honor the foreign killers of nearly 3,000 Americans on September 11, 2001, as agents of God's justice.

In the middle of the fourth paragraph Doctorow reveals his literary (rather than theological or sociological) credentials in a sentence rhetorically designed to persuade his readers with wit, rather than win them with logic: "And while it is precisely because of this principle of religious freedom that we enjoy such a continuous national uproar of praying and singing and studying and fasting and confessing and atoning and praising and preaching and dancing and dunking and vowing and quaking and shaking and abstaining and ordaining, a paradox arises from this expression of our religious democracy. . . ."

Mischievous teachers might generate a lively classroom discussion on the notion of religious tolerance. Why should any person committed to a religious position tolerate the practice of any other religious position? Which students approve of religious tolerance, and which reject it, and why? Which students agree that America is a "God-soaked" country? What emotional impact does the adjective carry? Is being "God-soaked" a good thing or a bad thing?

John Donne Meditation XVII, *from* Devotions upon Emergent Occasions (p. 1476)

Regardless of your students' religious convictions, this devotion can sensitize them to the power and possibilities of extended metaphor in the service of formal and deliberately exalted style. Consider the sequence: the church is a body to which we all belong; mankind is a volume, authored by God; death is a translation of that book produced by a variety of translators. Man is not an isolated island but part of the mainland, and every lost person diminishes the geography of Europe. Affliction and tribulation are potential treasures, gold still in the mine, but the awareness of another's affliction is like ready cash, because it brings one closer to God.

The extraordinary images are rendered in a prose made sonorous and exalted by syntactic inversions such as "he knows not" and "I know not that," and parallelism such as "who casts not up his eye . . . ," "but who takes off his eye . . . ," who bends not his ear. . . ." and "who can remove it from the bell. . . ." The rhetorical devices, together with the dazzling images, create an energy that poeticizes the prose and enables it to penetrate deeply into the awareness of an attentive reader.

The lyrical possibilities of this work attracted the attention of Simon and Garfunkel, who based their song "I Am a Rock" on this meditation from Donne's *Devotions upon Emergent Occasions*. The lyric's beleaguered speaker rejects Donne's invitation to connect, and desperately isolates himself from all human contact, noting that "A rock feels no pain / And an island never cries."

Erich Fromm   Is Love an Art?   (p. 1259)

This short piece is the introduction to Erich Fromm's celebrated book *The Art of Loving* (originally published in 1956, reissued in 1974). As a psychologist, Fromm moved away from Freudian emphasis on the "unconscious" and taught that social and economic considerations determine human behavior. Thus, he attempts to understand love dispassionately and pragmatically as one of the many "arts" that humans pursue as they move through life. It would be useful, he argues, to treat love as one might treat any other valuable commodity. He wants to demystify romantic love so that his readers will not only better understand just what love entails but also learn how to guard against the confusion and despair that often destroy love relationships. In short, he argues that love is an art—like any other—and is worthy of study because it "requires knowledge and effort."

Fromm laments the fact that people pursue love by attempting to be lovable rather than by learning to extend love. Such people feel there is nothing to be learned about loving others; we need only adopt behaviors that make us lovable. Attractive physical appearance, coupled with power, wit, charm, and wealth, makes for exceedingly desirable love objects. Men and women, in our western materialistic and capitalistic system, try to connect in these essentially commercial terms. They seek to become lovable *objects*, when they should be learning to project love as a human *function*. "Two persons," he asserts, "thus fall in love when they feel they have found the best object available on the market." We should not, then, be surprised to discover that "human love relations follow the same pattern of exchange which governs the commodity and the labor market."

Perhaps worse than this market-based view of love is the confusion of love with physical passion. The idea that we "fall" in love is perverse. We should "be" in love, or "stand"—not "fall"—in love. Fromm recognizes the exhilaration of sexual intimacy, but insists that such exhilaration soon diminishes, and should not be confused with love. Clear evidence—the divorce rate, the well-known anguish of ill-matched couples—mocks the widespread notion that "nothing is easier than to love." Yet few have the wisdom to examine the fundamental premises that brought them to this unhappy state. And such an examination is precisely the impetus for Fromm's book.

Avoiding the unhappiness generated by inappropriate ideas about the nature of love will require some effort. One must approach love as an art that requires, first, the mastery of a theory and, second, the mastery of practice (not unlike the education of a physician). But the energy invested in this enterprise will be wasted unless the would-be lovers realize that mastering the art of love "must be a matter of ultimate concern." Those who feel that "learning" is, principally, a tool to acquire wealth and prestige are not likely to understand that learning the art of love is worth the effort required, since it "only profits the soul."

Emma Goldman   Defense   (p. 636)

In examining the effectiveness of this speech, students need to keep in mind Goldman's audience. While she repeatedly addresses the presiding judge, her real audience lies beyond the courtroom. First, she is speaking to friends and followers who share her beliefs, reaffirming those beliefs and unflinchingly accepting the consequences of her acting on them. As well, she is speaking to the general public, those who might be indifferent or even hostile to her cause, fully conscious that she is a celebrity whose words and deeds will receive widespread media coverage.

She begins therefore with an appeal to the First Amendment protection of free speech, the rockbed principle of American democracy that is the first, both in order and arguably in importance, among the ten mighty guarantors of freedom in the Bill of Rights. (Historically, the Supreme Court has placed an especially heavy burden of proof on the government in any attempts to curtail First Amendment rights.) Her capricious arrest and conviction, she declares, amount to nothing less than an assault on a basic right.

Quoting from a then-popular drama playing in New York City, Goldman powerfully describes the "palpitating life" (para. 4) that has propelled her into crime. First she quotes government statistics on poverty and family size, then breathes life into them (and also establishes her own bona fides) by drawing on her personal experience (paras. 5 and 6).

Paragraphs 9 and 10 serve as a transition to the heart of her remarks: a class analysis of American society. She has been arrested and convicted of violating a "puritanic law" (para. 9) that directly serves the interests of the "Statesmen, politicians, men of the cloth, men who own the wealth of the world" (para. 12) who need a large underclass of underpaid workers for their factories as well as cannon fodder for their wars. Note, by the way, that the oppressors are not just the wealthy—but wealthy men. No, Goldman concludes, she is not a lawbreaker but a soldier in a worthy war.

Though a law such as that under which Goldman was convicted some ninety years ago would be struck down today as unconstitutional, the issues and the arguments she addresses remain much the same in the feverish contention between pro-life and pro-choice advocates.

Abeer Hoque   Ironed Blue Sky, 88°F   (p. 977)

A good way to present Hoque's piece is to have students search through it for incongruities. The central idea—that the borrowed pedagogy employed by teachers like Mr. Eze is ill-suited to this setting—is illustrated in numerous direct and indirect ways, by example and by analogy. Asking students to read the uniforms, the phonetically transcribed Nigerian-accented recitations of Blake, and other manifestations of Anglophilia as expressing incongruity can help them read the colonial situation in the way Hoque presents it here.

The effects of the imposition of cultural norms on another, far different culture is the subject of "Ironed Blue Sky, 88°F," and it might be worthwhile to ask students to think about what is gained by Hoque's decision to present this subject through the experience of schoolchildren. The importance of indoctrination through education is seen well from this angle, as is the inapplicability of the cultural norms so forced upon its targets, expressed on its most basic level by the inappropriateness of the British uniforms in a place that has, as the narrator says, "two seasons, wet heat and dry heat." Perhaps the piece's most painful and telling lines are those at the end, though, in which Hoque reflects on the tiger, subject of the Blake poem the students must recite. The students know the tiger from folktales, but see it through the lens of their colonizers' imaginations (even twenty years after independence), "pictured in textbooks, trapped and wilting in our little town zoo." "The tiger," it ends, "we understand." That they are seeing themselves trapped and wilting should not be difficult for students who have tracked Hoque's descriptions of the incongruities of British influence to comprehend.

Langston Hughes Salvation (p. 328)

While Hughes probably never left a freshman writing class with an assignment to write an essay on that hoary old topic "A Memorable Experience," the title would fit his piece perfectly. But Hughes was too good a writer to use such a flat, nondescript title. That's one of the first lessons students can learn from this essay. "Salvation" is decidedly unhackneyed and attention grabbing.

In the essay itself, from the intriguing paradox of the opening two sentences to the amusing pathos and paradox of the final one, Hughes's essay is a model of controlled, effective essay writing. Students can be shown how nicely that opening paradox sets up suspense and keeps the reader wondering how it will be resolved. They can observe how a good writer relies mostly on showing and lets the telling emerge from the details. The opening paragraph sets the scene and the second sets the problem (recognizing the signs of salvation). The following paragraphs then focus on the narrator and describe in vivid detail his futile attempts to feel saved, to recognize the signs described to him by his Auntie Reed. Finally, in desperation and piqued because "god had not struck Westley dead for taking his name in vain or for lying in the temple" (para. 11), Hughes stands up and brings joy to his aunt and the congregation but guilt upon himself for lying.

While the tone of the essay is serious, it is certainly not solemn. Indeed, it has comic undertones, especially in the figure of Westley, who is clearly made of coarser stuff than the narrator. But in the matter of salvation, there is no difference between him and Westley. It is this recognition that gives a comic tinge to the conclusion. The final sentence, like the opening one, embodies a paradox in the narrator's petulant implication that it is not his fault if the Jesus he no longer believes exists did not come to help him.

Zora Neale Hurston How It Feels to Be Colored Me (p. 953)

This sprightly essay shimmers with the verbal wit Hurston was famous for. Her title is catchy and intriguing: how does it feel to be someone else, especially, for a white audience, a "colored" someone else? The first sentence strikes the note of insouciance and lighthearted banter that carries through the essay: I make no apologies for being black, and I will certainly not claim, as so many of my race do, that I am descended from an Indian chief. The following paragraphs describe her childhood. in an all-black town, where the only whites she ever saw were passing through—sparing her, we can infer, the traumas and degradations of racism she would learn about when she was sent to school in Jacksonville at age thirteen (para. 5). This beginning would seem to announce another essay on a common black experience: a child's traumatic discovery of what it means to be black in America.

The opening sentence of the next paragraph disappoints the expectation: "But I am not tragically colored." Abandoning conventional narrative, she now writes impressionistically and poetically as she tries to make good on her title. She refuses to be defined by the color of her skin or the history of her race. As the metaphors accumulate, so do the ambiguities and perhaps even confusions. Are we to take as literal or metaphoric her declaration that "Slavery is the price I paid for civilization, and the choice was not with me. It is a bully adventure and worth all that I have paid through my ancestors for it" (para. 7)? When she goes on to say, "It is thrilling to think—to know that for any act of mine, I shall get twice as much praise or twice as much blame," how are we to understand this thrill? Is her reaction to listening to jazz a genuine emotional experience or a display of literary primitivism, the kind of stereotyping of black music that was common during the Harlem Renaissance?

The same questions can be asked about the concluding section as well, an almost feverish plunge into Emersonian mysticism as she feels herself become "the cosmic Zora," "a fragment of the Great Soul" (paras. 14–15). But the "cosmic Zora" collapses into the "brown bag of miscellany" in the brilliant and witty final paragraph, a grab bag of unrelated items with no discernible logic to bind them together.

Hurston's views on race and her refusal to engage in political action made her unpopular with her fellow black writers in the Harlem community. We can quibble with the logic, or lack of it, in this essay; we can disagree with her resolutely nonpolitical stance; we can accuse her of sacrificing seriousness to wit and flippancy. But Hurston, this essay amply demonstrates, is "a little world made cunningly." Her response no doubt would be, "Say what you will, that's how it feels to be colored me."

Note: "How It Feels to Be Colored Me" was published in *The World Tomorrow* in May 1928 and was not reprinted during Hurston's lifetime. From *Hurston: Folklore, Memoirs, and Other Writings* (Library of America, 1995), ed. Cheryl A. Wall.

Martin Luther King Jr.   Letter from Birmingham Jail   (p. 643)

The statement (reproduced below) that elicited King's letter appeared in the *Birmingham News* on April 13, 1963. It was signed by eight Christian and Jewish clergymen of Alabama, all of them white.

Aside from Donne's "Meditation XVII," King's letter is perhaps the most formal of the essays in the sense that he employs an elevated diction along with numerous rhetorical devices that lend a solemnity to his words. As one clergyman writing to others, King no doubt assumed that they would recognize the biblical parallels and rhetorical cadences (many of Paul's letters were written while he was in prison in Rome). King's biographer remarks:

> As King read over their statement, he had an inspiration. He was going to compose a rebuttal to those clergymen in the form of an open letter, a letter such as Paul might have sent them. He sensed a historic opportunity here, a chance not only to address the moral voice of the white South, but to produce a defense of the movement with profound symbolic import. Would not all America be stirred by a calm and reasonable disquisition on nonviolence, written by a Christian minister held in a jail in the most segregated city in the country?

These eight clergymen had stated the quintessential arguments of the so-called white moderates against even nonviolent direct action. In answering them, King could be confident that he would be addressing the majority of white Americans.

While King's lofty rhetoric and powerful metaphoric language lend to his prose the passion of pulpit persuasion, the letter never becomes merely an appeal to emotions. For King very carefully and systematically examines and refutes the criticisms leveled against him, bringing to bear logical, historical, and moral arguments.

King begins by taking up the charge that he is an outsider meddling in the affairs of others. Such a charge is, of course, a personal attack and gives King the opportunity to establish not only his right (as an individual and a U.S. citizen) but his duty (as a Christian and a minister) to intervene. With that charge disposed of, King is now able to turn to the substantive matter of why this intervention is necessary (paras. 6–9). He states the "four basic steps" (para. 6) in a nonviolent campaign and then proceeds to demonstrate how each of those steps has been taken: the racism of the city is beyond dispute, negotiations have failed, he and his people have undergone the self-purification necessary before taking direct action. Clearly and reasonably, King justifies the necessity for direct action, taking pains to explain (paras. 8, 9) the considerable care exercised in making such a momentous decision.

King then agrees with the ministers that negotiations are needed to improve race relations in Birmingham but rejects their implication that direct action and negotiations are alternative methods for achieving the same ends. Rather, King skillfully shows that direct action appears to be the only way to force a racist city to the negotiating table. To the ministers' admonition "Wait," King convincingly shows that African Americans have waited more than long enough.

Students should note that King's strategy is to begin with the simple and concrete and move to the complex and abstract. Having begun with the attack upon himself as an outsider and explained what he intends to do and his reasons for such action, he moves to the more complex questions of civil disobedience — its history, its meaning, its justification. In short, King now undertakes the difficult task of defining civil disobedience and providing its philosophical justification (paras. 15–22). At the heart of that justification is the critical distinction he makes between a just and an unjust law, the section most likely to provoke discussion (strangely, King fails to mention Henry David Thoreau's celebrated defenses of civil disobedience). A law is unjust, King says, if it satisfies three criteria: (1) it "degrades human personality" (para. 16), (2) it exempts a majority from obeying a law that the minority must obey (para. 17), and (3) the minority, denied the vote, "had no part in enacting or devising the law" (para. 18).

With these general principles now defined, King returns in paragraph 23 to a more personal level. He now addresses the clergymen as typical "white moderates" who confuse cause and effect by blaming the victims (paras. 23, 26) and who, in calling upon African Americans to go slow, adopt "the strangely irrational notion that there is something in the very flow of time that will inevitably cure all ills" (para. 26). Indeed, King goes on to say, time is running out as evidenced by the violent hatred and despair that has led many African Americans to embrace black nationalism (paras. 27–28). Contrary to what the clergymen say, nonviolent direct action has directly contributed to the avoidance of violence by giving African Americans an opportunity to release their frustration and anger (para. 30).

While King maintains an impressively equable and loving tone throughout the essay, in his discussion of white moderates and the failure of the white church, one senses a disappointment that borders on bitterness. For example, he wonders why these Christian ministers would praise a brutal police force rather than the peaceful protestors (paras. 45–47). But the loving tone is fully regained in the final paragraphs that express King's spirit of genuine Christian love and humility.

An interesting way to approach King's style might be to ask students what differences result if passages are stripped of their metaphors. Here are some examples:

Original: ". . . see ominous clouds of inferiority beginning to form in her little mental sky . . ." (para. 14)

Revision: . . . see a sense of inferiority beginning to form in her mind

Original: "Now is the time to lift our national policy from the quicksand of racial injustice to the solid rock of human dignity." (para. 26)

Revision: Now is the time to change our national policy from one that condones racial injustice to one that prohibits it.

Original: "They have carved a tunnel of hope through the dark mountain of disappointment." (para. 43)

Revision: They have given us hope in the most difficult times.

Original: "Let us all hope that the dark clouds of racial prejudice will soon pass away and the deep fog of misunderstanding will be lifted." (para. 50)

Revision: Let us hope that racial prejudice will soon end and misunderstanding will be overcome.

Finally, students might be asked to analyze the long periodic sentence that constitutes almost all of paragraph 14. Do they think it would make much difference to the sentence if the main clause came first?

Maxine Hong Kingston No Name Woman (p. 1263)

Maxine Hong Kingston's first book, *The Woman Warrior* (1976), examined the position of women in the Chinese society that produced her immigrant parents and sustained them in the New World. Her second, *China Men* (1980), inspired by her father's experiences, explored the lives of those Chinese men forced by economic necessity to leave their wives and families in China to search for sustenance both for themselves and their distant families. Though Kingston was born in Stockton, California, her traditional Chinese household provided the matter and the insights revealed in her work.

Doubtless, Kingston's mother told her the tragic story of her lost aunt, the No Name Woman, as a parable, warning the Americanized young Maxine about the perils of illicit sex. Later, the mature writer takes the story much further as she struggles to understand the life of her long-dead aunt. Along the way, her essay illuminates the dark side of Chinese village life as well as the debased status of women in such a culture.

Her father's sister was one of seventeen "hurry-up" brides, her marriage arranged quickly to a complete stranger from a neighboring village. These marriages were desined to tie the men leaving China to their ancestral homes and ensure some continuity to the traditional social patterns. Immediately after the marriage, her husband left the country. Years later, the illicit pregnancy of the No Name Woman results in the villagers' catastrophic attack on the entire household.

For Kingston's mother, her sister-in-law's sexual transgression is a source not only of shame but also of serious injury to the family. The punishment is appropriately severe. The murder/suicide of the outcasts—both child and mother—is exacerbated by the obliteration of their memory. Nothing could be worse in a society that venerates its ancestors and propagates in order to ensure that there will be a new generation to tend the graves and honor the spirits of the dead.

But Kingston tries to identify with her nameless aunt. First, she sees her as the victim of rape. As a woman trained to be subservient to men, she is powerless to resist the demands of her tormentor, who himself escapes guilt and punishment. Then the author imagines her as a coquette, relishing the attention her long hair and innocent beauty inspires in the men around her. After all, she spent only a single night with her technical "husband" before he disappeared from her life. But whether a pure victim or a willing accomplice, she, not her lover, suffers the humiliation of her pregnancy; her family suffers emotionally and physically at the hands of the pillaging villagers who enforce a morality made more urgent by hard economic times. But that morality is enforced against the woman, not the man.

And Kingston, defying her parents' determination to obliterate the No Name Woman, supports her aunt's right to the same honors accorded all worthy ancestors. To that end, she creates not the origami houses and clothing traditionally offered for the comfort of ancestral spirits, but these paper pages that insist on her aunt's existence.

Saadat Hasan Manto   Third Letter to Uncle Sam   (p. 684)

Students may at first be bewildered by "Third Letter to Uncle Sam." Historical background aside, questions about the piece's constantly shifting tone, subject matter, and even genre will present some obstacles. Rather than hoping these obstacles will disappear over the course of discussion, one good strategy might be to line them up at the start and use them to frame discussion. Why does the emotional tone change so quickly and so often? Why is Manto talking about "casual-wear shirts" in one breath and the atomic bomb in the next? Why does he begin by dismissing a national poetic tradition, saying "However, I think that is all poetry"? These questions and others will help students get past their initial confusion.

Once past that, students can move on to the feel of the speaker's voice, something they should more easily recognize. The "nephew" here is funny, sad, angry, and mocking, feelings and tones students are familiar with. The object of his satirical stance—his country's history and the hand of the United States both in pivotal events in that history and also in cultural changes—should become clear with minimal background provided by the instructor.

Jessica Mitford   The American Way of Death   (p. 1481)

One of the most fascinating differences among societies, ancient and modern, is the social response to death. And though the American way of death is not the most bizarre on a planet featuring Egyptian pyramids and guardian armies of terra cotta Chinese cavalry, it does exhibit some of the more unfortunate aspects of free economy capitalism. The undertaking industry is, after all, an industry. It has an enviable market—all of us. Worst, or best, of all—its customers are always overwrought with grief, generally inexperienced in the consumption of funeral products, and emotionally committed to preserving or acquiring the approval of the living by doing well by the dead.

In the tradition of muckraking journalism, Jessica Mitford takes aim at the undertakers who, for their own profit, have converted the solemn simplicity of death and burial into an exercise in conspicuous consumption. The four articles of faith that the funeral industry has sold itself are set down in paragraphs 8 through 11. The first argues that modern funeral procedures are an "American tradition," when, in fact, until fairly recently, funerals were much simpler, much cheaper, and managed by families and friends rather than funeral directors. The industry's second article of faith asserts that funeral establishments provide what the public wants, though Mitford argues that undertakers create an obligation to consume conspicuously by playing on the family's grief and guilt. Third, the funeral industry sees itself in a "dramaturgic role"—able to generate profit from services undreamed of in earlier and simpler times. And finally, as the industry insists upon its professional status, it has introduced euphemistic jargon to describe itself—among the more grotesque, "cremains" and "calcination—the *kindlier* heat."

Throughout, Mitford uses a breezy, sardonic tone. Her arguments are largely anecdotal and thus generate more outrage than an objective, scholarly study. In her peroration, she compares the arrogance of the funeral industry with that of the American automobile industry, and asks rhetorically whether future Americans might not demand funerals "without fins."

Underlying her wishfulness, of course, is a strong though tacit notion, suggested in paragraph 14, of how Americans *should* deal with death. They want "dignified funerals at reasonable cost." And her ideal of such dignity is suggested in paragraph 8 when she speaks of a past in which funerals were simple to "the point of starkness," characterized by "the plain pine box, the laying out of the dead by friends and family who also bore the coffin to the grave." The undertakers might reasonably reply that people do not live their lives with such stark simplicity—they buy expensive cars, ornate homes, jewelry. Whatever human tendency is served by such consumption can also be served by the ornate and expensive funeral.

Often the treatment of death reflects a society's beliefs about the nature of death. Hindus burn the dead—they believe the soul of the deceased is likely to be reincarnated. Zoroastrians (Parsees) feel that corpses pollute, so they neither burn, nor bury, for fear of polluting holy fire or the earth. The dead are left exposed in open towers for vultures to devour. A number of ancient civilizations saw death as the beginning of a perilous journey to another world, and provided furnishings—a boat, food and water, household implements, weapons—to ease the journey. In the West, some believe in the resurrection of the flesh, and thus forbid cremation. What belief system, finally, is served by the modern ornate funeral, with its lead-lined casket, cosmetically prepared corpse, innerspring mattress, and floral tributes?

Mitford's influential book changed the way Americans think about funerals and may even have inspired changes in the funeral industry, including an increase in the cremation rate and government regulation. She was at work on a new edition of *The American Way of Death* at the time of her own death in 1996. The new book's introduction retains the original's sense of outrage at morticians and the high price of dying.

Es'kia Mphahlele   African Literature: What Tradition?   (p. 982)

Mphahlele here makes many different points, and his argument is a subtle one. One good approach to an essay such as this is to ask not what the author's point is but rather what questions he asks, especially as he does raise topics in a way that opens rather than closes discussion. Asking students to find the explicit and implicit questions Mphahlele asks, from his subtitle on, will help them follow his essay and see what is at stake in what might seem a rather arcane topic, the African writer and intellectual.

Connecting the situation of the African intellectual to that of the African student by connecting this essay to Hoque's and Mnthali's pieces may help students better relate to Mphahlele's description of his betwixt-and-betweenness and his ambivalence about it. His point that he is of two minds about the influence of the West—almost literally—is crucial to his understanding of his situation, but hard for him to explain and for students to grasp. It might help to return to the opening paragraph, in which Mphahlele raises the question of the inevitability of Africa escaping the influence of a West "which was never going to let us be," if only to illustrate that these questions (Does it make sense to lament the inevitable? How should people feel about something that takes them away from the past but moves them toward the future?) are complicated and in some ways unanswerable.

George Orwell Shooting an Elephant (p. 957)

This essay can be compared profitably with Swift's "A Modest Proposal." Both are written by Englishmen, both attack British imperialism and both find colonial domination degrading for the rulers as well as the ruled. And while one employs satire and the other narrative, both have become classic statements. Students might be asked to contrast the different strategies each adopts to achieve roughly similar ends.

Whereas satire allows Swift to clothe his savage outrage in the garb of sweet reasonableness and scientific detachment, Orwell's straightforward autobiographical account expresses his unease and ambivalence as an agent of colonialism. The essay derives much of its force from the fact that Orwell is an agent, not a human being, driven by the imperatives of imperialism. As an individual, he would have remained anonymous and nondescript. But as the opening sentence makes clear, he is a symbol and thus a celebrity.

While in theory and in secret he is "all for the Burmese," as an agent of colonialism he must be their adversary. While he recognizes the justice of the Burmese hatred of him, he nevertheless sees them as "evil-spirited little beasts" for making his job so difficult (para. 2). That rending and ultimately insupportable disjunction reaches a crisis in the shooting of the elephant. As a sensible and compassionate human being, he recognizes that there is every reason *not* to shoot the elephant. But he is not acting as a human being. He is a representative of the oppressor and is thus compelled to do what is expected of him — not only by his government but by the colonial subjects as well. In this grotesque world, his overriding concern is not to be laughed at. Trapped in the abstractions of power and politics, he gains his central insight: "I perceived in this moment that when the white man turns tyrant it is his own freedoms that he destroys" (para. 7).

Students might be asked why Orwell interrupts his narrative to describe the lessons the episode taught him. While as an isolated episode the description of the shooting and the elephant's agonizingly slow death would be powerful enough, in the context of Orwell's reflections, it is immensely more significant. We witness the death of a "costly piece of machinery" (para. 6), the livelihood of a poor Burmese, and a magnificently huge beast; but the elephant's death becomes a metonymy for imperialism. Does the elephant symbolize only the suffering inflicted by colonialism for hundreds of years? Or does it represent also, in the author's eyes, both the imperialism that he hates and the Burmese who have enraged him?

Paul I Corinthians 13 (p. 1257)

Paul established a church that reflected the competing and disparate social and religious attitudes in Corinth, a wild, cosmopolitan seaport town. As a result, scholars maintain, Paul felt compelled to write at least four letters (edited and preserved in part as Corinthians I and II in the New Testament) to both chide and instruct a factional congregation. Corinthian Christians argued over the status conferred by their baptizers, among other things, and apparently fell into a vituperative contentiousness that threatened the stability of the church. In I Corinthians 13, the famous prose-poem on spiritual (not erotic) love, Paul attempts to persuade the fractious community to love one another and thus rise above petty disputes and jealousies and selfish childishness.

"Speaking in the tongues of men" is an allusion to the ecstatic glossolalia that marked the early church and still occurs in some modern charismatic communities. The unintelligible babble was, and is, thought to be a direct manifestation of religious experience. Elsewhere in I Corinthians, Paul caustically points out that he can speak in tongues as well as anyone — but that rational discourse is more useful. He chides those who seek status by speaking in tongues — he compares them to the noisy gongs and cymbals associated with pagan worship. The "prophesying" Paul alludes to was probably another form of ecstatic religious experience manifested in physical movement. The curious remark in verse 3 troubled some scribes who provided an alternative reading — "that I may glory" — for "burned." In either case, Paul argues that even martyrdom, without love, is futile.

Salman Rushdie "Imagine There's No Heaven": A Letter to the Six Billionth World Citizen (p. 670)

Though the 1988 *fatwa* (a religious injunction) issued by the Iranian Ayatollah Khomeini (offering $1 million to anyone who would execute Rushdie for blasphemy) might play some part in the author's antipathy to religion, his education and experience as a child in Bombay, a victimized schoolboy in England, a censored writer in Pakistan, would provide sufficient insight into his views. Students will probably recognize the title as a quote from John Lennon's celebrated lyric "Imagine," and those who don't know the song by heart will find it easily on the Web.

The occasion for this brief 1997 essay was a United Nations invitation to celebrated writers to propose a message to the six billionth living human who would be born that year. Rushdie's message is blunt and clear. He warns the newborn citizen of the world that, inevitably, priests of one kind or another, equipped with ancient creation myths, will compete for the privilege of explaining how he or she got here and how he or she must live. By cataloging a number of those myths side by side, Rushdie hopes to convey their absurdity. They may be good, even beautiful stories — but how can any thoughtful human, on the one hand, accept that they are true accounts, and, on the other hand, accept the absolute moral postulates based on the assumption that they are true? And so Rushdie urges his correspondent to refuse to let the keepers of these creation myths from ordering him or her around.

To the more difficult Socratic question, "How shall we live?," Rushdie proposes what might be considered an extraordinarily optimistic response. First, he rejects the notion of "cultural relativism," that is, the notion that since cultures differ from one another, their disparate views should be both tolerated and respected. For example, he has no respect for cultures that practice female circumcision (and, presumably, neither should his readers). Nor is he willing to accept a culture's privilege to ignore what he calls "the universality of human rights" (whatever those may be). Here we come to the optimistic part. Rushdie is quite willing to profess a code of ethical conduct that everyone should embrace — not because the priests of whatever religion require it, but because we have the "freedom" to embrace the "secular-ethical position."

This rather attractive-sounding notion, of course, fails to consider the darker aspects of the human condition — the greed, the lust, the aggression that writers have explored in works ancient and modern (think Cain and Abel, think *The Iliad* and *The Odyssey*, think Hobbes and Freud). And surely it is no coincidence that ethical systems engendered by religious doctrine address our darker urges. Rushdie recognizes the difficulty. He admits that the reasons for dismissing cultural relativism "aren't clear cut," but points out that only hard-line-ideology *is* clear cut — and anything "hard-line" is, presumably, by definition, bad. He prefers the admittedly "fuzzier" freedom, the never-ending debate about what constitutes morality in a "secular-ethical" social order, to a morality dictated by the diverse mythologies that be. Presumably, the fear of jail or execution is sufficient grounds for controlling our darker desires — we really don't need the fear of hell or the promise of heaven to keep us straight.

Finally, those who find Rushdie's views attractive (we include ourselves) are prepared to argue that the diversity of religious beliefs and the diverse moral absolutes that flow from them are more dangerous and damaging to the human condition than the optimistic hopefulness embedded in the idea of a "secular-ethical" code of behavior. After all, we all know right from wrong — don't we? Those whose behavior demonstrates a lack of clarity in the matter are destined to confront, in the absence of an angry god, a cold-eyed district attorney.

William Saroyan   Five Ripe Pears   (p. 331)

As in Dylan Thomas's "Fern Hill," Saroyan's narrator recreates a childhood experience whose significance he could only dimly and intuitively understand at the time.

In weaving together the past (innocence, intuition) with the present (rules, rationality), Saroyan creates a deceptively simple account about innocence and experience, about a child driven by the pure joy of his own body and the sensuous world around him in an act judged antisocial and requiring punishment by the adult world.

Using the device of explaining to "old Man Pollard" why he took the pears, the narrator begins his story. Impelled by a force far more powerful than the social conditioning that would brand his act a theft, he runs the two blocks to the waiting tree, its pears "fat and ready," in a "moment of numerous clarities, air, body, and mind " (para. 7). It is, we learn in the following paragraphs, the dramatic culmination of an entire elemental cycle the child had been observing, beginning with the bareness of winter, the leafing and blossoming of the tree, the appearance of the "hard green shapes of the unripe pears" (para. 9), and now the delectable ripeness of the pears. At this point, less than halfway into the narrative, the story reaches its climax. The pears are ripe, the child is ready. "But it was not to eat," the adult explains. "It was not to steal. It was to know: the *pear*. Of life—the sum of it—which *could* decay. I was determined to get to them, and remain innocent" (paras. 10 and 11).

Saroyan's child is overwhelmed by the rightness and readiness of everything. He must await adulthood to articulate what he could only intuit at the time: the intensity of the experience came from his recognition, like that of the young boy in Dylan Thomas's poem "Fern Hill," that time held him "green and dying." His act is an anguished and moving protest against change, decay, death.

The ringing of the school bell (para. 16) awakens him to the real world, where taking pears is considered stealing and leads to punishment, where an assertion that he "created" the pears (they are not so much fruit to eat as symbols of a joyous experience) would have no meaning.

Jonathan Swift   A Modest Proposal   (p. 625)

Any discussion of "A Modest Proposal" will have to deal centrally with irony and satire. But beyond that, there are numerous possibilities for analysis in such a rich and brilliant piece. A consideration of some of these possibilities will allow the class to focus on the essay itself, its major ideas, and its techniques.

The structure of Swift's essay falls into a number of sections: section 1 (paras. 1–7) introduces the problem and establishes the persona, the voice of the dispassionate but concerned observer. A transitional paragraph (para. 8) moves the essay to section 2 (paras. 9–16), in which the speaker offers his plan. Before he has laid out all the details, however, he interrupts himself with a digression, section 3 (paras. 17–19). In section 4 (paras. 20–28) the speaker returns to and completes the laying out of the details of his proposed solution. Section 5 (paras. 29–32) refutes the objections, actual and anticipated, to the plan. The speaker then ends the essay (para. 33) by stating explicitly what the tone of his voice has implied throughout, namely that he has no personal stake in seeing his clever solution adopted.

Ask students why the speaker characterizes section 3 as a digression. In a strict sense, of course, it is a digression because it interrupts the exposition of the plan to solve the problems of the poor. The three paragraphs of this section, by contrast, deal with "young lads and maidens" between the ages of twelve and fourteen, with "the vast number of poor people who are aged, diseased, or maimed" (presumably the elderly), as well as "the younger laborers." But these paragraphs constitute a digression only in a narrow, structural sense. In the broader, thematic sense, they contribute brilliantly to the speaker's arguments. Paragraph 17, for example, allows the speaker, in rejecting twelve- to fourteen-year-olds for consumption, to make the additional and supremely ironic observation that in any case even if they were edible, "some scrupulous people might be apt to censure such a practice (although indeed very unjustly) as a little bordering upon cruelty; which, I confess, hath always been with me the strongest objection against any project, how well soever intended" (para. 17). In paragraph 19, Swift takes up the problem of the adult poor who are such a "grievous" burden on the kingdom. The older among them, the speaker assures his readers, are "every day dying and rotting by cold and famine, and filth and vermin, as fast as can be reasonably expected." That final adverb encapsulates the savage irony of Swift's essay, as does the adjective "hopeful" in his allusion to the condition of "the younger laborers." The comfortable, fortunate, and well-fed readers are "hopeful" the young laborers will die because that will reduce the magnitude of the problem; the young laborers themselves no doubt wish to die in order to escape the misery of their existence.

Paragraph 29 is particularly noteworthy because it is a straightforward recital of the measures that must be taken by the Irish themselves if the misery of their land is to be ameliorated. The irony is maintained through the speaker's insistence that since Ireland is so devastatingly and uniquely oppressed by both the English and the failings of its own people, it is idle to talk of the measures a sensible nation would adopt.

Lewis Thomas   The Iks   (p. 964)

In this muscular and disturbing essay, Thomas rejects the anthropologist's conclusion and puts forward his own more hopeful view. Keep in mind that the Iks suffered *two* disasters—not only were they driven off their land, they were also visited by the anthropologist who wrote a book about them. The anthropologist (perhaps with a minor in cultural psychology) concluded that, deprived of their traditional culture, the Iks reverted to the primal savagery that civilized humans usually control through cultural institutions. If and when our own cultural traditions break down, we, too, will behave with the malice the Iks exhibit toward each other.

Thomas bases his rebuttal on the fact that the Iks seem altogether anomalous—other cultures have been violently upset, yet no peoples behave as the Iks do. Thus, the Iks do *not* illustrate fundamental human nature. Yet their behavior does seem familiar—it is the madness of individuals behaving as if they were committees, cities, nations. And Thomas gives a sobering account of committees that exhibit absolute selfishness, of cities that defecate in the rivers and lakes and detest their neighbors, of nations that defecate into whole oceans and live for the death of others. Such behavior is normal for groups of humans banded together to defend their turf, but when individuals behave with the same murderously selfish principles, they are judged insane. Man, Thomas concludes, is not a "sparse inhuman thing at his center"—he has simply not "yet learned how to stay human when assembled in masses." The essay finally indicts corporate civilization—not the Iks—by forcing readers to confront the insane behavior characteristic of groups.

James Thurber   Fables:
The Little Girl and the Wolf   (p. 639)
The Owl Who Was God   (p. 640)
The Unicorn in the Garden   (p. 641)
The Very Proper Gander   (p. 639)

Humor, certainly American humor and satire, thrives on exposing the hypocrisies of the official culture—its representatives and its cultural icons. Early in his career, Mark Twain wrote two hilarious sketches, "The Story of the Good Little Boy" and "The Story of the Bad Little Boy," ridiculing the Sunday School moral lessons taught in his day. The good little boy follows all the precepts and ends up a failure; the bad little boy violates them all and ends up a huge success.

The fable has long been the vehicle for conveying moral lessons and supreme among them are Aesop's. Thurber exploits the popularity of this form in the same way Twain exploited the Sunday School lessons. The fable, like the Sunday School lesson, is designed to inculcate (young) minds with the values a culture prizes. Since the discrepancies between what a culture teaches and what it practices are often glaring, satirists have found the official values an irresistible target.

"Little Red Riding Hood" is the celebrated cautionary tale for girls on the dangers of talking to strangers. In Thurber's modern rewriting, the tables are turned, warning the wolf, or the wolves that may be, not to mess with little girls. In "The Owl Who Was God," President Abraham Lincoln's celebrated aphorism, "You can fool some of the people all of the time, and all of the people some of the time, but you cannot fool all of the people all of the time" is reduced to a lethal bromide, not so much to skewer politicians as those who mindlessly follow politicians and mobs.

Many of Thurber's works, "The Unicorn in the Garden" among them, are peopled by seemingly docile husbands and predatory wives. In Thurber's more innocent time, the conflict was, often affectionately, dubbed "the battle of the sexes." Whether the subject plays as well in our postfeminist era, students will have to decide. If we can put aside objections to stereotyping, certainly the wife deserves the come-uppance she receives. The husband may be docile but he is not insensitive. He has his revenge, which, in our more therapeutic times, would be diagnosed as "passive-aggressive behavior."

"The Very Proper Gander" exposes the way a jingoistic patriotism joined to ignorance (and poor hearing) can generate a mob frenzy. It is a somber fable, the only one of the four that is not funny.

Mark Twain Little Bessie Would Assist Providence (p. 1478)

This gleeful attack on certain popular theological assumptions provides an opportunity for students to examine literary treatments of religious positions. The essay would have troubled publishers during the first decade of the twentieth century; it first appeared (after Twain's death) in Albert Bigelow Paine's biography of Twain (1912). Compare it to "Design," Frost's sonnet questioning the theory that the design of the universe implies the existence of a designer.

Both pieces raise the issues addressed by Job in the Old Testament, Frost's tone embodies a high seriousness, spiced by the ironic suggestion that God is responsible not only for what is good and beautiful but also for what is sinister and deadly. Twain's tone, emerging from the unsophisticated but devastating innocence of a nearly three-year-old child, is comic, but nonetheless serious. Bessie clearly out-debates her mother (leaving the question: Who is the innocent here?). In both pieces, readers are asked to confront the paradoxical presence of evil in a world created by a presumably just and loving God. You might have students contrast Twain's (and Frost's) view with Donne's remarkable "Meditation XVII" and his sonnet "Death, Be Not Proud." The Anglican priest confronts and diminishes the terror of death with an altogether different sensibility that reflects his faith and his conviction that we are all immortal.

Twain was a masterful stand-up comedian, and that skill is nicely reflected in this dialogue's rhythm. After discussing Billy Norris's death from typhus, Bessie's mother proclaims her certainty that God "does nothing that isn't right and wise and merciful." Bessie pauses thoughtfully (a count of five perhaps?) before dropping the roof "on the stranger that was trying to save the crippled old woman from the fire." Then a rising crescendo of calamities leads to unspeakable horror — an attack on God that leaves Bessie's mother no alternative but unconsciousness.

Mark Twain The War Prayer (p. 633)

Twain's essay opens with a short generalizing sentence followed by a paragraph underscoring the timelessness of the subject. He describes the familiar elements of a people preparing for war: the beating drums, the martial music of marching bands, the waving flags, the young men — they are always the young men, "gay and fine in their new uniforms" (para. 1) — cheered on by their countrymen as they march off to die. Above all, the pastors in churches call upon the God of Battles to bless "our good cause." The few dissenters and doubters are quickly intimidated into silence. The description of the war fervor continues, but now with more specificity. The Sunday morning service in a single church builds to a resounding, climactic invocation and the "long prayer," a passionate plea that "our" fighting men be favored and "theirs" be crushed.

The pastor's sermon is interrupted by a mysterious stranger (a figure, incidentally, who appears throughout Twain's works, as Colonel Sherburn in *Huckleberry Finn* and as Satan in *The Mysterious Stranger*, for example). Announcing himself as the messenger of God, the stranger delivers a sermon on "the unspoken part of the prayer" the congregation has just heard. Every prayer for victory, he thunders, in a passage marked by its biblical diction, rhetorical parallelism, and repetition, is inescapably also a prayer for defeat. "Our" victory can be achieved only at the cost of "their" misery and death. Is this, the stranger asks, what you wish "Him Who is the Source of Love" to grant?

The bitter final sentence provides the answer. A patriotism whipped into fury brooks no opposition. Those who are foolish enough "to disapprove of the war and cast a doubt upon its righteousness" (para. 1) are silenced. The rare doubter who refuses to be silenced, such as the mysterious stranger, is dismissed as a lunatic. This lunacy consists, of course, in exposing the murderous illogic of political and religious absolutism.

While "The War Prayer" makes no reference to any specific historical events, its genesis is to be found in Twain's response to America's colonial activities during the end of the nineteenth and the beginning of the twentieth centuries. Twain initially applauded America's victory over Spain in Cuba and the Philippines in 1898 as a step in bringing democracy and self-determination to oppressed people. But when it became clear that the United States intended to turn these countries into colonies, Twain attacked the U.S. government's imperialist designs. The Philippine-American war (1899–1902), which some historians view as America's first real colonial war as a world power, ended with the defeat of the Philippine rebels. It was not until July 4, 1946, that the Philippines became an independent nation.

An excellent recent book on the history of American imperialism is Warren Zimmerman's *First Great Triumph: How Americans Made Their Country a World Power* (2002).

Virginia Woolf What If Shakespeare Had Had a Sister? (p. 944)

The graceful writing of this personal yet erudite essay is perhaps a good place to begin. Having failed to turn up information on women "throughout the ages," Woolf will now report, her opening paragraph announces, the results of her more modest attempt to discover some facts about women during the Elizabethan period.

The essay is driven by a series of straightforward and simple questions that lead to anything but straightforward and simple answers. The first one, "why no women wrote a word of that extraordinary literature when every other man, it seemed, was capable of song or sonnet," leads her to the historians, for surely the answer must lie in the conditions under which women lived. The definition of fiction Woolf provides in the second paragraph is crucial to the entire essay in its insistence upon the inseparable relationship between the creation of art and the material conditions of the artist. But little is known beyond the bare fact that women were (often brutally) subjugated to men and to the imperatives of a society made by and for men.

Since women were oppressed in real life, how then, Woolf asks, does one account for the fact that women are portrayed in literature to be "as great as . . . man . . ." (para. 3)? At this point, Woolf's inquiry broadens, for in the quiet statement, "I turned to Professor Trevelyan again to see what history meant to him" (para. 5), and her reference shortly thereafter to the celebrated Elizabethan biographer John Aubrey, she makes plain that the condition of women in society at any given moment and the "condition" of women in history are merely two facets of the same male domination and brutality that women have always suffered.

The final lines of paragraph 6 referring to the bishop are an interesting moment in the development of the essay. Of course no woman could have written Shakespeare's plays in a society that degraded her, a society typified by the pompous bishop who pronounced with equal dogmatic confidence on the souls of cats and the minds of women. In these sentences, especially in the wonderful juxtaposition of the last two, Woolf's voice (for the only time) becomes ironic, her tone satiric as she gives form to the anger she feels in recalling the good bishop's insulting, ignorant dismissal of women. She now moves to her account of the life of Shakespeare's hypothetical sister (para. 7), providing out of her aroused and powerful imagination the facts that history has failed to record.

She argues that "it is unthinkable that any woman of Shakespeare's day should have had Shakespeare's genius" because no woman of his day was allowed a room of her own. And here, beginning with paragraph 8, Woolf develops her central thesis that literary, intellectual achievements are not "born among labouring, uneducated, servile people." Though Woolf is here proposing an elitist view of things, she argues that genius among the laboring classes is mostly doomed to wither and die for lack of material support. When to the disadvantage of poverty are added the disabilities of being female, the odds are hopeless. A man might do what he wished — travel, write, work, seduce women — the world was largely indifferent. A woman who stepped beyond the narrow path society defined for her was sure to incur the world's hostility. Above all, to leave that path was to put at risk the virtue whose unsanctioned loss condemned her not just in the world's eyes but in her own as well.

In the final paragraph, Woolf brings her essay to a powerful and effective conclusion. She restates her major points and strikes a note of cautious optimism by appealing to her primarily female audience and invoking the spirit of "many other women who are not here tonight," suggesting that only women can alter the conditions that have historically thwarted and often destroyed them.